THE EGYPT OF THE HEBREWS AND HERODOTOS

The Rev. A. H. SAYCE
PROFESSOR OF ASSYRIOLOGY AT OXFORD

ISBN: 978-1-63923-689-3

All Rights reserved. No part of this book maybe reproduced without written permission from the publishers, except by a reviewer who may quote brief passages in a review to be printed in a newspaper or magazine.

Printed: February 2023

Published and Distributed By:
Lushena Books
607 Country Club Drive, Unit E
Bensenville, IL 60106
www.lushenabks.com

ISBN: 978-1-63923-689-3

THE EGYPT OF THE HEBREWS
AND HERODOTOS

PREFACE

A FEW words of preface are needful to justify the addition of another contribution to the over-abundant mass of literature of which Egypt is the subject. It is intended to supplement the books already in the hands of tourists and students, and to put before them just that information which either is not readily accessible or else forms part of larger and cumbrous works. The travels of Herodotos in Egypt are followed for the first time in the light of recent discoveries, and the history of the intercourse between the Egyptians and the Jews is brought down to the age of the Roman Empire. As the ordinary histories of Egypt used by travellers end with the extinction of the native Pharaohs, I have further given a sketch of the Ptolemaic period. I have moreover specially noted the results of the recent excavations and discoveries made by the Egypt

Exploration Fund and by Professor Flinders Petrie, at all events where they bear upon the subject-matter of the book. Those who have not the publications of the Fund or of Professor Petrie, or who do not care to carry them into Egypt, will, I believe, be glad to have the essence of them thus extracted in a convenient shape. Lastly, in the Appendices I have put together information which the visitor to the Nile often wishes to obtain, but which he can find in none of his guide-books. The Appendix on the nomes embodies the results of the latest researches, and the list will therefore be found to differ here and there from the lists which have been published elsewhere. Those who desire the assistance of maps should procure the very handy and complete *Atlas of Ancient Egypt*, published by the Egypt Exploration Fund (price 3s. 6d.). It makes the addition of maps to this or any future work on Ancient Egypt superfluous.

Discoveries follow so thickly one upon the other in these days of active exploration that

Preface ix

it is impossible for an author to keep pace with them. Since my manuscript was ready for the press Dr. Naville, on behalf of the Egypt Exploration Fund, has practically cleared the magnificent temple of Queen Hatshepsu at Dêr el-Bâhari, and has discovered beneath it the unfinished sepulchre in which the queen fondly hoped that her body would be laid; Professor Petrie has excavated in the desert behind Zawêdeh and opposite Qoft the tombs of barbarous tribes, probably of Libyan origin, who settled in the valley of the Nile between the fall of the sixth and the rise of the eleventh dynasty; Mr. de Morgan has disinterred more jewellery of exquisite workmanship from the tombs of the princesses of the twelfth dynasty at Dahshûr; and Dr. Botti has discovered the site of the Serapeum at Alexandria, thus obtaining for the first time a point of importance for determining the topography of the ancient city.

The people whose remains have been found by Professor Petrie buried their dead in open graves without mummifying them, and made use of implements and weapons of polished stone. Their pottery, which is frequently ornamented with concentric rings of red on a whitish ground, has been already found at Khozâm, north of Karnak, and elsewhere, and the figures of giraffes, ostriches, and other creatures scratched on the sandstone rocks of Silsilis and its neighbourhood seem to have been in great measure their work. In the midst of their cemetery are the ruins of a temple built by Thothmes III. to 'Set the lord of Nubti,' the Ombos near Denderah to which Juvenal refers. As for the jewellery discovered in the spring of this year by Mr. de Morgan, it is even more marvellous than that which he found a year ago. Among it are two crowns of delicately-worked gold, one of which is ornamented with stars or forget-me-nots formed of precious stones inlaid so exquisitely as to look like enamel, while between the sprays are gold ornaments in the shape of what we should call St. Cuthbert's crosses.

The Serapeum at Alexandria, where the last of its great libraries was established, is now marked by the lofty column known as Pompey's Pillar. The column stood in the middle of a great central court, on one side of which were porticoes opening into the shrines of Serapis and his fellow deities, while to the east it led into a hall with a cupola, which again opened into a propylæum. From this there was a descent of a hundred steps into the lower ground at the foot of the rock on which the building stood. There was no other access to the edifice, which, like the other temples of Egypt, was used as a fortress as well as a sanctuary, and is accordingly called the Acropolis of Alexandria by Aphthonios, a Greek orator who visited it about A.D. 315 and gave a minute description of it. Dr. Botti has found remains of the gilding and sculptures with which, according to Aphthonios, the great court was adorned, as well as inscriptions dedicated to Serapis, and the basin of a sacred fountain which the Greek orator tells us was situated in the central court. But his most interesting discovery is that of long subterranean passages, once faced with masonry, and furnished with niches for lamps, where the mysteries of Serapis were celebrated. At the entrance of one of them pious visitors to the shrine have scratched their vows on the wall of rock. Those who are interested in the discovery should consult Dr. Botti's memoir on *L'Acropole d'Alexandrie et le Sérapeum*, presented to the Archæological Society of Alexandria, 17th August 1895.

Two or three other recent discoveries may also find mention here. A Babylonian seal-cylinder now in the Metropolitan Museum of Art at New York has at last given me a clue to the native home of the Hyksos leaders. This was in the mountains of Elam, on the eastern frontier of Chaldæa. It was from these mountains that the Kassi descended upon Babylonia and founded a dynasty there which lasted for nearly 600 years, and the same movement which brought them into Babylonia may have sent other bands of them across Western Asia into Egypt. At all events, the inscription upon the seal shows that it belonged to a certain Uzi-Sutakh, 'the son of the Kassite,' and 'the servant of Burna-buryas,' who was the Kassite king of Babylonia in the age of the Tel el-Amarna correspondence. As the name of Sutakh is preceded by the determinative of divinity, it is clear that we have in it the name of the Hyksos deity Sutekh.

In a hieroglyphic stela lately discovered at Saqqârah, and now in the Gizeh Museum, we read of an earlier parallel to the Tyrian Camp at Memphis seen by Herodotos. We learn from the stela that, in the time of King Ai, in the closing days of the eighteenth dynasty, there was already a similar 'Camp' or quarter at Memphis which was assigned to the Hittites. The inscription is further interesting as showing that the authority of Ai was acknowledged at Memphis, the capital of Northern Egypt, as well as in the Thebaid.

Lastly, Professor Hommel seems to have

found the name of the Zakkur or Zakkal, the kinsfolk and associates of the Philistines, in a broken cuneiform text which relates to one of the Kassite kings of Babylonia not long before the epoch of Khu-n-Aten. Here mention is made not only of the city of Arka in Phœnicia, but also of the city of Zaqqalû. In Zaqqalû we must recognise the Zakkur of Egyptian history. I may add that Khar or Khal, the name given by the Egyptians to the southern portion of Palestine, is identified by Professor Maspero with the Horites of the Old Testament.

By way of conclusion, I have only to say that those who wish to read a detailed account of the manner in which the great colossus of Ramses II. at Memphis was raised and its companion statue disinterred must refer to the Paper published by Major Arthur H. Bagnold himself in the *Proceedings* of the Society of Biblical Archæology for June 1888.

A. H. SAYCE.

October 1895.

CONTENTS

CHAPTER I
	PAGE
THE PATRIARCHAL AGE	1

CHAPTER II
| THE AGE OF MOSES | 52 |

CHAPTER III
| THE EXODUS AND THE HEBREW SETTLEMENT IN CANAAN | 80 |

CHAPTER IV
| THE AGE OF THE ISRAELITISH MONARCHIES | 104 |

CHAPTER V
| THE AGE OF THE PTOLEMIES | 134 |

CHAPTER VI
| HERODOTOS IN EGYPT | 175 |

CHAPTER VII
| IN THE STEPS OF HERODOTOS | 206 |

CHAPTER VIII
| MEMPHIS AND THE FAYYÛM | 242 |

APPENDICES

	PAGE
I. THE EGYPTIAN DYNASTIES ACCORDING TO MANETHO (AS QUOTED BY JULIUS AFRICANUS, A.D. 220), ETC.	287
II. THE PTOLEMIES	315
III. BIBLICAL DATES	316
IV. THE NOMES (HESEPU)	318
V. THE GREEK WRITERS UPON EGYPT	326
VI. ARCHÆOLOGICAL EXCURSIONS IN THE DELTA	*331
INDEX	335

THE EGYPT OF THE HEBREWS AND HERODOTOS

CHAPTER I

THE PATRIARCHAL AGE

'ABRAM went down into Egypt to sojourn there.' When he entered the country the civilisation and monarchy of Egypt were already very old. The pyramids had been built hundreds of years before, and the origin of the Sphinx was already a mystery. Even the great obelisk of Heliopolis, which is still the object of an afternoon drive to the tourist at Cairo, had long been standing in front of the temple of the Sun-god.

The monuments of Babylonia enable us to fix the age to which Abraham belongs. Arioch of Ellasar has left memorials of himself on the bricks of Chaldæa, and we now know when he and his Elamite allies were driven out of Babylonia and the

Babylonian states were united into a single monarchy. This was 2350 B.C.

The united monarchy of Egypt went back to a far earlier date. Menes, its founder, had been king of This (or Girgeh) in Upper Egypt, and starting from his ancestral dominions had succeeded in bringing all Egypt under his rule. But the memory of an earlier time, when the valley of the Nile was divided into two separate sovereignties, survived to the latest age of the monarchy. Up to the last the Pharaohs of Egypt called themselves 'kings of the two lands,' and wore on their heads the crowns of Upper and Lower Egypt. The crown of Upper Egypt was a tiara of white linen, that of Lower Egypt a throne-like head-dress of red. The double crown was a symbol of the imperial power.

To Menes is ascribed the building of Memphis, the capital of the united kingdom. He is said to have raised the great dyke which Linant de Bellefonds identifies with that of Kosheish near Kafr el-Ayyât, and thereby to have diverted the Nile from its ancient channel under the Libyan plain. On the ground that he thus added to the western bank of the river his new capital was erected.

Memphis is the Greek form of the old Egyptian Men-nefer or 'Good Place.' The final *r* was dropped in Egyptian pronunciation at an early date, and thus arose the Hebrew forms of the name, Moph and Noph, which we find in the Old Testament,[1] while 'Memphis' itself—Mimpi in the cuneiform inscriptions of Assyria—has the same origin. Another name by which it went in old Egyptian times was Anbu-hez, 'the white wall,' from the great wall of brick, covered with white stucco, which surrounded it, and of which traces still remain on the northern side of the old site. Here a fragment of the ancient fortification still rises above the mounds of the city; the wall is many feet thick, and the sun-dried bricks of which it is formed are bonded together with the stems of palms.

In the midst of the mounds is a large and deep depression, which is filled with water during the greater part of the year. It marks the site of the sacred lake, which was attached to every Egyptian temple, and in which the priests bathed themselves and washed the vessels of the sanctuary. Here, not long ago, lay the huge colossus of limestone which represented Ramses II. of the nineteenth dynasty, and had been presented by the Egyptian Khedive to the British Government. But it was too heavy and unwieldy for modern engineers to carry across the sea, and it was therefore left lying with its face prone in the mud and water of the ancient lake, a prey to

---

[1] Hosea ix. 6; Isaiah xix. 13; Jeremiah ii. 16.

the first comer who needed a quarry of stone. It was not until after the English occupation of Egypt that it was lifted out of its ignoble position by Major Bagnold and placed securely in a wooden shed. While it was being raised another colossus of the same Pharaoh, of smaller size but of better workmanship, was discovered, and lifted beyond the reach of the inundation.

The two statues once stood before the temple of the god Ptah, whom the Greeks identified with their own deity Hephæstos, for no better reason than the similarity of name. The temple of Ptah was coeval with the city of Memphis itself. When Menes founded Memphis, he founded the temple at the same time. It was the centre and glory of the city, which was placed under the protection of its god. Pharaoh after Pharaoh adorned and enlarged it, and its priests formed one of the most powerful organisations in the kingdom.

The temple of Ptah, the Creator, gave to Memphis its sacred name. This was Hâ-ka-Ptah, 'the house of the double (or spiritual appearance) of Ptah,' in which Dr. Brugsch sees the original of the Greek Aigyptos.

But the glories of the temple of Ptah have long since passed away. The worship of its god ceased for ever when Theodosius, the Roman Emperor, closed its gates, and forbade any other religion save the Christian to be henceforth publicly professed in the empire. Soon afterwards came the Mohammedan conquest of Egypt. Memphis was deserted; and the sculptured stones of the ancient shrine served to build the palaces and mosques of the new lords of the country. Fostât and Cairo were built out of the spoils of the temple of Ptah. But the work of destruction took long to accomplish. As late as the twelfth century, the Arabic writer 'Abd el-Latîf describes the marvellous relics of the past which still existed on the site of Memphis. Colossal statues, the bases of gigantic columns, a chapel formed of a single block of stone and called 'the green chamber'— such were some of the wonders of ancient art which the traveller was forced to admire.

The history of Egypt, as we have seen, begins with the record of an engineering feat of the highest magnitude. It is a fitting commencement for the history of a country which has been wrested by man from the waters of the Nile, and whose existence even now is dependent on the successful efforts of the engineer. Beyond this single record, the history of Menes and his immediate successors is virtually a blank. No dated monuments of the first dynasty have as yet been discovered. It may be, as many Egyptologists think, that the Sphinx is older than

Menes himself; but if so, that strange image, carved out of a rock which may once have jutted into the stream of the Nile, still keeps the mystery of its origin locked up in its breast. We know that it was already there in the days of Khephrên of the fourth dynasty; but beyond that we know nothing.

Of the second dynasty a dated record still survives. Almost the first gift received by the Ashmolean Museum at Oxford was the lintel-stone of an ancient Egyptian tomb, brought from Saqqârah, the necropolis of Memphis, by Dr. Greaves at the end of the seventeenth century. When, more than a century later, the hieroglyphics upon it came to be read, it was found that it had belonged to the sepulchre of a certain Sheri who had been the 'prophet' of the two Pharaohs Send and Per-ab-sen. Of Per-ab-sen no other record remains, but the name of Send had long been known as that of a king of the second dynasty.

The rest of Sheri's tomb, so far as it has been preserved, is now in the Gizeh Museum. Years after the inscription on the fragment at Oxford had been deciphered, the hinder portion of the tomb was discovered by Mariette. Like the lintel-stone in the Ashmolean Museum, it is adorned with sculptures and hieroglyphics. Already, we learn from it, the hieroglyphic system of writing was complete, the

The Patriarchal Age

characters being used not only to denote ideas and express syllables, but alphabetically as well. The name of Send himself is spelt in the letters of the alphabet. The art of the monument, though not equal to that which prevailed a few generations later, is already advanced, while the texts show that the religion and organisation of the empire were already old. In the age of the second dynasty, at all events, we are far removed from the beginnings of Egyptian civilisation.

With Snefru, the first king of the fourth dynasty, or, according to another reckoning, the last king of the third, we enter upon the monumental history of Egypt. Snefru's monuments are to be found, not only in Egypt, but also in the deserts of Sinai. There the mines of copper and malachite were worked for him, and an Egyptian garrison kept guard upon the Bedouin tribes. In Egypt, as has now been definitely proved by Professor Petrie's excavations, he built the pyramid of Medûm, one of the largest and most striking of the pyramids. Around it were ranged the tombs of his nobles and priests, from which have come some of the most beautiful works of art in the Gizeh Museum.

The painted limestone statues of Ra-nefer and his wife Nefert, for instance, are among the finest existing specimens of ancient Egyptian workmanship. They are clearly life-like portraits, executed with a delicacy and finish which might well excite the envy of a modern artist. The character, and even the antecedents of the husband and wife, breathe through their features. While in the one we can see the strong will and solid common-sense of the self-made man, in the other can be traced the culture and refinement of a royal princess.

The pyramids of Gizeh are the imperishable record of the fourth dynasty. Khufu, Khaf-Ra and Men-ka-Ra, the Kheops, Khephrên and Mykerinos of Herodotos, were the builders of the three vast sepulchres which, by their size and nearness to Cairo, have so long been an object of pilgrimage to the traveller. The huge granite blocks of the Great Pyramid of Khufu have been cut and fitted together with a marvellous exactitude. Professor Petrie found that the joints of the casing-stones, with an area of some thirty-five square feet each, were not only worked with an accuracy equal to that of the modern optician, but were even cemented throughout. 'Though the stones were brought as close as $\frac{1}{500}$ inch, or, in fact, into contact, and the mean opening of the joint was $\frac{1}{50}$ inch, yet the builders managed to fill the joint with cement, despite the great area of it and the weight of the stone to be moved—some sixteen tons. To merely place such stones in exact contact at the sides would be careful work; but to do so with cement in the joints seems almost impossible.'[1]

Professor Petrie believes that the stones were cut with tubular drills fitted with jewel points—a mode of cutting stone which it was left to the nineteenth century to re-discover. The lines marked upon the stone by the drills can still be observed, and there is evidence that not only the tool but the stone also was rotated. The great pressure needed for driving the drills and saws with the requisite rapidity through the blocks of granite and diorite is indeed surprising. It brings before us the high mechanical knowledge attained by the Egyptians in the fourth millennium before our era even more forcibly than the heights to which the blocks were raised. The machinery, however, with which this latter work was effected is still unknown.

The sculptured and painted walls of the tombs which surround the pyramids of Gizeh tell us something about the life and civilisation of the period. The government was a highly organised bureaucracy, under a king who was already regarded as the representative of the Sun-god upon earth. The land was inhabited by an industrious people, mainly agricultural, who lived in peace and plenty. Arts

[1] *Pyramids and Temples of Gizeh* (first edition), p. 44.

and crafts of all kinds were cultivated, including that of making glass. The art of the sculptor had reached a high perfection. One of the most striking statues in the world is that of Khaf-Ra seated on his imperial throne, which is now in the Museum of Gizeh. The figure of the king is more than life-size; above his head the imperial hawk stretches forth its wings, and on the king's face, though the features bear the unmistakable impress of a portrait, there rests an aspect of divine calm. And yet this statue, with its living portraiture and exquisite finish, is carved out of a dioritic rock, the hardest of hard stone.

The fourth dynasty was peaceably succeeded by the fifth and the sixth. Culture and cultivation made yet further progress, and the art of the painter and sculptor reached its climax. Those whose knowledge of Egyptian art is derived from the museums of Europe have little idea of the perfection which it attained at this remote period. The hard and crystallised art of later ages differed essentially from that of the early dynasties. The wooden figure of the 'Sheikh el-Beled'—the sleek and well-to-do farmer, who gazes complacently on his fertile fields and well-stocked farm—is one of the noblest works of human genius. And yet it belongs to the age of the fifth or the sixth dynasty, like the pictures in low relief, resembling exquisite embroidery on stone,

The Patriarchal Age

which cover the walls of the tombs of Ti and Ptah-hotep at Saqqârah.

The first six dynasties constitute what Egyptologists call the Old Empire. They ended with a queen, Nit-aqer (the Greek Nitôkris), and Egypt passed under sudden eclipse. For several centuries it lies concealed from the eye of history. A few royal names alone are preserved; other records there are as yet none. What befell the country and its rulers we do not know. Whether it was foreign invasion or civil war, or the internal decay of the government, certain it is that disaster overshadowed for a while the valley of the Nile. It may be that the barbarian tribes, whose tombs Professor Petrie has lately discovered in the desert opposite Qoft, and whom he believes to have been of Libyan origin, were the cause. With the tenth dynasty light begins again to dawn. Mr. Griffith has shown that some at least of the tombs cut out of the cliffs behind Siût belonged to that era, and that Ka-meri-Ra, whose name appears in one of them, was a king of the tenth dynasty. The fragmentary inscription, which can still be traced on the walls of the tomb, seems to allude to the successful suppression of a civil war.

The eleventh dynasty arose at Thebes, of which its founders were the hereditary chiefs. It introduces us to the so-called Middle Empire. But the Egypt of the Middle Empire was no longer the Egypt of the Old Empire. The age of the great pyramid-builders was past, and the tomb carved in the rock begins to take the place of the pyramid of the earlier age. Memphis has ceased to be the capital of the country; the centre of power has been transferred to Thebes and the south. The art which flourished at Memphis has been superseded by the art with which our museums have made us familiar. With the transfer of the government, moreover, from north to south, Egyptian religion has undergone a change. Ptah of Memphis and Ra of Heliopolis have had to yield to Amon, the god of Thebes. The god of the house of the new Pharaohs now takes his place at the head of the pantheon, and the older gods of the north fall more and more into the background.

The Egypt of the Middle Empire was divided among a number of great princes, who had received their power and property by inheritance, and resembled the great lords of the feudal age. The Pharaoh at first was little more than the chief among his peers. But when the sceptre passed into the vigorous hands of the kings of the twelfth dynasty, the influence and authority of the feudal princes was more and more encroached upon. A firm government at home and successful campaigns abroad restored the supreme rule of the Pharaoh and made

The Patriarchal Age

him, perhaps more than had ever been the case before, a divinely-instituted autocrat.

The wars of the twelfth dynasty extended the Egyptian domination far to the south. The military organisation of the Middle Empire was indeed its most striking point of contrast to the Old Empire. The Egypt of the first six dynasties had been self-contained and pacific. A few raids were made from time to time against the negroes south of the First Cataract, but only for the sake of obtaining slaves. The idea of extending Egyptian power beyond the natural boundaries of Egypt had as yet never presented itself. The Pharaohs of the Old Empire did not need an army, and accordingly did not possess one. But with the Middle Empire all this was changed. Egypt ceases to be isolated: its history will be henceforth part of the history of the world. Foreign wars, however, and the organisation of a strong government at home, did not absorb the whole energies of the court. Temples and obelisks were erected, art was patronised, and the creation of the Fayyûm, whereby a large tract of fertile land was won for Egypt, not only proved the high engineering skill of the age of the twelfth dynasty, but constituted a solid claim for gratitude to its creator, Amon-em-hat III., on the part of all succeeding generations.

The thirteenth dynasty followed in the footsteps of

its predecessor. We possess the names of more than one hundred and fifty kings who belonged to it, and their monuments were scattered from one end of Egypt to the other. The fourteenth dynasty ended in disaster. Egypt was invaded by Asiatic hordes, and the line of native Pharaohs was for a time extinct.

The invaders were called by Manetho, the Egyptian historian, the Hyksos or Shepherd Princes: on the monuments they are known as the Aamu or 'Asiatics.' At first, we are told, their progress was marked by massacre and destruction. The temples were profaned and overthrown, the cities burned with fire. But after a while the higher culture of the conquered people overcame the conquerors. A king arose among the invaders who soon adopted the prerogatives and state of the Pharaohs. The fifteenth, sixteenth, and seventeenth dynasties were Hyksos.

Recent discoveries have proved that at one time the dominion of the Hyksos extended, if not to the first cataract, at all events far to the south of Thebes. Their monuments have been found at Gebelên and El-Kab. Gradually, however, the native princes recovered their power in Upper Egypt. While the seventeenth Hyksos dynasty was reigning at Zoan, or Tanis, in the north, a seventeenth Egyptian dynasty was ruling at Thebes. But the princes of Thebes did not as yet venture to claim the imperial title. They still acknowledged the supremacy of the foreign Pharaoh.

The war of independence broke out in the reign of the Hyksos king Apopi. According to the Egyptian legend, Apopi had sent messengers to the prince of Thebes, bidding him worship none other god than Baal-Sutekh, the Hyksos divinity. But Amon-Ra of Thebes avenged the dishonour that had been done him, and stirred up his adorers to successful revolt. For five generations the war went on, and ended with the complete expulsion of the stranger. Southern Egypt first recovered its independence, then Memphis fell, and finally the Hyksos conquerors were driven out of Zoan, their capital, and confined to the fortress of Avaris, on the confines of Asia. But even here they were not safe from the avenging hand of the Egyptian. Ahmes I., the founder of the eighteenth dynasty, drove them from their last refuge and pursued them into Palestine.

The land which had sent forth its hordes to conquer Egypt was now in turn to be conquered by the Egyptians. The war was carried into Asia, and the struggle for independence became a struggle for empire. Under the Pharaohs of the eighteenth dynasty, Egypt, for the first time in its history, became a great military state. Army after army poured out of the gates of Thebes, and brought back to it the spoils of the known world. Ethiopia and Syria alike felt the tread of the Egyptian armies, and had alike to bow the neck to Egyptian rule. Canaan became an Egyptian province, Egyptian garrisons were established in the far north on the frontiers of the Hittite tribes, and the boundaries of the Pharaoh's empire were pushed to the banks of the Euphrates.

It is probable that Abraham did not enter Egypt until after the Hyksos conquest. But before the rise of the eighteenth dynasty Egyptian chronology is uncertain. We have to reckon it by dynasties rather than by years. According to Manetho, the Old Empire lasted 1478 years, and a considerable interval must be allowed for the troublous times which intervened between its fall and the beginning of the Middle Empire. We learn from the Turin papyrus—a list of the Egyptian kings and dynasties compiled in the time of Ramses II., but now, alas! in tattered fragments—that the tenth dynasty lasted 355 years and 10 days, the eleventh dynasty 243 years. The duration of the twelfth dynasty is known from the monuments (165 years 2 months), that of the thirteenth, with its more than one hundred and fifty kings, cannot have been short. How long the Hyksos rule endured it is difficult to say. Africanus,

The Patriarchal Age

quoting from Manetho, as Professor Erman has shown, makes it 953 years, with which the fragment quoted by Josephus from the Egyptian historian also agrees. In this case the Hyksos conquest of Egypt would have taken place about 2550 B.C.

Unfortunately the original work of Manetho is lost, and we are dependent for our knowledge of it on later writers, most of whom sought to harmonise its chronology with that of the Septuagint. When we further remember the corruptions undergone by numerical figures in passing through the hands of the copyists, it is clear that we cannot place implicit confidence in the Manethonian numbers as they have come down to us. Indeed, the writers who have recorded them do not always agree together, and we find the names of kings arbitrarily omitted or the length of their reigns shortened in order to force the chronology into agreement with that of the author. The twelfth dynasty reigned 134 years according to Eusebius, 160 years according to Africanus; its real duration was 165 years, 2 months, and 12 days.

With the help of certain astronomical data furnished by the monuments, Dr. Mahler, the Viennese astronomer, has succeeded in determining the exact date of the reigns of the two most famous monarchs of the eighteenth and nineteenth dynasties,

Thothmes III. and Ramses II. Thothmes III. reigned from the 20th of March B.C. 1503 to the 14th of February B.C. 1449, while the reign of Ramses II. lasted from B.C. 1348 to B.C. 1281. The date of Thothmes III. enables us to fix the beginning of the eighteenth dynasty about B.C. 1570.

The dynasties of Manetho were successive and not contemporaneous. This fact was one of the main results of the excavations and discoveries of Mariette Pasha. The old attempts to form artificial schemes of chronology—which, however, satisfied no one but their authors—upon the supposition that some of the dynasties reigned together are now discredited for ever. Every fresh discovery made in Egypt, which adds to our knowledge of ancient Egyptian history, makes the fact still more certain. There were epochs, indeed, when more than one line of kings claimed sway in the valley of the Nile, but when such was the case, Manetho selected what he or his authorities considered the sole legitimate dynasty, and disregarded every other. Of the two rival twenty-first dynasties which the monuments have brought to light, the lists of Manetho recognise but one, and the Assyrian rule in Egypt at a subsequent date is ignored in favour of the princes of Sais who were reigning at the same time.

If, then, any reliance is to be placed on the length

of time ascribed to the Hyksos dominion in the valley of the Nile, and if we are still to hold to the old belief of Christendom and see in the Hebrew wanderer into Egypt the Abram who contended against Chedor-laomer and the subject kings of Babylonia, it would have been about two centuries after the settlement of the Asiatic conquerors in the Delta that Abraham and Sarah arrived at their court. The court was doubtless held at Zoan, the modern Sân. Here was the Hyksos capital, and its proximity to the Asiatic frontier of Egypt made it easy of access to a traveller from Palestine. We are told in the Book of Numbers (xiii. 22) that Hebron was built seven years before Zoan in Egypt; and it may be that the building here referred to was that which caused Zoan to become the seat of the Hyksos power.

Asiatic migration into Egypt was no new thing. On the walls of one of the tombs of Beni-Hassan there is pictured the arrival of thirty-seven Aamu or Asiatics 'of Shu,' in the sixth year of Usertesen II. of the twelfth dynasty. Under the conduct of their chief, Ab-sha, they came from the mountains of the desert, bringing with them gazelles as well as kohl for the ladies of the court. Four women in long bright-coloured robes walk between groups of bearded men, and two children are carried in a pannier on a donkey's back. The men are armed with bows, their feet are shod with sandals, and they wear the vari-coloured garments for which the people of Phœnicia were afterwards famed.

After the Hyksos conquest Asiatic migration must naturally have largely increased. Between northern Egypt and Palestine there must have been a constant passage to and fro. The rulers of the land of the Nile were now themselves of Asiatic extraction, and it may be that the language of Palestine was spoken in the court of the Pharaoh. At all events, the emigrant from Canaan no longer found himself an alien and a stranger in 'the land of Ham.' His own kin were now supreme there, and a welcome was assured to him whenever he might choose to come. The subject population tilled their fields for the benefit of their foreign lords, and the benefit was shared by the inhabitants of Canaan. In case of famine, Palestine could now look to the never-failing soil of Egypt for its supply of corn.

If, therefore, Abraham lived in the age when northern Egypt was subject to the rule of the Hyksos Pharaohs, nothing was more natural than for him, an Asiatic emigrant into Canaan, to wander into Egypt when the corn of Palestine had failed. He would but be following in the wake of that larger Asiatic migration which led to the rise of the Hyksos dynasties themselves.

There is, however, a statement connected with his residence at the court of the Pharaoh which does not seem compatible with the evidence of the monuments. We are told that among the gifts showered upon him by the king were not only sheep and oxen and asses, but camels as well. The camel was the constant companion of the Asiatic nomad. As far back as we can trace the history of the Bedouin, he has been accompanied by the animal which the old Sumerian population of Babylonia called the beast which came from the Persian Gulf. Indeed, it would appear that to the Bedouin belongs the credit of taming the camel, in so far as it has been tamed at all. But to the Egyptians it was practically unknown. Neither in the hieroglyphics, nor on the sculptured and painted walls of the temples and tombs, do we anywhere find it represented. The earliest mention of it yet met with in an Egyptian document is in a papyrus of the age of the Exodus, and there it bears the Semitic name of *kamail*, the Hebrew *gamal*.[1] Naturalists have shown that it was not introduced into the northern coast of Africa until after the beginning of the Christian era.

Nevertheless it does not follow that because the camel was never used in Egypt by the natives of the country, it was not at times brought there by

[1] *Pap. Anastasi*, i. p. 23, line 5.

nomad visitors from Arabia and Palestine. It is difficult to conceive of an Arab family on the march without a train of camels. And that camels actually found their way into the valley of the Nile has been proved by excavation. When Hekekyan Bey, in 1851-54, was sinking shafts in the Nile mud at Memphis for the Geological Society of London, he found, among other animal remains, the bones of dromedaries.[1]

The name of the Pharaoh visited by Abraham is not told to us. As elsewhere in Genesis, the king of Egypt is referred to only by his official title. This title of 'Pharaoh' was one which went back to the early days of the monarchy. It represents the Egyptian Per-âa, or 'Great House,' and is of repeated occurrence in the inscriptions. All power and government emanated from the royal palace, and accordingly, just as we speak of the 'Sublime Porte' or 'Lofty Gate' when we mean the Sultan of Turkey, so the Egyptians spoke of their own sovereign as the Pharaoh or 'Great House.' To this day the king of Japan is called the Mi-kado, or 'Lofty Gate.'

That the Hyksos princes should have assumed the title of their predecessors on the throne of Egypt

---

[1] Horner, in the *Philosophical Transactions of the Royal Society*, 1855-58.

The Patriarchal Age 23

is not surprising. The monuments have shown us how thoroughly Egyptianised they soon became. The court of the Hyksos Pharaoh differed but little, if at all, from that of the native Pharaoh. The invaders rapidly adopted the culture of the conquered people, and with it their manners, customs, and even language. The most famous mathematical treatise which Egypt has bequeathed to us was written for a Hyksos king. It may be that the old language of Asia was retained, at all events for a time, by the side of the language of the subject population; but if so, its position must have been like that of Turkish by the side of Arabic in Egypt during the reign of Mohammed Ali. For several centuries the Hyksos could be described as Egyptians, and the dynasties of the Hyksos Pharaohs are counted by the Egyptian historian among the legitimate dynasties of his country.

It was only in the matter of religion that the Hyksos court kept itself distinct from its native subjects. The supreme god of the Hyksos princes was Sutekh, in whom we must see a form of the Semitic Baal. As has already been stated, Egyptian legend ascribed the origin of the war of independence to a demand on the part of the Hyksos Pharaoh Apopi that the prince and the god of Thebes should acknowledge the supremacy of the

Hyksos deity. But even in the matter of religion the Hyksos princes could not help submitting to the influence of the old Egyptian civilisation. Ra, the sun-god of Heliopolis, was identified with Sutekh, and even Apopi added to his name the title of Ra, and so claimed to be an incarnation of the Egyptian sun-god, like the native Pharaohs who had gone before him.

When next we hear of Egypt in the Old Testament, it is when Israel is about to become a nation. Joseph was sold by his brethren to merchants from Arabia, who carried him into Egypt. There he became the slave of Potiphar, 'the eunuch of Pharaoh and chief of the executioners,' or royal body-guard. The name of Potiphar, like that of Potipherah, the priest of On, corresponds with the Egyptian Pa-tu-pa-Ra, 'the Gift of the Sun-god.' It has been asserted by Egyptologists that names of this description are not older than the age of the twenty-second dynasty, to which Shishak, the contemporary of Rehoboam, belonged; but because no similar name of an earlier date has hitherto been found, it does not follow that such do not exist. As long as our materials are imperfect, we cannot draw positive conclusions merely from an absence of evidence.

That Potiphar should have been an eunuch and yet been married seems a greater obstacle to our acceptance of the story. This, however, it need not be. Eunuchs in the modern East, who have risen to positions of power and importance, have possessed their harems like other men. In ancient Babylonia it was only the service of religion which the eunuch was forbidden to enter. Such was doubtless the case in Egypt also.

Egyptian research has brought to light a curious parallel to the history of Joseph and Potiphar's wife. It is found in one of the many tales, the equivalents of the modern novel, in which the ancient Egyptians delighted. The tale, which is usually known as that of 'The Two Brothers,' was written by the scribe Enna for Seti II. of the nineteenth dynasty when he was still crown-prince, and it embodies the folk-lore of his native land. Enna lived under Meneptah, the probable Pharaoh of the Exodus, and his work was thus contemporaneous with the events which brought about the release of the Israelites from their 'house of bondage.' How old the stories may be upon which it is based it is impossible for us to tell.

Here is Professor Erman's translation of the commencement of the tale :—

'Once upon a time there were two brothers, born of one mother and of one father; the elder was called Anup, the younger Bata. Now Anup possessed a house and had a wife, whilst his younger brother lived with him as a son. He it was who wove (?) for him, and drove his cattle to the fields, who ploughed and reaped; he it was who directed all the business of the farm for him. The younger brother was a good (farmer); the like of whom was not to be found throughout the country.' One day Anup sent Bata from the field to the house to fetch seed-corn. 'And he sent his younger brother,[1] and said to him: Hasten and bring me seed-corn from the village. And his younger brother found the wife of his elder brother occupied in combing her hair. And he said to her: Rise up, give me seed-corn that I may return to the field, for thus has my elder brother enjoined me, to return without delaying. The woman said to him: Go in, open the chest, that thou mayst take what thine heart desires, for otherwise my locks will fall to the ground. And the youth went within into the stable, and took thereout a large vessel, for it was his will to carry out much seed-corn. And he loaded himself with wheat and dhurra and went out with it. Then she said to him: How great is the burden in thy arms? He said to her: Two measures of dhurra and three measures of wheat make together five measures which rest on my arms. Thus he spake to her. But she spake to

---

[1] Brugsch's translation, *Egypt under the Pharaohs*, Eng. trans. first edition, i. p. 266.

the youth and said: How great is thy strength! Well have I remarked thy power many a time. And her heart knew him. . . . And she stood up and laid hold of him and said unto him: Come let us celebrate an hour's repose; the most beautiful things shall be thy portion, for I will prepare for thee festal garments. Then was the youth like unto the panther of the south for rage on account of the wicked word which she had spoken to him. But she was afraid beyond all measure. And he spoke to her and said: Thou, oh woman, hast been like a mother to me and thy husband like a father, for he is older than I, so that he might have been my begetter. Wherefore this great sin that thou hast spoken unto me? Say it not to me another time, then will I this time not tell it, and no word of it shall come out of my mouth to any man at all. And he loaded himself with his burden and went out into the field. And he went to his elder brother, and they completed their day's work. And when it was evening, the elder brother returned home to his house. And his younger brother followed behind his oxen, having laden himself with all the good things of the field, and he drove his oxen before him to bring them to the stable. And behold the wife of his elder brother was afraid because of the word which she had spoken, and she took a jar of fat and was like to one to whom an evil-doer had offered violence, since she wished to say to her husband: Thy younger brother has offered me violence. And her husband returned home at evening, according to his daily custom, and found his wife lying stretched out and suffering from injury. She poured no water over his hands, as was her custom; she had not lighted the lights for him, so that his house was in darkness, and she lay there ill. And her husband said to her: Who has had to do with thee? Lift thyself up! She said to him: No one has had to do with me except thy younger brother, since when he came to take seed-corn for thee, he found me sitting alone and said to me, "Come, let us make merry an hour and repose: let down thy hair!" Thus he spake to me; but I did not listen to him (but said), "See! am I not thy mother, and is not thy elder brother like a father to thee?" Thus I spoke to him, but he did not hearken to my speech, but used force with me that I might not tell thee. Now if thou allow him to live I will kill myself.

'Then the elder brother began to rage like a panther: he sharpened his knife and took it in his hand. And the elder brother stood behind the door of the stable in order to kill the youth when he came back in the evening to bring the oxen into the stable. Now when the sun was setting and he had laden

The Patriarchal Age 29

himself with all the good things of the field, according to his custom, he returned (to the house). And his cow that first entered the stable said to him: Beware! there stands thy elder brother before thee with his knife in order to kill thee; run away from him! So he heard what the first cow said. Then the second entered and spake likewise. He looked under the door of the stable, and saw the feet of his brother, who was standing behind the door with his knife in his hand. He threw his burden on the ground and began to run away quickly. His elder brother ran after him with his knife in his hand.'

Ra, the sun-god, however, came to the help of the innocent youth, and interposed a river full of crocodiles between him and his pursuer. All night long the two brothers stood on either side of the water; in the morning Bata convinced his brother that he had done no wrong, and reproached him for having believed that he could be guilty. Then he added: 'Go home now and see after thine oxen thyself, for I will no longer stay with thee, but will go to the acacia valley.' So Anup returned to his house, put his wife to death, and sat there in solitude and sadness.

Joseph, more fortunate than Bata, rose from his prison to the highest office of state. The dreams, through which this was accomplished, were in full keeping with the belief of the age. Dreams even to-day play an important part in the popular faith of Egypt. In the days of the Pharaohs it was the same. Thothmes IV. cleared away the sand that had overwhelmed the Sphinx, and built a temple between its paws, in consequence of a dream in which Ra-Harmakhis had appeared to him when, wearied with hunting, he had lain down to sleep under the shadow of the ancient monument. A thousand years later Nut-Amon of Ethiopia was summoned by a dream to march into Egypt. In Greek days, when the temple of Abydos had fallen into ruin, an oracle was established in one of its deserted chambers, and those who consulted it received their answers in the 'true dreams' that came to them during the night. The dreams, however, needed at times an interpreter to explain them, and of such an interpreter mention is made in a Greek inscription from the Serapeum at Memphis. At other times the dreamer himself could interpret his vision by the help of the books in which the signification of dreams had been reduced to a science.

The dreams of Pharaoh and 'his two eunuchs,' however, 'the chief butler' and 'the chief baker,' were of a strange and novel kind, and there were no books that could explain them. Even the 'magicians' and 'wise men' of Egypt failed to understand the dream

The Patriarchal Age

of Pharaoh. And yet, when the Hebrew captive had pointed out its meaning, no doubt remained in the mind of Pharaoh and his servants that he was right. From time immemorial the Nile had been likened to a milch-cow, and the fertilising water which it spread over the soil to the milk that sustains human life. The cow-headed goddess Hathor or Isis watched over the fertility of Egypt. It was said of her that she 'caused the Nile to overflow at his due time,' and the 'seven great Hathors' were the seven forms under which she was worshipped. In the seven kine, accordingly, which stood 'upon the bank of the river' the Egyptian readily saw the life-giving powers of the Nile.

It needed but the word of the Pharaoh to change the Hebrew slave into an Egyptian ruler, second only to the monarch itself. His very name ceased to be Semitic, and henceforth became Zaphnath-paaneah. He even allied himself with the exclusive priesthood of Heliopolis or On, marrying Asenath, the daughter of the priest of Ra. By name and marriage, as well as by position, he was thus adopted into the ranks of the native aristocracy.

Such changes of name are not unknown to the inscriptions. From time to time we meet with the records of foreigners who had settled down in the valley of the Nile and there received new names of

Egyptian origin. Thus a monument found at Abydos tells us of a Canaanite from Bashan called Yu-pa-â, whose son Ben-Azan received in Egypt the new name of Ramses-em-per-Ra and was a vizier of Meneptah, the Pharaoh of the Exodus. The Hittite wife of Ramses II. similarly adopted an Egyptian name, and the tombstones of two Karians are preserved, in which the Karian names of the dead are written in the letters of the Karian alphabet, while a hieroglyphic text is attached which gives the Egyptian names they had borne in Egypt.

The exact transcription in hieroglyphics of the Egyptian name of Joseph is still doubtful. But it is plain that it contains the Egyptain words *pa-ânkh*, 'the life,' or 'the living one,' which seem to be preceded by the particle *nti*, 'of.' The term *pa-ânkh* is sometimes applied to the Pharaoh, and since Kames, the last king of the seventeenth dynasty, assumed the title of Zaf-n-to, 'nourisher of the land,' it is possible that in Zaphnath-paaneah we may see an Egyptian Zaf-nti-pa-ânkh, 'nourisher of the Pharaoh.' But the final solution of the question must be left to future research.

It is now more easy to explain the cry which was raised before Joseph when he went forth from the presence of the Pharaoh with the golden chain around his neck and the royal signet upon his finger.

'*Abrêk!*' they shouted before him, and an explanation of the word has been vainly sought in the Egyptian language. It really is of Babylonian origin. In the primitive non-Semitic language of Chaldæa *abrik* signified 'a seer' or 'soothsayer,' and the term was borrowed by the Semitic Babylonians under the two forms of *abrikku* and *abarakku*. Joseph was thus proclaimed a seer, and his exaltation was due to his power of foreseeing the future. It was as a divinely-inspired seer that the subjects of the Pharaoh were to reverence him.

How a Babylonian word like *abrek* came to be used in Egypt it is idle for us to inquire. Those who believe in the late origin and fictitious character of the story of Joseph would find an easy explanation of it. But easy explanations are not necessarily true, either in archæology or in anything else. And since we now know that Canaan, long before the time of Joseph, had fallen under Babylonian influence, that the Babylonian language and writing were employed there, and that Babylonian words had made their way into the native idiom, it does not require much stretch of the imagination to suppose that such words may have also penetrated to the court of the Asiatic rulers of northern Egypt. Up to the era of the Exodus, Egypt and Canaan were for several centuries as closely connected with each other as were England and the north of France in the age of the Normans and Plantagenets.

The prosperity of Egypt depends upon the Nile. If the river rises to too great a height during the period of inundation, the autumn crops are damaged or destroyed. If, on the other hand, its rise is insufficient to fill the canals and basins, or to reach the higher ground, the land remains unwatered, and nothing will grow. Egypt, in fact, is the gift of the Nile; let the channel of the great river be diverted elsewhere, and the whole country would at once become an uninhabited desert.

A low Nile consequently brings with it a scarcity of food. When provisions cannot be imported from abroad, famine is the necessary result, and the population perishes in thousands. Such was the case in the eleventh and twelfth centuries of our era, when the inundation was deficient for several successive years. The Arabic writers, El-Makrîzî and Abd-el-Latîf, describe the famines that ensued in terrible terms. Abd-el-Latîf was a witness of that which lasted from A.D. 1200 to 1202, and of the horrors which it caused. After eating grass, corpses, and even excrement, the wretched inhabitants of the country began to devour one another. Mothers were arrested in the act of cooking their own children, and it was unsafe to walk in the streets for fear of being murdered for food.

The Patriarchal Age

The famine described by El-Makrîzî lasted, like that of Joseph, for seven years, from A.D. 1064 to 1071, and was similarly occasioned by a deficient Nile. A hieroglyphic inscription, discovered in 1888 by Mr. Wilbour in the island of Sehêl, contains a notice of another famine of seven years, which occurred at an earlier date. The island of Sehêl lies in the Cataract, midway between Assouan and Philæ, and the inscription is carved on a block of granite and looks towards the south. It is dated in the eighteenth year of a king, who was probably one of the Ethiopian princes that reigned over southern Egypt in the troublous age of the fourth and fifth Ptolemies. According to Dr. Brugsch's translation, it states that the king sent to the governor of Nubia saying : 'I am sorrowing upon my high throne over those who belong to the palace. In sorrow is my heart for the vast misfortune, because the Nile flood in my time has not come for seven years. Light is the grain ; there is lack of crops and of all kinds of food. Each man has become a thief to his neighbour. They desire to hasten and cannot walk; the child cries, the youth creeps along and the old man ; their souls are bowed down. Their legs are bent together and drag along the ground, and their hands rest in their bosoms. The counsel of the great ones of the court is but emptiness. Torn open are the chests of provisions, but instead of contents there is air. Everything is exhausted.' The text then goes on to declare how Khnum the Creator came to the help of the Pharaoh, and caused the Nile once more to inundate the lands. In return for this the king gave the priests of Khnum at Elephantine twenty miles of river bank on either side of the island, together with tithes of all the produce of the country.

Dr. Brugsch has brought to light yet another record of a famine in Upper Egypt which belongs to an older period. Among the rock-cut tombs of El-Kab, where the princes of Thebes held their court in the days of the Hyksos, is one which commemorates the name of a certain Baba. The name occurs elsewhere at El-Kab, and was that of the father of 'Captain Ahmes,' whose tomb is one of the most interesting there, and who, in his youthful days, assisted Ahmes of the eighteenth dynasty in driving the Hyksos from their last fortress in Egypt. Baba enumerates his wealth and many good deeds, and adds: 'When a famine arose, lasting many years, I issued out corn to the city.'

It may be that the famine here referred to is the famine of Joseph. All we know about the date of Baba is that he lived in the age of the Hyksos. If he flourished before the war of independence and in

The Patriarchal Age 37

days when the authority of the Hyksos Pharaoh was still paramount in Upper Egypt, we should have good reason for believing that the famine of which he speaks was the same as that described in Genesis. One of the results of the latter was that the Egyptians parted with their lands and stock to Joseph, so that henceforth they became the tenants of the Pharaoh, to whom they paid a fifth of all their produce. If this statement is historical, the administration of Joseph must have extended from one end of Egypt to the other. His Hyksos master must have been like Apopi, of whom the Sallier Papyrus tells us that 'the entire country paid him tribute, together with its manufactured products, and so loaded him with all the good things of Egypt.'

The account of Joseph's famine, however, betrays in one respect a sign of later date. The famine is said to have extended to Caanan. But a famine in Egypt and a famine in Caanan were not due to the same cause, and the failure of the waters of the Nile would have no effect upon the crops of Palestine. In Canaan it was the want of rain, not of the inundation of the Nile, which produced a failure of corn. We hear from time to time, in the inscriptions, of corn being sent from Egypt to Syria, but it was when there was plenty on the banks of the Nile and a scarcity of rain on the Syrian coast. The Hebrew writer has regarded the history of the past from a purely Asiatic rather than an Egyptian point of view.

Joseph must have entered Egypt when it was still under Hyksos domination. The promise made to Abraham (Gen. xv. 13) is very explicit: 'Know of a surety that thy seed shall be a stranger in a land that is not theirs, and shall serve them; and they shall afflict them four hundred years.' Equally explicit is the statement of the book of Exodus (xii. 40, 41): 'The sojourning of the children of Israel who dwelt in Egypt was four hundred and thirty years. And it came to pass at the end of the four hundred and thirty years, even the self-same day it came to pass, that all the hosts of the Lord went out from the land of Egypt.' Here thirty years—the length of a generation—are added to the four hundred during which the Israelites were to be afflicted in the land of the foreigner. If the Exodus took place in the latter years of the nineteenth dynasty—and, as we shall see, the Egyptian monuments forbid our placing it elsewhere—the four hundred and thirty years of the Biblical narrative bring us to the beginning of the last Hyksos dynasty.

It is a curious fact that Egyptian history also knows of an epoch of four hundred years which covers almost the same period as the four hundred years of Genesis. Mariette Pasha, when excavating at Sân, the ancient Zoan, found a stela which had been erected in the reign of Ramses II. by one of his officers, the governor of the Asiatic frontier. The stela commemorates a visit to Sân made by the governor, on the fourth day of the month Mesori, in the four hundredth year of 'the king of Upper and Lower Egypt, Set-âa-pehti, the son of the Sun who loved him, also named Set-Nubti.' Since Set or Sutekh was the god of the Hyksos, while Sân was the Hyksos capital, it is clear that Set-âa-pehti or Set-Nubti was a Hyksos prince who claimed rule over the whole of Egypt, and with whom a Hyksos era commenced. Professor Maspero and Dr. de Cara consider the prince in question to have been really the god Sutekh himself; this, however, is not the natural interpretation of the titles assigned to him, and it is not improbable that Professor Wiedemann is right in identifying him with a certain Hyksos Pharaoh, Set-[Nub?]ti, mentioned on a monument discovered by Mariette at Tel-Mokdam. This latter Pharaoh is entitled 'the good god, the star of Upper and Lower Egypt, the son of the Sun, beloved by Sutekh, the lord of Avaris.'

But whether or not the Hyksos Pharaoh of Tel-Mokdam is the same as Set-Nubti of Sân, it would seem probable that the era connected with his name marked the rise of the last Hyksos dynasty. According to Eusebius, the leader of this dynasty was Saitês, a name which reminds us of Set-âa-[pehti]. Eusebius makes the length of the dynasty 103 years, but Africanus, a more trustworthy authority, gives it as 151 years. This would assign the rise of the seventeenth dynasty, the last of Hyksos rule, to about B.C. 1720, a date which agrees very well with that of the monument of Sân.[1] The Exodus of the Israelites, if it took place in the reign of Meneptah, would have happened about B.C. 1270 (or B.C. 1250, if it occurred in the reign of Seti II., as Professor Maspero maintains); in this case the 430 years of sojourning in the land of Egypt brings us to B.C. 1700 (or 1680). This would be about twenty years after the establishment of the last Hyksos line of Pharaohs, and one hundred and thirty years before the foundation of the eighteenth dynasty. Joseph would thus have been vizier of the country long before the war of independence broke out, and there would have been time in abundance for him to have lived and died before his friends and protectors were driven from the land they had so long occupied.

Chronologically, therefore, the Biblical narrative

---

[1] Ramses II. reigned from B.C. 1348 to 1281; if the stela of Sân had been erected in the twenty-eighth year of his reign, four hundred years would take us back to B.C. 1720. The Syrian wars were concluded by the treaty with the Hittites in the twenty-first year of his reign.

fits in with the requirements of Egyptian history, and allows us to see in the Hebrew captive the powerful minister of a race of kings who, like himself, had come from the highlands of Asia. But it must be remembered that it was only in the north of Egypt that Hyksos rule made itself actually visible to the eyes of the people. Southern Egypt was nominally governed by its native princes, though they did not assume the title of king or Pharaoh. They were *hiqu*, 'hereditary chieftains,' the last representatives of the royal families of earlier days. They acknowledged the supremacy of the Hyksos Pharaoh, and tribute was sent to him from Thebes and El-Kab.

Though Memphis, the ancient capital of the country, was in the hands of the strangers, Zoan, the Tanis of classical geography, was rather the seat of Hyksos power. Protected by the marshes which surrounded it, Zoan, the modern Sân, lay on the eastern side of the Delta at no great distance from the frontier of Asia and the great Hyksos fortress of Avaris. From Zoan, the 'road of the Philistines,' as it is called in the Pentateuch, ran almost in a straight line to Pelusium and the south of Palestine, skirting on one side the Mediterranean Sea, and leaving to the right the lofty fortress-rock of El-Arîsh on the waterless 'river of Egypt.'

Tanis had existed in the days of the Old Empire, but either the Hyksos conquest or earlier invasions had caused it to decay, and when the Hyksos court was established there its ancient temple was already in ruins. The restoration of the city was due to the Hyksos kings, who have left in it memorials of themselves. The Hyksos sphinxes in the Museum of Gizeh, on one of which the name of Apopi is engraved, were found there by Mariette, as well as a curious group of two persons with enormous wigs holding fish and water-fowl in their laps. When it is stated in the book of Numbers (xiii. 22) that 'Hebron was built seven years before Zoan,' it is probable that the building of Zoan by the Shepherd kings is meant.

In journeying from southern Palestine to Zoan, Jacob and his sons had no very long distance to traverse. Nor had they to pass through a long tract of Egyptian territory. From the desert, with its roving bands of kindred Bedouin, to the Pharaoh's court at Zoan, was hardly more than a day's journey. There was little fear that the Semitic traveller would meet with insult or opposition from the Egyptian *fellahin* on the way. The *fellahin* themselves were doubtless then, as now, mixed with Semitic elements; it was needful to go westward of Zoan in order to find Egyptians of pure blood.

The Patriarchal Age 43

Nor was the land of Goshen, the modern Wadi Tumilât, far from the Hyksos capital. It lay to the south of Zoan, on the banks of a canal whose course is now marked by the Freshwater Canal of Lesseps. The tourist who takes the train from Ismailîyeh to Zagazig traverses the whole length of the land of Goshen. The tradition that here was the territory assigned by Joseph to his brethren lingered long into the Christian centuries, and had been revived by more than one Egyptologist in later years. But the question was finally settled by Dr. Naville, and the excavations he undertook for the Egypt Exploration Fund. In 1883 he disinterred the remains of Pa-Tum, or Pithom, one of the two 'store-cities' which the children of Israel were forced to build. The ruins are now known as Tel el-Maskhuteh, 'the mound of the Statue,' about twelve miles to the south-east of Ismailîyeh, and the monuments discovered there show that the Pharaoh for whom the city was built was Ramses II. There was more than one Pa-Tum, or temple-city of the Sun-god of the evening, and the Pa-Tum of the eastern Delta is referred to in papyri of the nineteenth dynasty. Thus, in the eighth year of Meneptah II., an official report speaks of the passage of certain Shasu or Bedouin from Edom through the frontier-fortress of Thukut or Succoth, to 'the pools of the city of

Pa-Tum of Meneptah-hotep-hir-ma, in the district of Thukut.'

In 1884 Dr. Naville excavated, at Saft el-Henneh, an ancient mound close to the railway between Zagazig and Tel el-Kebîr. His excavations resulted in the discovery that Saft el-Henneh marks the site of the ancient Qesem or˙ Qos (Pha-kussa in the Greek geographers), the capital of the nome of the Egyptian Arabia. Qesem corresponds exactly with Geshem, which represents in the Septuagint the Hebrew Goshen, and points to the fact that the Egyptian Jews, to whom the Greek translation of the Old Testament was due, recognised in the Biblical Goshen the Qeshem of Egyptian geography.

The district immediately around Saft el-Henneh is fertile, but the name of the Egyptian Arabia which it once bore shows unmistakably who its cultivators must have been. They were the Semitic nomads from the East who, like their descendants to-day, occasionally settled on the frontier-lands of Egypt, and became more or less unwilling agriculturists. But the larger part of them remained shepherds, leading a nomad life with their flocks and camels, and pitching their tents wherever the monotony of the desert was broken by water and vegetation. The Wadi Tumilât, into which the district of Saft el-Henneh opened, was thus eminently suited for the residence of the Hebrew Bedouin. Here they had food for their flocks, plenty of space for their camping-grounds, and freedom from interference on the part of the Egyptians, while in the background was a fertile district, in close connection with the capital, where those of them who cared to exchange a pastoral for an agricultural life could find rich soil to sow and cultivate.

Hard by Zagazig are the mounds of the ancient Bubastis, and here the excavations carried on by the Egypt Exploration Fund have brought to light remains of the Hyksos Pharaohs, including one of Apopi. Bubastis, therefore, must have been a Hyksos residence, and its temple was adorned by the Hyksos kings. Between Bubastis and Heliopolis stood Pa-Bailos, and of this town Meneptah II says at Thebes that 'the country around was not cultivated, but left as pasture for cattle because of the strangers, having been abandoned since the times of old.' What better proof can we have that the Arabian nome was in truth what the land of Goshen is represented to be?

By a curious coincidence, the Wadi Tumilât, the old land of Goshen, has, in the present century, again been handed over to Bedouin and Syrians, and again been the scene of an Exodus. Mohammed Ali was anxious to establish the culture of the silk-worm in Egypt, and accordingly planted mulberry-trees in the Wadi Tumilât, and settled there a large colony of Syrians and Bedouin. The Bedouin were induced to remain there, partly by the pasturage provided for their flocks, partly by a promise of exemption from taxes and military conscription. When Abbas Pasha became Khedive, however, the promise was forgotten; orders were issued that the free Bedouin of the Wadi Tumilât should be treated like the enslaved *fellahin*, compelled to pay the tax-gatherer, and to see their children driven in handcuffs and with the courbash to serve in the army. . But the orders were never carried out. Suddenly, in a single night, without noise or warning, the whole Bedouin population deserted their huts, and with their flocks and other possessions disappeared into the eastern desert. The Pasha lost his slaves, the culture of the silk-worm ceased, and when the Freshwater Canal was cut not a single mulberry-tree remained.

In the land of Goshen, the Israelitish settlers throve and multiplied. But a time came when a new king arose 'which knew not Joseph,' and when the descendants of Jacob seemed to the Egyptians a source of danger. Like Abbas Pasha in a later century, the Pharaoh determined to reduce the free-born Israelites into the condition of public slaves, and by every means in his power to diminish their number. The male children were destroyed, the adults compelled to labour at the cities the Egyptian monarch was building in their neighbourhood, and the land in which they lived was surrounded by Egyptian garrisons and controlled by Egyptian officers.

The slaves, however, succeeded in escaping from their 'house of bondage.' Under the leadership of Moses they made their way into the eastern desert, and received, at Sinai and Kadesh-Barnea, the laws which were henceforth to govern them. The army sent to pursue them was swallowed up in the waters of the sea, and the district they had occupied was left desolate.

A variety of reasons had led Egyptologists to the belief that in the Pharaoh of the Oppression we were probably to see Ramses II. Ramses II., the Sesostris and Osymandyas of Greek story, was the third king of the nineteenth dynasty, and one of the most striking figures of Egyptian history. His long reign of sixty-seven years was the evening of Egyptian greatness. With his death the age of Egyptian conquests passed away, and the period of decay set in. Like Louis XIV. of France, the *grand monarque* of ancient Egypt exhausted in his wars the resources and fighting population of his country.

But it was as a builder rather than as a conqueror

that Ramses II. was famous. Go where we will in Egypt or Nubia, we find traces of his architectural activity. There is hardly a place where he has not left his name. His whole reign must have been occupied with the construction of cities and temples, or the restoration and enlargement of previously existing ones, and, in spite of its length, it is difficult to understand how so vast an amount of work could have been accomplished in the time. Much of the work, however, is poor and scamped; it bears, in fact, marks of the feverish haste with which it was carried through. Much of it, on the other hand, is grandiose and striking in its colossal proportions and boldness of design. The shattered granite colossus at the Ramesseum, once nearly sixty feet in height, the fragment of a standing figure of granite found by Professor Flinders Petrie at Sân, which must originally have been over a hundred feet high, the great hall of columns at Karnak, the temple of Abu-Simbel in Nubia, are all so many witnesses of vast conceptions successfully realised. Abu-Simbel, indeed, where a mountain has been hollowed into a temple, and a cliff carved into the likeness of four sitting figures, each with an unrivalled expression of divine calm upon its countenance, justly claims to be one of the wonders of the world.

Apart from the colossal proportions of so many of

The Patriarchal Age

them, the buildings of Ramses II. are distinguished by another trait. They were erected to the glory of the Pharaoh rather than of the gods. It is the name and titles of Ramses that everywhere force themselves upon our notice, and often constitute the chief decoration of the monument. He must have been vainglorious above all other kings of Egypt, filled with the pride of his own power and the determination that his name should never be forgotten upon the earth.

It is not strange, therefore, that Ramses II. should be the most prominent figure in ancient Egyptian history. His name and the shattered relics of his architectural triumphs force themselves upon the attention of the traveller wherever he goes.. His long reign, moreover, was a period of great literary activity, and a considerable portion of the literary papyri which have survived to us was written during his lifetime. He was, furthermore, the last of the conquering Pharaohs; the last of the Theban monarchs whose rule was obeyed from the mountains of Lebanon and the plateau of the Haurân to the southern frontiers of Ethiopia. With his death the empire, which had been founded by the military skill and energy of the kings of the eighteenth dynasty, began to pass away. His son and successor, Meneptah, had to struggle for bare existence against an invasion of barbarian hordes, and the sceptre dropped from the feeble hands of Seti II., who next followed, into those of rival kings. The nineteenth dynasty ended in the midst of civil war and foreign attack: for a while Egypt submitted to the rule of a Syrian stranger, and when Setnekht, the founder of the twentieth dynasty, restored once more the native line of kings, he found a ruined and impoverished country, scarcely able to protect itself from hostile assault.

But the age of the twentieth dynasty was still distant when Jacob and his sons journeyed into Egypt, or even when his descendants, under the leadership of Moses, succeeded in escaping from the land of their slavery. Before that age arrived more than one revolution was destined to pass over the valley of the Nile, which had momentous consequences for the foreign settlers in Goshen. The Hyksos were driven back into Asia, and a united Egypt once more obeyed the rule of a native Pharaoh.

But the centre of power had been shifted from the north to the south. Memphis and Zoan had to make way for Thebes, and it is probable that the monarchs of the eighteenth dynasty, under whom Egypt recovered its independence, had Nubian blood in their veins. A new life was breathed into the ancient kingdom of Menes, and for the first time in its history Egypt became a great military power. The war was transferred from the Delta to Asia itself;

The Patriarchal Age

Canaan and Syria were conquered, and an Egyptian empire established, which extended as far as the Euphrates. With this empire in Asia, however, came Asiatic influences, ideas, and beliefs. The Pharaohs intermarried with the royal families of Asia, and little by little their court became semi-Asiatic. Then followed reaction and counter-revolution. A new king arose—the founder of the nineteenth dynasty—'who knew not Joseph,' representing the national antagonism to the Asiatic foreigner and his religious faith. For a while the Asiatic was proscribed; and the expulsion of the stranger and his religion, which Arabi endeavoured to effect in our time, was successfully effected in the troublous days which saw the fall of the eighteenth dynasty. In this war against the hated Asiatic the Israelites were involved; their children were destroyed lest they should multiply, and they themselves were degraded into public slaves. We have now to trace the events which led to such a result, and to show how the political history of Egypt was the ultimate cause of the Israelitish Exodus.

CHAPTER II

THE AGE OF MOSES

ON the eastern bank of the Nile, about midway between Minieh and Assiout, the traveller from Cairo to Assouan passes a line of mounds which are known by the name of Tel el-Amarna. *Tel* is the name given to the artificial mounds which cover the remains of ancient cities, while *el-Amarna* denotes the Bedouin tribe of Beni-Amrân whose descendants inhabit the district in which the line of mounds is found. Between the mounds and the Nile is a fertile strip of bank, green with corn in the winter and spring, and shaded with groves of lofty palms. On the other side of them is a tawny desert plain, shut in by an amphitheatre of hills. The limestone cliffs of the latter are broken in three places, where ravines lead through them to the Arabian plateau beyond. The central ravine is short and rugged; that to the north, however, though its lofty walls of rock seem at times almost to meet, eventually carries the explorer by a slow ascent into the heart of the Arabian desert. About three miles from its mouth, and in a side-valley, the tomb has lately been discovered of the founder of the city, of which the mounds of Tel el-Amarna are now the sole representatives. The tomb is worthy of the monarch for whom it was intended. In the distant solitude of the desert gorge, it is cut deep into the solid rock. Steps first convey the visitor downwards to the huge door of the sepulchre. Within is a broad sloping passage, to the right of which are the sculptured chambers in which the body of one of the Pharaoh's daughters once rested, while at the end of it is a vast columned hall, within which the sarcophagus of the Pharaoh himself was placed.

The Pharaoh had been named by his father, Amenôphis III., after himself, but Amenôphis IV. had not long mounted the throne before he gave himself a new name, and was henceforth known as Khu-n-Aten, 'the Glory of the Solar Disk.' The change of name was the outward sign and token of a religious revolution. The king publicly renounced the ancient religion of Egypt, of which he was the official representative, and declared himself a convert to an Asiatic form of faith. The very name of Amon, the supreme god of Thebes and of the royal family to which Khu-n-Aten belonged, was proscribed, and erased from the monuments wherever it occurred. In the temples and tombs and quarries alike it was defaced; even the name of the king's own father, which contained it, was not spared. When the arm of the persecutor was thus extènded to the written and sculptured monument, we cannot suppose that the adherents of the ancient cult would be treated with a gentle hand.

It was not long before the Pharaoh and the powerful hierarchy of Thebes were at open war. But the priesthood proved too strong for the king. He quitted the capital of his fathers and built himself a new city farther north. It is the site of this city which is now covered by the mounds of Tel el-Amarna.

Towards the northern side of it rose the palace of the Pharaoh, whose ruins have been explored by Professor Flinders Petrie. It was one of the most gorgeous edifices ever erected by man. The walls and columns were inlaid with gold and bronze and stones of various colours, and adorned with statuary and painting. Even the floors were frescoed; and, if we may judge from the one discovered by Professor Petrie, the art was of the highest order. The plants and animals and fish depicted on it are drawn with a perfection and a truthfulness to nature which seem to belong to the nineteenth century of our era rather than to the fifteenth century before Christ.

The public offices of the government adjoined the palace, and around it were the houses of the nobles and officers of the court. They too reflected the gay and brilliant adornment of the royal palace, and their walls were enlivened by frescoes, which represented the scenes of every-day life. Among the public offices was the archive-chamber, to which the documents of state had been transferred from Thebes, as well as the foreign office, where scribes were busily engaged in correspondence with the governors of the Asiatic provinces of the empire and the princes of foreign states.

In the centre of the city rose the great temple of Aten, the solar disk, the new object of the Pharaoh's adoration. Though the name was Egyptian, the deity and his cult were alike of Asiatic origin. The Aten, in fact, to whom the temple had been reared, was the Asiatic Baal. He was the Sun-god, whose visible manifestation was the solar disk. But it was a Sun-god who was not only supreme over all other gods; they were absorbed into him, and existed only in so far as he endowed them with divine life. It is thus that Aten-Ra, the solar disk of the Sun-god, is addressed by the Pharaoh's queen: 'Thou disk of the Sun, thou living god, there is none other beside thee! Thou givest health to the eyes through thy beams, Creator of all things!' One of Khu-n-Aten's officers, on the walls of his tomb, speaks in similar terms: 'Thou, O god, who in truth art the living one, standest before the two eyes. Thou art he which createst what never was, which formest everything, which art in all things: we also have come into being through the word of thy mouth.'

The new faith of Egypt was a combination of the worship of Baal with the philosophic conceptions which had gathered round the worship of the Egyptian Sun-god, Ra, at Heliopolis. The worship of Baal had lost its grossness, and been refined into a form of monotheism. But the monotheism was essentially pantheistic; there was, indeed, but one god to whom adoration was paid, but he was universally diffused throughout nature. The personal character of the Asiatic Baal seems to have disappeared in the Aten worship of Egypt.

Along with the new religion came a new style of art. Asiatic artists and workmen manufactured the variegated glass and bright-coloured porcelain of Tel el-Amarna, or discarded the conventionalism of Egyptian art in their delineation of animal and vegetable life, while architecture branched out in new directions, and the sculptor exaggerated the peculiarities of the king's personal appearance. Every effort, in fact, was made to break away from the past, and from the mannerisms and traditions of Egyptian art. That art had been closely associated with the ancient religion of the country, and

The Age of Moses 57

with the change of religion came a change in all things else.

The causes of the change can now in great measure be traced. To some extent it was due to the character of the king himself. A plaster cast of his face, taken immediately after death, has been found by Professor Petrie, and is an eloquent witness of what the man himself was like. It is the face of a philosopher and a mystic, of one whose interest lay rather in the problems of religious belief than in the affairs of state. In studying it we feel that the man to whom it belonged was destined to be a religious reformer.

But this destiny was assisted by the training and education which Khu-n-Aten had received. His mother, Teie, bore a foremost part in the introduction of the cult of Aten. She must have been a woman of strong character, and her influence over her son must also have been great. If, as is probable, Khu-n-Aten was very young when he ascended the throne, the religious reform he endeavoured to effect must have been in great measure his mother's work. That she had aroused deep feelings of hatred among the adherents of the older creed may be gathered from the condition of Khu-n-Aten's tomb. Though the body of the Pharaoh was despoiled, and the sarcophagus in which it rested shattered into fragments, they had nevertheless been deposited in the sepulchre that had been constructed to receive them. But no trace of the queen-mother's mummy has been met with, and the corridor in the royal tomb, which seems to have been excavated for her, has never been finished, any more than the two or three tombs which were cut in the immediate neighbourhood. After the death of her son, Queen Teie seems to have found no protector from the vengeance of her enemies.

It is probable that Teie was of Asiatic birth, though no certain proof of it has yet been found. Her husband, Amenôphis III., was fond of connecting himself by marriage with the royal houses of Asia, and more than one of the wives who occupied a secondary rank in the Pharaoh's household were of Asiatic extraction. His own mother had been an Asiatic princess, the daughter of the king of Mitanni, the Aram-Naharaim of the Old Testament. From Mitanni also had come two of his own wives, as well as the wife of his son and successor, Amenophis IV. (Khu-n-Aten).

There is little room for wonder that, with their Asiatic proclivities and half-Asiatic descent, the later Pharaohs of the eighteenth dynasty should have surrounded themselves with Asiatic officials and courtiers. The conquest of Western Asia by Thothmes III. had brought Asiatic fashions into Egypt. Thothmes himself, on the walls of his temple at Karnak, shows the spirit of an Asiatic rather than of an Egyptian conqueror. The inscriptions engraved upon them differ wholly from those which usually adorn the walls of an Egyptian temple. There are no praises or lists of the gods, no description of the offerings made to them, no interminable catalogue of the empty titles of the Pharaoh; we have, on the contrary, a businesslike account of his campaigns, much of it copied from the memoranda of the scribes who accompanied the army on its march. It reads like an inscription on the walls of an Assyrian palace rather than one belonging to an Egyptian temple. It is, in fact, unique, the solitary example of a historical text which the great monuments of Egypt have bequeathed to us. It is, of itself, an eloquent testimony to the influence which Asia had already acquired in the valley of the Nile.

The conquests of Thothmes III. placed the northern boundary of the Egyptian empire at the banks of the Euphrates. The kingdoms to the east, including Assyria, offered tribute to the Egyptian monarch, and those of northern Syria and eastern Asia Minor paid him homage. Farther south, Palestine, Phœnicia, and the land of the Amorites, which lay to the north of Palestine, became Egyptian provinces, garrisoned by Egyptian troops and administered by Egyptian officers. Even the country beyond the Jordan, Bashan and the Haurân, formed part of the Egyptian empire. In many cases the native princes were left to manage the affairs of their several states, like the protected princes of modern India, but they were controlled by 'commissioners' sent from the valley of the Nile. More frequently their place was taken by Egyptian governors, a very considerable number of whom, however, were of Canaanitish descent. This, indeed, is one of the most remarkable facts connected with the Egyptian empire in Asia; it was governed for the Pharaoh by natives rather than by Egyptians. But this was not all. Under Khun-Aten Egypt itself was invaded by the Asiatic stranger. The high places about the court were filled with foreigners whose names proclaim their Canaanitish origin; even the Vizier was called Dudu, the Biblical Dodo, to which the name of David is akin. The adherents of the cult of Aten who gathered round the Pharaoh at Tel el-Amarna seem largely to have belonged to Asia instead of Egypt.

Even the official language and writing were of Asiatic derivation. The language was that of Babylonia, the script was the cuneiform syllabary of the same country. The Babylonian script and language

The Age of Moses

were used from the banks of the Euphrates to those of the Nile. They were the common medium of intercourse throughout the civilised world. It is in these that an Egyptian official writes to his master, and it is again in these that the reply is sent from the Egyptian foreign office.

The fact is a very surprising one, but recent discoveries have tended to explain it. At a very remote epoch Babylonian armies had made their way to the west, and Palestine was a province of Babylonia long before it became a province of Egypt. The long-continued and deep-seated influence of Babylonia brought to it the culture and civilisation of the Babylonian cities. The Babylonian system of writing formed a very important element in this ancient culture, and, along with the language of which it was the expression, took deep root in Western Asia. How long it continued to be employed there may be gathered from the fact that each district of Western Asia developed its own peculiar form of cuneiform script.

All this we have learned from a discovery made in 1887 in the mounds of Tel el-Amarna. Among the ruins of the foreign office of Khu-n-Aten, which adjoined the royal palace, the *fellahin* found a collection of clay tablets inscribed with cuneiform or wedge-shaped characters. They turned out to be the foreign correspondence of Khu-n-Aten and his father. When Khu-n-Aten quitted Thebes he took with him the archives of his father, and to these were subsequently added the official letters which he himself received.

Altogether, about three hundred tablets were discovered. But no one was on the spot who could appreciate their value, and, owing to a series of deplorable accidents, several of them were injured or destroyed before they fell into European hands. Eighty-two found their way to the British Museum, more than 160 fragments are at Berlin, the Gizeh Museum possesses 56, and a few are in the hands of private individuals.

The tablets have thrown a new and unexpected light on the history of the past. To find that the language and script of Babylonia were the common medium of literary and official intercourse throughout Western Asia in the century before the Exodus was sufficiently startling; it was much more startling to find that this early period was emphatically a literary era. Letters passed to and fro along the high-roads upon the most trifling subjects, and a constant correspondence was maintained between the court of the Pharaoh and the most distant parts of Western Asia. The Bedouin chiefs beyond the Jordan send letters protesting their loyalty to the

Egyptian monarch, and declaring that their forces were at his disposal; the vassal-king of Jerusalem begs for help from Egypt to protect him against his personal enemies; the governors of Phœnicia and the land of the Amorites describe the threatening attitude of the Hittites in the north; the king of Mitanni or Aram-Naharaim dwells with pride on his relationship to the ruler of the Egyptian empire; while the kings of Assyria and Babylonia ask that gold may be sent them from Egypt, where it is as plentiful as 'the dust,' or discuss questions of international policy or commercial interest. We are suddenly transported to a world much like our own; —a world in which education is widely spread, where schools and scholars abound, and libraries and archive-chambers exist.

The nature of the cuneiform system of writing would of itself indicate that schools were numerous. It was a system which was extraordinarily difficult to learn. Unlike the hieroglyphs of Egypt, no assistance was afforded to the memory by any resemblance between the characters and external objects; like the Chinese characters of to-day, they consisted merely of groups of conventionally arranged lines or wedges. Like the Egyptian hieroglyphs, however, the number of characters was extremely large, and each character not only represented more than one phonetic value, but it could also be used ideographically to express ideas. Thus the same character may not only represent the phonetic values *kur*, *mat*, *nat*, *lat*, *sat*, and *gin*; it may also denote the ideas of 'country,' 'mountain,' and 'conquest.' But this was not all. The original picture-writing out of which the cuneiform syllabary developed, had been invented by the primitive non-Semitic population of Chaldæa, from whom it had been afterwards adopted and adapted by their Semitic successors. Accordingly, whole groups of characters which denoted a particular word in Sumerian—the non-Semitic language of ancient Chaldæa—were taken over by the Semites and used by them to denote the same word, though, of course, with a totally different pronunciation. In Sumerian, for example, *mer-sig* signified 'trousers,' but though the two characters *mer* and *sig* continued to be written in Semitic times in order to express the word, the pronunciation attached to them was *sarbillu*, the modern Arabic *shirwâl*.

The pupil, therefore, who wished to learn the cuneiform syllabary at all thoroughly was compelled to know something of the old Sumerian language of Chaldæa. It was far more necessary in his case than a knowledge of Latin would be in our own. Moreover, it was necessary for him to learn the various forms which the same cuneiform character assumed in different countries or at different periods in the same country. These various forms were very numerous, and they often differed more than black letter differs from ordinary modern type.

The fact, then, that the cuneiform syllabary was studied and used from the banks of the Euphrates to those of the Nile, brings with it the further fact that throughout this area there must have been numerous schools and teachers. Time and persevering labour were needed for its acquisition, while a knowledge of the Babylonian language which accompanied its study could not have been obtained without the help of teachers. It is accordingly a matter of no small astonishment that the letters received at the Egyptian foreign office were written, not only by professional scribes, but also by officials and soldiers.

Naturally the study of the foreign syllabary and language was facilitated in every possible way. In his excavations at Tel el-Amarna, Professor Flinders Petrie has discovered fragments of lists of cuneiform characters, as well as of comparative dictionaries of Semitic Babylonian and Sumerian. Moreover, a Babylonian mythological text has been found, in which the words have been divided from one another by dots of red paint, in order to assist the learner in making his way through the legend.

This mythological text is not the only one which

has been met with among the tablets of Tel el-Amarna. The existence of such texts is a proof that the literature of Babylonia, as well as its language and script, was carried to the West. From very remote times public libraries, consisting for the most part of clay-books, were to be found in the Babylonian and Assyrian cities, and when Babylonian culture made its way to the West, similar libraries must have sprung up there also. The revelations made to us by the tablets of Tel el-Amarna show that these libraries, like those of Babylonia, were stocked with books written upon clay, many of which contained copies of Babylonian legends and myths.

One of the mythological tales discovered at Tel el-Amarna is the latter portion of a story which described the creation of the first man, Adapa or Adama, and the introduction of death into the world. Adapa had broken the wings of the south wind, and was accordingly ordered to appear before Anu, the lord of the sky. There he refused to touch the food and water of 'death' that were offered him, and when subsequently the heart of Anu was 'softened ' towards him, he refused also the food and water of 'life.' Whereupon ' Anu looked upon him and raised his voice in lamentation : " O Adapa, wherefore eatest thou not ? wherefore drinkest thou not ? The gift of life cannot now be thine." '

The Age of Moses

The beginning of the story has been in the British Museum many years. It is a fragment of a copy of the myth which was made for the library of Nineveh some eight centuries after the rest of the story, which has now been disinterred on the banks of the Nile, had been buried under the ruins of Khu-n-Aten's city. I copied it nearly twenty years ago, but had to wait for the discovery of the tablets of Tel el-Amarna before ascertaining its true meaning and significance. Nineveh and Tel el-Amarna had to unite in the restoration of the old Babylonian myth.

Canaan was the country in which the two streams of Babylonian and Egyptian culture met together, and we now know that Canaan was the centre of that literary activity which the Tel el-Amarna tablets have revealed to us. Canaan, in the age of the eighteenth dynasty, was emphatically the land of scribes and letter-writers. If libraries existed anywhere in Western Asia, they would surely have done so in the cities of Canaan.

One of these cities, Kirjath-Sepher, or 'Book-town,' is mentioned in the Old Testament. It was also called called Kirjath-Sannah, or 'City of Instruction,' doubtless from the school which was attached to its library. The site of it is unfortunately lost: should it ever be recovered, we may expect to find beneath it literary treasures similar to those which the mounds of Assyria and Babylonia have yielded. Perhaps some day the papyri of Egypt will tell us where exactly to look for it. A reference to it has already been met with. In the time of Ramses II., an Egyptian scribe composed an ironical account of the adventures of a military officer in Palestine. The officer in question was called a Mohar, a word borrowed from the Babylonians, in whose language it signified 'an envoy.'

The Egyptian work is consequently usually known as *The Travels of a Mohar*, and it gives us an interesting picture of Canaan shortly before the Israelitish Exodus. The author was clearly very proud of his geographical knowledge, and has therefore introduced the names of a large number of places. In one passage he asks : ' Hast thou not seen Kirjath-Anab together with Beth-Sopher? Dost thou not know Adullam and Zidiputha?' Dr. W. Max Müller, to whom the correct reading of the passage is due, points out that the scribe has interchanged the words Kirjath, 'city,' and Beth, 'house,' and that he ought to have written Beth-Anab and Kirjath-Sopher. That he was acquainted, however, with the meaning of the Canaanitish word Sopher (in Egyptian Thupar) is shown by his adding to it the determinative of 'writing.' *Sopher*, in fact, means 'scribe,' just as *sepher* means 'book,' and indicates the fact that

Kirjath-Sepher was not only a town of books, but of book-writers as well. It will be remembered that Beth-Anab, 'the house of grapes,' in the abbreviated form of Anab, is associated with Kirjath-Sepher in the Old Testament (Josh. xi. 21 ; xv. 49, 50), just as it is in the Egyptian papyrus.

In the Tel el-Amarna tablets we have a picture of Canaan in the century which preceded the Exodus of the Israelites out of Egypt. As we have seen, it was at that time an Egyptian province. We can thus understand why, in the tenth chapter of Genesis, Canaan is made a brother of Mizraim, or Egypt. For a while it obeyed the same sovereign and was administered by the same laws ; the natives of Canaan held office in the court of the Pharaoh, and Egyptian governors ruled in the Canaanitish cities. It was not until after the death of Ramses II., of the nineteenth dynasty, and about the very time when the Israelites were escaping from their house of bondage, that Canaan ceased to be an Egyptian dependency. From that time forward it was politically and geographically severed from the valley of the Nile, and the geographer could never again couple it with the land of Egypt.

When Khu-n-Aten was Pharaoh, the cities of Canaan were numerous and wealthy. The people were highly cultured, and excelled especially as workers in gold and silver, as manufacturers of porcelain and vari-coloured glass, and as weavers of richly-dyed linen. Their merchants already traded to distant parts of the known world. The governors appointed by the Pharaoh were for the most part of native origin, and at times a representative of the old line of kings was left among them, though an Egyptian prefect was often placed at his side. The governors were controlled by the presence of Egyptian garrisons, as well as by the visits of an Egyptian 'commissioner.' Their rivalries and quarrels form the subject of many of the letters which have been found at Tel el-Amarna, both sides appealing to the Pharaoh for protection and help, and alike protesting their loyalty to him. It seems to have been the part of Egyptian policy to encourage these quarrels, or at all events to hold an even balance between the rival governors.

As long as the power of Egypt remained intact, these quarrels, which sometimes resulted in open war, offered no cause for alarm. Egyptian troops could always be sent to the scene of disturbance before it could become dangerous. But in the troublous days of Khu-n-Aten's reign, when Egypt itself was restless and inclined for revolt, the position of affairs was changed. The Egyptian forces were needed at home, and the Pharaoh was compelled to turn a deaf ear

The Age of Moses

to the piteous appeals that were made to him for assistance. The enemies of Egyptian rule began to multiply and grow powerful. In the south the Khabiri or 'Confederates' threatened the Egyptian domination; in the north, Amorite rebels intrigued with the Hittites and with the kings of Naharaim and Babylonia, while in all parts of Palestine the Sute or Bedouin were perpetually on the watch to take advantage of the weakness of the government.

It was the vassal-king of Jerusalem, Ebed-tob by name, who was especially menaced by the Khabiri. In his letters he describes himself as unlike the other governors, in that he had been appointed to his office by the 'arm' or 'oracle' of 'the Mighty King,' the supreme deity of his city. It was not from his father or his mother, consequently, that he had derived his royal dignity. He was, in fact, a priest-king, like his predecessor Melchizedek, to whom Abram had paid tithes. Ebed-tob, however, was unable to make head against his enemies the Khabiri. One by one the towns which were included in the territory of Jerusalem, from Keilah and Gath-Karmel to Rabbah, fell into their hands; the Pharaoh was unable to send him the help for which he so earnestly begged, and we finally hear of his having fallen into the hands of his Bedouin enemy, Labai, along with the cities of which he was in charge. Labai was in alliance with a certain Malchiel, who also writes letters to the Egyptian monarch, as well as with Tagi of Gath and the Khabiri. The latter seem to have given the name of Hebron, 'the Confederacy,' to the old city of Kirjath-Arba.

Megiddo was the seat of an Egyptian governor, like Gaza, near Shechem. The name of Shechem has not been found in the Tel el-Amarna tablets, but a reference is made to its 'mountain,' in the *Travels of a Mohar*. Either Mount Ebal or Mount Gerizim must consequently have been already well known in Egypt. Another Egyptian governor was in command of Phœnicia. Gebal, north of Beyrût, was his chief residence, but he had palaces also at Tyre and Zemar, in the mountains of the interior. In one of his letters he alludes to the wealth of Tyre, which must therefore have been already famous.

Phœnicia and Palestine are alike included under the name of 'Canaan' in the cuneiform documents, though in the hieroglyphic records they are called Zahi and Khal (or Khar). North of Palestine came 'the land of the Amorites,' of which Ebed-Asherah and his son, Aziru or Ezer, were governors, and to the east of the Jordan was 'the field of Bashan.' The Egyptian supremacy was acknowledged as far south as the frontier of Edom; the latter country preserved its independence.

The Age of Moses

Such was the condition of Canaan when the cuneiform correspondence of Tel el-Amarna comes suddenly to an end. The death of Khu-n-Aten had been the signal for a revolt against the faith which he had endeavoured to impose upon Egypt, as well as against the Asiatic influences by which he had been surrounded. He left daughters only behind him. One of them was married to a prince who, in order to secure the throne, was forced to return to the old religion of the country, and to call himself by the name of Tutânkh-Amon. But his reign was short, like those of one or two other relations and followers of Khu-n-Aten who have left traces of themselves upon the monuments. A rival king, Ai by name, held possession of Egypt for a while, and after his death Hor-m-hib, the Armais of Manetho, ruled once more at Thebes over a united Egypt, and the worship of the solar disk was at end.

But the ruins of Tel el-Amarna show that the restoration of the old creed and the overthrow of Khu-n-Aten's adherents had not been without a struggle. Most of the tombs in the cliffs and sandhills which surround the old city have been unfinished: the followers of the new cult for whom they were intended have never been allowed to occupy them. The royal sepulchre itself, as we have seen, is in an equally unfinished condition, and the sarcophagus in which the body of the king rested was violated soon after his mummy had been placed in it. Indeed, it had never been deposited in the niche that had been cut to receive it; its shattered fragments were discovered far away on the floor of the great columned hall. The capital of the 'heretic king' was destroyed by its enemies soon after his death, and never inhabited again. The ruins of its palace and houses were full of broken statues and other objects which their owners had no time to carry away. The city lasted only for about thirty years, and the sands of the desert then began to close over its fallen greatness. How sudden and complete must have been its overthrow is proved by the cuneiform tablets; not only were these imperial archives not carried elsewhere, the correspondence contained in them breaks off suddenly with a half-told tale of disaster and dismay. The Asiatic empire of Egypt is falling to pieces, its enemies are enclosing it on every side; the Hittites have robbed it of its northern provinces, and revolt is shaking it from within. The governors and vassals of the Pharaoh send more and more urgent requests for instant aid: 'If troops come this year, then there will remain both provinces and governors to the king, my lord; but if no troops come, no provinces or governors will remain.' But no answer was returned to these pressing appeals, and the sudden cessation of the correspondence under the ruins of the Egyptian foreign office itself gives us the reason why.

One of the first acts of Hor-m-hib after the settlement of affairs at home was to chastise the Asiatics, who had doubtless taken advantage of the momentary weakness of Egypt. With the death of Hor-m-hib, after a reign of five years,[1] the eighteenth dynasty came to an end. Ramses I., the founder of the nineteenth dynasty, introduced a new type of royal name, and also, as we learn from the monuments, a new type of royal face. After a short reign of two years, he was succeeded by his son, Seti I., in whose name we have an evidence that the proscribed worship of the god Set—the god of the Delta—was again taken under royal patronage. It was an indication that the new dynasty traced its descent from northern Egypt.

Seti I. once more led the Egyptian armies to victory in Asia. With the spoils of conquest temples were built and decorated, and the names of conquered nations engraved upon their walls. One of these temples was at Abydos, the most beautiful of

[1] This is the length of the reign as given by Manetho, and with this agree all the dated monuments of Hor-m-hib, with the exception of a fragment in the British Museum (*Egyptian Inscriptions*, 5624), which has been supposed to refer to his seventh and twenty-first years. But the king to whom these dates refer is uncertain, and Dr. Birch may be right in considering that Amenôphis is meant.

all those which have been left to us in Egypt. But Seti's fame as a builder was far eclipsed by that of his son and successor, Ramses II., and even the temples which he had raised at Abydos and Qurnah were completed, and to a certain extent appropriated, by his better-known son.

We are told in the Book of Exodus that two of the 'treasure cities' which the Israelites built for the Pharaoh of the Oppression were 'Pithom and Raamses.' The discovery of Pithom was, as we have already seen, the inaugural work of the Egypt Exploration Fund. The discovery, as has been already stated, was made by Dr. Naville, who was led to the site by certain monuments of Ramses II., which had been found there by the French engineers of M. de Lesseps. These monuments consisted of a great tablet and monolith of red granite, two sphinxes of exquisitely polished black granite, and a broken shrine of red sandstone which had been transported to Ismailîyeh, where they formed the chief ornament of the little public garden. As they all showed that Tum, the setting sun, was the supreme deity of the place from which they had come, Dr. Naville concluded that it would prove to be Pi-Tum, 'the abode of Tum,' the Pithom of Scripture, and not the companion city of Raamses, as Lepsius had believed.

The Age of Moses

The mounds from which the monuments had been disinterred are about twelve miles to the west of Ismailîyeh, and are called Tel el-Maskhuteh, 'the Mound of the Image.' In the last century, however, they were known as Abu Kêshêd, and were famous for a half-buried monolith of granite representing Ramses II. seated between Tum and Râ, the hieroglyphic inscription on the back of which has been published by Sir Gardner Wilkinson. The canal made by the Pharaohs for uniting the Nile with the Red Sea, and afterwards cleared of the sand that choked it by Darius, by Trajan, and by the Arab conqueror 'Amru, skirted the southern side of the mounds. At present the modern Freshwater Canal runs along their northern edge, to the north of which again is the line of the railway from Cairo to Suez. The fortifications erected by Arabi, however, hide the site of the old city from the traveller in the train.

Dr. Naville's excavations proved him to have been right in identifying Tel el-Maskhuteh with Pithom. The inscriptions he found there showed that its ancient name was Pi-Tum, and that it stood in the district of Thukut, the Succoth of the Old Testament. The name of this district was already known from papyri of the age of the nineteenth dynasty, and Dr. Brugsch had pointed out its identity with the Biblical Succoth.

But the discovery of the ancient name was not the only result of the explorer's work. It turned out that the city had been built by Ramses II., and that it contained a number of large brick buildings which seem to have been intended for magazines. Here, then, at last was a proof that the Egyptologists were correct in making Ramses II. the Pharaoh of the Oppression.

The site of Raamses or Ramses, the companion city of Pithom, has still to be discovered. But it cannot be far distant from Tel el-Maskhuteh, and, like the latter, must have been in that land of Goshen in which the Israelites were settled. The discoveries which enabled Dr. Naville to determine the boundaries of the land of Goshen and to fix the site of its ancient capital have already been described. The site of Zoan, the modern Sân, had long been known, and the excavations, first of Mariette Pasha and then of Professor Flinders Petrie, have laid bare the foundations of its temple and brought to light the monuments of the kings who enriched and adorned it. Built originally in the age of the Old Empire, it was restored by the Hyksos conquerors of Egypt, and became under them a centre of influence and power.

Goshen, Zoan and Pithom, the sites around which the early history of Israel gathered, have thus been brought to light. The disputes which have raged

The Age of Moses 79

about them are at last ended. Here and there a persistent sceptic, who has been reared in the traditions of the past, may still express doubts concerning the discoveries of recent years, but for the Egyptologist and the archæologist the question has been finally settled. We can visit 'the field of Zoan' and explore the mounds of Pithom with no misgivings as to their identity. When the train carries us from Ismailîyeh to Cairo, we may feel assured that we are passing through the district in which Jacob and his family were settled, and where the kinsfolk of Moses had their homes. The Egypt of the patriarchs and the Exodus was an Egypt narrow in compass and easily traversed in these days of steam; it represented the western part of the Delta, more especially the strip of cultivable land which stretches along the banks of the Freshwater Canal from Zagazig to Ismailîyeh: that is all. The eastern and northern Delta, Upper Egypt—even the district in which Cairo now stands—lay outside it. The history which attaches itself to them is not the history of the early Israelites.

CHAPTER III

THE EXODUS AND THE HEBREW SETTLEMENT IN CANAAN

RAMSES II. was the last of the conquering Pharaohs of native Egyptian history. The Asiatic empire of Thothmes III. was in some measure restored by the victories of his father and himself. The cities of Palestine yielded him an unwilling obedience. Gaza, and the other towns in what was afterwards the territory of the Philistines, were garrisoned by Egyptian troops, and on the walls of the Ramesseum were depicted his conquest of Shalem or Jerusalem, Merom, Beth-Anath, and other Canaanite states, in his eighth year. Egyptian armies again marched northward into Syria along the highroad that led past the Phœnician cities, and on the banks of the Nahr el-Kelb, or Dog's River, near Beyrût, the Pharaoh erected a tablet in commemoration of his successes. On the eastern side of the Jordan also Egyptian authority once more prevailed. In front of the northern pylon of the temple of Luxor, Ramses

The Exodus and Hebrew Settlement in Canaan 81

erected six colossal figures of himself, and on their recently-uncovered bases are inscribed the names of the various nations he claimed to have subdued. Among them we find, for the first time in the Egyptian records, the name of Moab, following immediately upon that of Assar, the Asshurim of Genesis xxv. 3. That the insertion of the name was not an idle boast we learn from a discovery lately made by Dr. Schumacher. On the eastern side of the Jordan, but at no great distance from the Lake of Tiberias, is a monolith called the 'Stone of Job.' On this the German explorer has found Egyptian sculptures and hieroglyphs. Above the figure of the Pharaoh are the cartouches of Ramses II., and opposite the king, on the left, a local deity is represented with a full face and the crown of Osiris, over whom is written the name of Akna-zapn, or 'Yakin of the North.' The monument is an evidence of a permanent occupation of the country by the Egyptians, as the name and figure of the god indicate that it was erected, not by the Egyptians themselves, but by the Egyptianised natives of the land.

Along the Syrian coast Seti I. had already carried his arms. His campaigns were followed by those of his son. Arvad, the shores of the Gulf of Antioch, and even Cilicia, are enumerated among the conquests of the Pharaoh. He even claims to have

F

defeated the armies of Assyria, of Matena or Mitanni, the Aram-Naharaim of Scripture, and of Singar in Mesopotamia. At Luxor, on the western walls of the newly excavated court, we hear of his having been at Tunip (now Tennib), 'in the land of Naharaim,' of his capture of a fortress of the Kati in the same district, and of how 'the Pharaoh' had taken a city in 'the land of Satuna.' Satuna was one of those countries in the far north whose name is never mentioned elsewhere in the Egyptian texts.

The Syrian conquests, however, could never have been long in the Pharaoh's possession. Between them and Palestine lay the southern outposts of the Hittite race. In the troublous times which followed the death of Khu-n-Aten, the Hittites had overrun 'the land of the Amorites' to the north of Canaan, and fixed their southern capital in the holy city of Kadesh, on the Orontes. It was a stronghold against which the forces of Ramses were hurled in vain. For twenty years did the struggle continue between the Pharaoh of Egypt and 'the great king of the Hittites,' and at last, exhausted by the long conflict, in which neither party had gained the advantage, the two enemies agreed upon peace. A treaty was signed on the twenty-first of the month Tybi, in the twenty-first year of the reign of Ramses (B.C. 1327), 'in the city of Ramses,' to which the Hittite

The Exodus and Hebrew Settlement in Canaan 83

ambassadors had come. Ramses, on the one side, and Khita-sir, the son of Mul-sir, the Hittite prince, on the other, bound themselves in it to eternal friendship and alliance. In case of war they were to send troops to one another's help, and they agreed to put to death any criminals who might fly from the one country to the other. Political offenders, however, who had taken refuge in the territory of one or other of the two contracting parties, were not to be injured. It was of course the Canaanitish subjects of the Pharaoh, who adjoined the Hittite kingdom, that were principally affected by these stipulations. It was further determined that on no pretext whatever should any change be made in the boundaries of the two monarchies. The treaty was placed under the protection of the deities of Egypt and the Hittites, and a Hittite copy of it was engraved on a silver plate. The agreement was cemented by the marriage of Ramses to a daughter of the Hittite king, who thereupon assumed an Egyptian name.

Northern Syria was thus formally conceded to the powerful conquerors who had descended from the mountains of Kappadokia, while Palestine remained under Egyptian dominion. But it was not destined to do so long. Ramses was succeeded by Meneptah, the fourteenth of his many sons, who had reigned only four years when the very existence of his kingdom was threatened by a formidable invasion from the west and north. 'The peoples of the north' swarmed out of their coasts and islands, and a great fleet descended upon Egypt, in conjunction with the Libyans and Maxyes of northern Africa. Aqaiush or Achæans, Shardana or Sardinians, Tursha or Tyrsenians appear among them, as well as Leku from Asia Minor, and Zakkur, who a little later are the colleagues and brethren of the Philistines. Part of the Delta was overrun and devastated before the Pharaoh could make head against his foes. But a decisive battle was at length fought at Pa-Alu-sheps, not far from Heliopolis, which ended in the complete overthrow of the invading hordes. Egypt was saved from the danger which had threatened it, but it seems never to have recovered from the shock. The power of the government was weakened in the valley of the Nile itself, and one by one the foreign conquests passed out of its grasp. The sceptre of Seti II., who followed Meneptah, seems to have dropped into the hands of a usurper, Amon-messu by name: the history of the period is, however, involved in obscurity, and all that is certain is that the empire of Ramses II. was lost, and that Egypt itself fell into a state of decadence. With Si-Ptah the nineteenth dynasty came to an inglorious end.

The Exodus and Hebrew Settlement in Canaan 85

Its fall was the signal for internal confusion and civil war. A Syrian foreigner, Arisu by name, possessed himself of the throne of the Pharaohs, and Egypt for a while was compelled to submit to Canaanitish rule. Its leading nobles were in banishment, its gods were deprived of their customary offerings, and famine was added to the horrors of war. A deliverer came in the person of Set-nekht, the founder of the twentieth dynasty. He drove the stranger out the country, and restored it again to peace and prosperity. Hardly had his task been completed when he died, and was succeeded by his son, Ramses III. Under him a transient gleam of victory and conquest visited once more the valley of the Nile.

It was well for Egypt that she possessed an energetic general and king. The same hordes which had threatened her in the reign of Meneptah now again attacked her with increased numbers and greater chances of success. In the fifth year of Ramses III., the fair-skinned tribes of the western desert poured into the Delta. The Maxyes, under their chieftains Mdidi, Mâshakanu, and Mâraiu, and the Libyans, under Ur-mâr and Zut-mâr, met the Pharaoh in battle at a place which ever afterwards bore a name commemorative of their defeat. The victory of the Egyptians was, in fact, decisive. As many as 12,535 slain were counted on the field of battle, and captives and spoil innumerable fell into the hands of the victors.

But Ramses was allowed only a short breathing-space. Three years after the Libyan invasion, and doubtless in connection with it, came a still more formidable invasion on the part of the barbarians of the north. This time they came partly by land, partly by sea. Vast hordes of them had marched out of Asia Minor, overrunning the kingdoms of the Hittites, of Naharaim, of Carchemish, and of Arvad, and carrying with them adventurers and recruits from the countries through which they passed. First they pitched their camp in 'the land of the Amorites,' and then marched southward towards the frontiers of Egypt. The place of the Aqaiush was taken by the Daanau or Danaans, but the Zakkur again formed part of the invading host, this time accompanied by Pulsata or Philistines, and Shakalsh or Siculians. By the side of the land army moved a fleet of ships, and fleet and army arrived together at the mouths of the Nile. The cities in the extreme south of Palestine, once occupied by Egyptian garrisons, were captured by the Philistines, and became henceforward their assured possession.

But the main body of the invaders were not so fortunate. The Egyptian forces were ready to

The Exodus and Hebrew Settlement in Canaan 87

receive them, and their ships had scarcely entered the mouth of the Nile before they were attacked by the Egyptian fleet. The battle ended in the complete annihilation of the attacking host. A picture of it is sculptured on the walls of Medînet Habu at Thebes, the temple-palace which Ramses built to commemorate his victories, and we can there study the ships of the European barbarians and the features and dress of the barbarians themselves. In the expressive words of the Egyptian scribe, 'they never reaped a harvest any more.'

Ramses, however, was even now not left at rest. Three years later the Maxyes again assailed Egypt under Mashashal, the son of Kapur, but once more unsuccessfully. Cattle, horses, asses, chariots and weapons of war in large quantities fell into the hands of the Egyptians, as well as 2052 captives, while 2175 men were slain. From this time forward Egypt was secure from attack on its western border.

Freed from the necessity of defending his own territories, Ramses now carried the war into Asia. What in later days was the land of Judah was overrun by his forces; Gaza and the districts round Hebron and Salem or Jerusalem were occupied, and the name of the Dead Sea appears on the walls of Medînet Habu for the first time in Egyptian history. The Egyptian army even crossed to the eastern side of the Jordan and captured the Moabite capital. Another campaign led it along the Phœnician coast into northern Syria. Hamath was taken, and Ramses seems to have penetrated as far as the slopes of the Taurus. He even claims to have defeated the people of Mitanni or Aram-Naharaim on the eastern bank of the Euphrates. The kings of the Hittites and the Amorites, like the chiefs of the Zakkur and the Philistines, were already prisoners in his hands.

But the northern campaigns of Ramses were intended to strike terror rather than to re-establish the Asiatic empire of Egypt. No attempt was made to hold the cities and districts which had been overrun. Though a temple was erected to Amon on the frontiers of the later Judæa, even Gaza was given up, and the fortress which had. so long defended the road from Canaan into Egypt was allowed to pass into Philistine hands. It was the same with the campaign which the Pharaoh conducted at a later date against the 'Shasu' or Bedouin of Edom. For the first time an Egyptian army succeeded in making its way into the fastnesses of Mount Seir, slaying the warriors of Edom, and plundering their 'tents.' The Edomite chief himself was made a prisoner. The expedition

The Exodus and Hebrew Settlement in Canaan 89

had the effect of protecting the Egyptian mining establishments in the Sinaitic peninsula as well as the maritime trade with southern Arabia. Large quantities of malachite were brought year by year from the Egyptian province of Mafka or Sinai, and the merchant-vessels of Ramses coasted along the Red Sea, bringing back with them the precious spices of Yemen and Hadhramaut.

Ramses III. died after a reign of more than thirty-two years, and the military renown of Egypt expired with him. His exact date is still a matter of doubt, but his accession must have fallen about B.C. 1200. The date is important, not only because it closes the history of Egypt as a conquering power, but also as it marks a great era of migration among the northern populations of the Mediterranean, as well as the permanent settlement of the Philistines in Palestine. It was, moreover, the period to which the Israelitish invasion of Canaan must belong.

When Ramses III. overran the southern portion of Palestine, and built the temple of the Theban god at the spot now known as Khurbet Kan'an, not far from Hebron, the Israelites could not as yet have entered the Promised Land. There is no reference to the Egyptians in the Pentateuch, and there is no reference to the Israelites in the hieroglyphic texts of Medînet Habu. Hebron, Migdal, Karmel of Judah, Ir-Shemesh and Hadashah, all alike fell into the hands of the Egyptian invaders, but neither in the Egyptian nor in the Hebrew records is there any allusion to a struggle between Egypt and Israel. When Joshua entered Canaan all these cities belonged to the Canaanites, and when Ramses III. attacked them this was also the case. The Palestinian campaign of Ramses must have prepared the way for the Israelitish conquest; it could not have followed after it.

Moreover, 'the five lords of the Philistines' seem to have already been settled in the extreme south when the Israelitish invasion took place (Josh. xiii. 3). Yet it also seems clear from the Egyptian monuments that the settlement was not fully completed until after the Asiatic campaigns of the Pharaoh had occurred. The Philistines indeed formed part of the great invading host which poured through Syria and assailed Egypt in the early part of his reign, but Gaza was one of his conquests, and its possession enabled him to march into Canaan. Before Gaza could become a Philistine city it was needful that its Egyptian garrison should be withdrawn. Professor Prášek believes that the Philistine occupation of southern Canaan took place in the year B.C. 1209, since the Roman historian Justin tells us that in this year a king of Ashkelon stormed the city of

Sidon, and that the Sidonians fled to a neighbouring part of the coast, and there founded Tyre. However this may be, the Philistine settlement in Canaan must be ascribed to the age of Ramses III., and it was already with the Philistines that the Israelites came into conflict under almost the earliest of their judges.

But the date of the Israelitish conquest of Canaan is closely bound up with that of the Exodus out of Egypt. It is true that when we are told of the forty years' wandering in the desert, the word 'forty' is used, as it is elsewhere in the Old Testament, as well as upon the Moabite Stone, to denote an indeterminate period of time. It was a period during which the greater part of the generation that had left Egypt had time to die. Joshua and Caleb indeed remained, and Othniel, the brother of Caleb, lived to deliver Israel from the king of Aram-Naharaim, and to be the first of the judges. But otherwise it was a new generation which was led to conquest by Joshua.

If Ramses II. was the Pharaoh of the Oppression, the Pharaoh of the Exodus must have been one of his immediate successors. Egyptologists have hesitated between Meneptah, Seti II., and Si-Ptah. There is much to be said in favour of each. None of them reigned long, and after the death of Meneptah the sceptre fell into feeble hands, and the Egyptian monarchy went rapidly to decay.

Native tradition, as reported by the historian Manetho, made Meneptah the Pharaoh under whom the children of Israel escaped from their house of bondage. Amenôphis or Meneptah, it was said, desired to see the gods. He was accordingly instructed by the seer Amenôphis, the son of Pa-apis, to clear the land of the leprous and impure. This he did, and 80,000 persons were collected from all parts of Egypt, and were then separated from the other inhabitants of the country and compelled to work in the quarries of Tûra, on the eastern side of the Nile. Among them there happened to be some priests, one of whom was Osarsiph, a priest of On, and the sacrilegious act of laying hands on them was destined to be avenged by the gods. The seer prophesied that the impure lepers would find allies, and with their help would govern Egypt for thirteen years, when a saviour should arise in the person of Amenôphis himself. Not daring to tell the king of this prediction, he put it in writing and then took away his own life. After a time the workers in the quarries were removed to Avaris, the deserted fortress of the Hyksos, on the Asiatic frontier of the Egyptian kingdom. Here they rose in rebellion under Osarsiph, who organised them into a

The Exodus and Hebrew Settlement in Canaan 93

community, and gave them new laws, forbidding them to revere the sacred animals, and ordering them to rebuild the walls of Avaris. He also sent to the descendants of the Hyksos at Jersualem, begging for their assistance. A force of 200,000 men was accordingly despatched to Avaris, and the invasion of Egypt decided on. Amenôphis retired into Ethiopia without striking a blow, carrying with him his son Sethos, who was also called Ramesses after his grandfather, as well as the sacred bull Apis, and other holy animals. The images of the gods were concealed, lest they should be profaned by the invaders. Amenôphis remained in Ethiopia for thirteen years, while Osarsiph, who had taken the name of Moses, together with his allies from Jerusalem, committed innumerable atrocities. At last, however, Amenôphis and his son Sethos returned, each at the head of an army; the enemy were defeated and overthrown, and finally pursued to the borders of Syria.

The tradition is a curious mixture of fact and legend. Osarsiph is but an Egyptianised form of Joseph, the first syllable of which has been explained as representing the god of Israel (as in Ps. lxxxi. 5), and has accordingly been identified with Osar or Osiris. The ancient Egyptian habit of regarding the foreigner as impure has been interpreted to mean that the followers of Osarsiph were lepers. The

Exodus of the Israelites has been confounded with the invasion of the northern barbarians in the reign of Meneptah, as well as with the troublous period that saw the fall of the nineteenth dynasty when the throne of Egypt was seized by the Syrian Arisu. And, lastly, the hated Hyksos have been introduced into the story; their fortress Avaris is made the rallying-place of the revolted lepers, and it is through the help they send from Jerusalem that the rule of Osarsiph or Moses is established in the valley of the Nile.

An interesting commentary on the legend has been furnished by a papyrus lately acquired by M. Golénischeff, and dating from the age of Thothmes III. On the last page is a sort of Messianic prophecy, the hero of which has the name of Ameni, a shortened form of Amenôphis. 'A king,' it says, 'will come from the south, Ameni the truth-declaring by name. He will be the son of a woman of Nubia, and will be born in . . . He will assume the crown of Upper Egypt, and will lift up the red crown of Lower Egypt. He will unite the double crown. . . . The people of the age of the son of man (*sic*) will rejoice and establish his name for all eternity. They will be far from evil, and the wicked will humble their mouths for fear of him. The Asiatics (Âmu) will fall before his blows, and the Libyans before his flame. The wicked will wait on his judgments, the rebels on his power. The royal serpent on his brow will pacify the revolted. A wall shall be built, even that of the prince, so that the Asiatics may no more enter into Egypt. In this Ameni we should probably see the Amenôphis of the Manethonian story.

Against the identification of Meneptah with the Pharaoh of the Exodus it has, however, been urged that he seems on the whole to have been a successful prince. His kingdom passed safely through the shock of the Libyan and northern invasions, and notices which have survived to us show that, at all events in the earlier part of his reign, Gaza and the neighbouring towns still acknowledged his authority. At Zaru, on the Asiatic frontier of Egypt, a young scribe, Pa-ebpasa by name, was stationed, whose duty it was to keep a record of all those who entered or left the country by 'the way of the Philistines.' Some of his notes, made in the third year of Meneptah, are entered on the back of his school copybook, which is now in the British Museum. One of them tells us that on the fifteenth of Pakhons Baal-... the son of Zippor of Gaza, passed through with a letter to Baal-marom(?)-ga[b]u, the prince of Tyre; another that Thoth, the son of Zakarumu, and the policeman Duthau, the son of Shem-baal, as well as Sutekh-mes, the son of Epher-dagal, had come from Gaza with a message to the king.

A curious despatch, dated in Meneptah's eighth year, goes to show that at that time the kinsfolk of the Israelites still had liberty to pass from the desert into the land of Goshen and there find pasturage for their flocks. One of his officials informs him that certain Shasu or Bedouin from Edom had been allowed to pass the Khetam or fortress of Meneptah Hotep-hima in the district of Succoth, and make their way to the lakes of the city of Pithom, in the district of Succoth, 'in order to feed themselves and their herds on the possessions of Pharaoh, who is there a beneficent sun for all peoples.' The document may be interpreted in two ways. It may be taken as a proof that the Israelites had not yet fled from Egypt, and that there was consequently as yet no restraint placed by the Egyptians upon the entrance of the Asiatic nomads into their country, or it may be regarded as implying that the land of Goshen was already deserted, so that there was abundance of room for both shepherds and flocks. On behalf of this view a passage may be quoted from the great inscription of Meneptah at Karnak, in which we read that 'the country around Pa-Bailos (the modern Belbeis) was not cultivated, but left as pasture for cattle because of the strangers. It was abandoned since the time of the ancestors.' More probably, however, this means that the land in question was not inhabited by Egyptian *fellahin*, but given over to the Hebrew shepherds and the 'mixed multitude' of their Bedouin kinsmen.

A more serious objection to making Meneptah the Pharaoh of the Exodus is the fact that his son Seti II. was already acknowledged as heir to the throne during his father's lifetime. The 'tale of the two brothers,' to which we have already had to refer, was dedicated to him while he was still crown-prince. Indeed, it would even appear that he was associated with his father on the throne, since the cartouches of Meneptah and Seti II. are found side by side in the rock-temple of Surarîyeh. It would seem, therefore, that the first-born of the Pharaoh, who was destroyed on the night of the Passover, could not have been a son of Meneptah—at all events, if his heir and future successor were his first-born son. That Meneptah should have been buried in one of the royal tombs of Bibân el-Molûk at Thebes, and received divine honours after his death, is of less consequence. As has often been remarked, no mention is made in the narrative of the Exodus that the Pharaoh himself was drowned, and though Meneptah's tomb (No. 8) is unfinished, the cult that was paid to his memory indicates that his mummy was deposited in it. It was plundered centuries ago, and the numerous Greek inscriptions on its walls make it clear that it was open to visitors in the Roman age.

Professor Maspero has suggested that the Pharaoh of the Bible was Seti II. We know that Seti must have been a weak prince, and that his rule was disputed. A usurper, Amon-messu by name, seized the crown either during his lifetime or at his death, and governed at Thebes, while the authority of the lawful line of princes was still acknowledged in the north. We also know that he must have died suddenly, for his tomb at Thebes (No. 15), though begun magnificently, was never finished. Its galleries and halls were hewn out of the rock, but never adorned with sculptures and paintings, and, except at the entrance, we have merely outline sketches, which were never filled in. His cartouches, however, are found in another tomb, not far off (No. 13), and after his death worship was paid to him and his wife.

A despatch, written during his reign, relates to the escape of two fugitives who had travelled along the very road which the Israelites attempted to take. The scribe tells us that he set out in pursuit of them from the royal city of Ramses on the evening of the 9th of Epiphi, and had arrived at the Khetam or fortress of Succoth the following day. Two days later he reached another Khetam, and there learned that the slaves were already safe in the desert, having passed

The Exodus and Hebrew Settlement in Canaan 99

the lines of fortification to the north of the Migdol of King Seti. The account is an interesting illustration of the flight, on a far larger scale, that must have taken place about the same time. The geography of the despatch is in close harmony with that of the Book of Exodus, and bears witness to the contemporaneousness of the latter with the events it professes to record. It is a geography which ceased to be exact after the age of the nineteenth dynasty.

It is thus possible that Seti II., instead of Meneptah, is the Pharaoh whose host perished in the waves of the Red Sea. But there is yet another claimant in Si-Ptah, with whom the nineteenth dynasty came to an end. Dr. Kellogg has argued ably on behalf of him, and it is possible that the views of this scholar are correct. Si-Ptah's right to the throne was derived from his wife, Ta-user, and he reigned at least six years. That he followed Seti II. has long been admitted, on the authority of Manetho, though doubts have been cast on it in consequence of a statement of Champollion that he found the name of Seti written over that of Si-Ptah in the tomb of the latter at Bibân el-Molûk (No. 14). All doubts, however, are now set at rest by an inscription I copied at Wadi Halfa two years ago, in which the writer, Hora, the son of Kam, declares that he had formerly belonged to the palace of Seti II., and had engraved the inscription in the third year of Si-Ptah. In another inscription in the same place, dated also in Si-Ptah's reign, the author states that he had been an ambassador to the land of Khal or Syria. Intercourse with Asia was therefore still maintained.

Si-Ptah's tomb at Thebes was usurped by Setnekht, the founder of the twentieth dynasty. It is even doubtful whether the king for whom it was made was ever buried in it. In the second sepulchral hall the lid of his sarcophagus was discovered, but of the sarcophagus itself there was no trace. Perhaps it had been appropriated by Set-nekht. At any rate, those who believe that the Pharaoh of the Exodus perished in the Red Sea will find in Si-Ptah a better representative of him than in Meneptah or Seti. And the period of anarchy which followed upon his death may be regarded as the natural sequel of the disasters that befel Egypt before the children of Israel were permitted to go.

However this may be, the question of the date of the Exodus is reduced to narrow limits. The three successors of Ramses II. reigned altogether but a short time. Manetho gives seven years only to Si-Ptah, five years to Amon-messu, and we know from the monuments that Meneptah and Seti II. can have reigned but a very few years. Thirty or forty years at most will have covered the period that elapsed between the death of the great Ramses and the downfall of his dynasty. Then came a few years of confusion and anarchy, followed by the reign of Setnekht. If we place the accession of Ramses III. in B.C. 1230, we cannot be far wrong.

When that happened, the Israelites were hidden out of the sight of the great nations of the world among the solitudes of the desert. They were pitching their tents on the frontiers of Mount Seir, in the near neighbourhood of their kinsmen in Edom and Midian. There, at Sinai and Kadesh-barnea, they were receiving a code of laws, and being fitted to become a nation and the conquerors of Canaan. Were they included among the Shasu of Mount Seir whose overthrow is commemorated by Ramses III.?

For an answer we must turn to the twenty-first chapter of the Book of Numbers. There we read how 'it is said in the book of the wars of the Lord: 'Waheb in Suphah and the brooks of Arnon, and the stream of the brook that goeth down to the dwelling of Ar, and lieth upon the border of Moab.' Of the war against the Amorites on the banks of the Arnon we know something, but the Old Testament has preserved no record of the other war, which had its scene in Suphah. Where Suphah was we know from the opening of the Book of Deuteronomy, which tells us that the words of Moses were addressed to the people 'in the plain over against Suph.' Suph, in fact, was the district which gave its name to the *yâm Sûph* or 'Sea of Suph,' the Red Sea of the authorised version, the modern Gulf of Akabah. Here were the Edomite ports of Eloth and Ezion-geber, where Solomon built his fleet of merchantmen (1 Kings ix. 26), and here too was the region which faced 'the plain' on the southern side of Moab.

The barren ranges of Mount Seir run down southward to Ezion-geber and Eloth, at the head of the Gulf of Akabah. And it was just in the ranges of Mount Seir that Ramses III. tells us he smote the Shasu and plundered their tents. When he made this expedition, the Israelites were probably still encamped on the borders of Edom. They had not as yet entered Canaan when he marched through the later Judæa, and crossed the Jordan into Moab, and his campaign against the Shasu of the desert did not take place many years later. At Medînet Habu, the 'chief of the Shasu' figures among his prisoners by the side of the kings of the Hittites and the Amorites.

Was 'the war of the Lord' in Suphah waged against the Pharaoh of Egypt? Chronology is in favour of it, and if the enemies of the Israelites were not the Egyptian army, it is hard to say who else they could have been. We know from the

Pentateuch that they were not the people of Edom; 'meddle not with them,' the Israelites were enjoined; the children of Esau were their 'brethren,' and God had 'given Mount Seir unto Esau for a possession.'

But whether or not Ramses III. and the tribes of Israel ever came into actual conflict, it must have been during his reign that the first Israelitish conquests in Canaan were made. The settlement of the twelve tribes in Palestine was coeval with the final decay of the Egyptian monarchy.

CHAPTER IV

THE AGE OF THE ISRAELITISH MONARCHIES

RAMSES III. was the last of the great Pharaohs in whose veins ran native Egyptian blood. His successors all bore the same name as himself, but they possessed neither his energy nor his power to rule. He had saved Egypt from further attack from without, and it was well he had done so, for the feeble monarchs of the twentieth dynasty would have been unable to resist the foe. They ceased even to build or to erect the monuments which testified to the prosperity of the country and the progress of its art. The high-priests of Amon gradually usurped their authority, and a time came at length when the last of the Ramses fled into exile in Ethiopia, and a new dynasty governed in his stead. But the rule of the new monarchs was hardly acknowledged beyond the Delta; Thebes was practically independent under its priest-kings, and though they acknowledged the authority of the Tanite Pharaohs in name, they acted, in real fact, as if they were independent sovereigns. One of them, Ra-men-kheper, built fortresses not only at Gebelên in the south, but also at El-Hîbeh in the north, and thus blocked the river against the subjects of the Tanite princes, as well as against invaders from the south. At times, indeed, the Tanite Pharaohs of the twenty-first dynasty exercised an actual sovereignty over Upper Egypt, and Smendes, the first of them, quarried stone at Dababîyeh, opposite Gebelên, with which to repair the canal of Luxor; but, as a general rule, so far as the south was concerned, they were Pharaohs only in name. The rival dynasty of Theban high-priests was at once more powerful and more king-like. They it was who, in some moment of danger, concealed the mummies of the great monarchs of the eighteenth and nineteenth dynasties in the pit at Dêr el-Bahâri, and whose own mummies were entombed by the side of those of a Thothmes and a Ramses.

The Egyptian wife of Solomon was the daughter of one of the last Pharaohs of the twenty-first dynasty. She brought with her as a dowry the Canaanitish city of Gezer. Gezer had been one of the leading cities of Palestine in the days of the Tel el-Amarna correspondence, and through all the years of Israelitish conquest it had remained in Canaanitish hands. It was a Pharaoh of Tanis, and not an Israelite, into whose possession it was destined finally to fall.

The waning power of Solomon in Israel coincided with the waning power of the twenty-first dynasty. Long before the death of the Hebrew monarch, a new dynasty was reigning over Egypt. Shishak, its founder, was of Libyan origin. His immediate forefathers had commanded the Libyan mercenaries in the service of the Pharaoh, and inscriptions lately discovered in the Oasis of El-Khargeh write the name Shashaka. The Egyptians slightly changed its pronunciation and made it Shashanq, but in the Old Testament the true form is preserved.

Shishak brought new vigour into the decaying monarchy of the Nile. The priest-kings of Thebes went down before him, along with the effete Pharaohs of Tanis.. It may be that Solomon attempted to assist his father-in-law; if he did so, the only result was to bring trouble upon himself. His rebel subject Jeroboam fled to Egypt, and found shelter and protection in Shishak's court.

Shishak must have looked on with satisfaction while the neighbouring empire of Israel fell to pieces, until eventually the central power itself was shattered in twain. The rebel he had so carefully nurtured at his own court was the instrument which relieved him of all further fear of danger on the side of Asia. So far from being a menace to Egypt, Jerusalem now lay at the mercy of the Egyptian armies, and in the fifth year of Rehoboam, Shishak led his forces against it. The strong walls Solomon had built were of no avail; its temple and palace were plundered, and the golden shields in its armoury were carried away. A record of the campaign was engraved by the conqueror on the southern wall of the temple of Amon at Karnak. There we read how he had overthrown the Amu or Asiatics, and the Fenkhu or people of Palestine, and underneath are the cartouches, each with the head of a captive above it, which contain the names of the conquered places. At the outset come the names of towns in the northern kingdom of Israel. But, as Professor Maspero remarks, this does not prove that they were actually among the conquests of Shishak. If Jeroboam had begged his aid against Judah, and thereby acknowledged himself the vassal of the Pharaoh, it would have been a sufficient pretext for inserting the names of his cities among the subject states of Egypt. But it may be that the campaign was directed quite as much against Israel as against Judah, and that Judah suffered most, simply because it had to bear the brunt of the attack.

In any case, the list of vanquished towns begins first with Gaza, the possession of which was necessary before the Egyptian army could force its way into Palestine; then come Rabbith of Issachar, Taanach, near Megiddo, Hapharaim and Beth-Horon, while

Mahanaim, on the eastern side of the Jordan, is also included among them. But after this the list deals exclusively with the towns and villages of Judah, and of the Bedouin tribes in the desert to the south of it. Thus we have Ajalon and Makkedah, Socho and Keilah, Migdol and Beth-anoth. Then we read the names of Azem and Arad, farther to the south, as well as of the Hagaraim or 'Enclosures' of Arad, and Rabbith 'Aradai, 'Arad the capital.' Next to Arad comes the name of Yurahma, the Jerahme-el of the Old Testament, the brother of Caleb the Kenizzite (1 Chron. ii. 42) whose land was ravaged by David (1 Sam. xxx. 29). But the larger portion of the list is made up of the names of small villages and even Bedouin encampments, or of such general terms as Hagra, 'enclosure,' Negebu, 'the south,' 'Emeq, 'the valley,' Shebbaleth, 'a torrent,' Abilim, 'fields,' Ganat, 'garden,' Haideba, 'a quarry,' and the Egyptian Shodinau, 'canals.'[1] Among them we look in vain even for names like those of Gezer and Beer-sheba. Jerusalem, too, is conspicuous by its absence, unless we agree with Professor Maspero in seeing it in the last name of the list (No. 133), of which only the first syllable is preserved. Were it not for the record in

---

[1] See Maspero's exhaustive paper 'The List of Sheshonq at Karnak,' in the *Journal of the Transactions of the Victoria Institute*, xxvii. (1893-94).

The Age of the Israelitish Monarchies 109

the First Book of Kings, we should never have known that the campaign of Shishak had inflicted such signal injury on the kingdom of Judah.

Champollion, indeed, the first discoverer of the list and of its importance, believed that he had found in it the name of the Jewish capital. The twenty-ninth cartouche reads Yaud-hamelek, which he explained as signifying 'the kingdom of Judah,' while Rosellini made it 'the king of Judah.' But both interpretations are impossible. *Melek*, it is true, means 'king' in Hebrew, but 'king of Judah' would have to be *melek-Yaudah*; 'kingdom of Judah,' *malkûth-Yaudah*. In the Semitic languages the genitive must follow the noun that governs it.

Yaud-hamelek is the Hebrew Ye(h)ud ham-melech 'Jehud of the king.' Jehud was a town of Dan (Josh. xix. 45), which Blau has identified with the modern El-Yehudîyeh, near Jaffa, and the title attached to it in the Egyptian list implies that it was an appanage of the crown. The faces of the prisoners who surmount the cartouches are worthy of attention. The Egyptian artists were skilled delineators of the human features, and an examination of their sculptures and paintings has shown that they represented the characteristics of their models with wonderful truth and accuracy. For ethnological purposes their portraits of foreign races are of considerable importance. Now the prisoners of Shishak have the features, not of the Jew, but of the Amorite. The prisoners who served as models to the Egyptian sculptors at Karnak must therefore have been of Amorite descent. It is a proof that the Amorite population in southern Palestine was still strong in the days of Rehoboam and Shishak. The Jews would have been predominant only in Jerusalem and the larger cities and fortresses of the kingdom. Elsewhere the older race survived with all its characteristic features; the Israelitish conquest had never rooted it out. Hence it is that it still lives and flourishes in its ancient home. The traveller in the country districts of Judah looks in vain for traces of the Jewish race, but he may still see there the Amorite just as he is depicted on the monuments of Egypt. The Jews, in fact, were but the conquering and dominant caste, and with the extinction of their nationality came also in Judah the extinction of their racial type. The few who remained were one by one absorbed into the older population of the country.

Shishak died soon after his Jewish campaigns. None of his successors seem to have possessed his military capacity and energy. One of them, however, Osorkon II., appears to have made an expedition against Palestine. Among the monuments disinterred at Bubastis by Dr. Naville for the Egyptian

Exploration Fund are the inscribed blocks of stone which formed the walls of the second hall of the temple. This hall was restored by Osorkon, who called it the 'Festival Hall' of Amon, which was dedicated on the day of Khoiak, in the twenty-second year of the king's reign. On one of the blocks the Pharaoh declares that 'all countries, the Upper and Lower Retennu, are hidden under his feet.' The Upper Retennu denoted Palestine, the Lower Retennu Northern Syria, and though the boast was doubtless a vainglorious one, it must have had some foundation in truth.

In the Second Book of Chronicles (xiv. 9-15) we are told that when Asa was on the Jewish throne, 'there came out against them Zerah the Ethiopian with an host of a thousand thousand and three hundred chariots.' The similarity between the names Zerah and Osorkon has long been noticed, and the reign of Osorkon II. would coincide with that of Asa. Dr. Naville, therefore, is probably right in believing that some connection exists between the campaign of Zerah and the boast of Osorkon. It is true that the Chronicler calls Zerah an Ethiopian, and describes his army as an Ethiopian host; but this seems due to the fact that the next kings of Egypt who interfered in the affairs of Palestine, So and Tirhaḳah, were of Ethiopian descent. In the time of Asa, at any rate, when the twenty-second dynasty was ruling over Egypt, no Ethiopian army could have entered Judah without the permission of the Egyptian monarch. However, Dr. Naville draws attention to the fact that Osorkon seems to have had some special tie with Ethiopia. His great festival at Bubastis was attended by natives of Ethiopia, the Anti came with their gifts from 'the land of the negroes,' and are depicted like the priests on the walls of the hall.

But troublous times were in store for Egypt. The twenty-second dynasty came to an end, and a period followed of confusion, civil war, and foreign invasion. The kings of Ethiopia sailed down the Nile and swept the country from Assuan to the sea. Petty princes reigned as independent sovereigns in the various cities of Egypt, and waged war one against the other. Pi-ankhi the Ethiopian was content with their momentary submission; he then retired to his ancestral capital at Napata, midway between Dongola and Khartûm, carrying with him the spoils of the Nile. Another Ethiopian, Shabaka or Sabako, the son of Kashet, made a more permanent settlement in Egypt. He put to death the nominal Pharaoh, Bak-n-ran-f or Bokkhoris, and founded the twenty-fifth dynasty. Order was again restored, the petty princes suppressed, and Egypt

The Age of the Israelitish Monarchies

as well as Ethiopia obeyed a single head. The roads were cleared of brigands, the temples and walls of the cities were rebuilt, and trade could again pass freely up and down the Nile.

An Egyptian civilisation and an Egyptian religion had been established in Ethiopia since the days of the eighteenth dynasty. For some centuries, even after they had become independent of Egypt, the ruling classes boasted of the purity of their Egyptian descent. But before the age of Sabako the Egyptian element had been absorbed by the native population. We have learned from a monument of the Assyrian king, Esar-haddon, lately found at Sinjerli, in northern Syria, that Sabako and his successors had all the physical characteristics of the negro. But no sign of this is allowed to appear on the Egyptian monuments. With the contempt for the black race which still distinguishes them, the Egyptians refused to acknowledge that their Pharaohs could be of negro blood. In the sculptures and paintings of the Nile, accordingly, the kings of the Ethiopian dynasty are represented with all the features of the Egyptian race.

In spite, however, of all attempts to conceal the fact, we now know that they were negroes in reality. But they brought with them a vigour and a strength of will that had long been wanting among the rulers of Egypt. And it was not long before their Asiatic neighbours found that a new and energetic power had arisen on the banks of the Nile. Assyria was now extending its empire throughout Western Asia, and claiming to control the politics of Syria and Palestine. The Syrian princes looked to Egypt for help. In B.C. 720, Assyria and Egypt met face to face for the first time. Sib'e, the Tartan, or commander-in-chief, of the Egyptian armies, with Hanno of Gaza and other Syrian allies, blocked the way of the Assyrian invaders at Raphia, on the border of Palestine. The victory was won by the Assyrian Sargon. Hanno was captured, and Sib'e fled to the Delta. But Sargon turned northward again, and did not follow up his success. He was content with receiving the tribute of Pharaoh (Pir'u) 'king of Egypt,' of Samsi, the queen of Arabia, and of Ithamar the Sabæan.

In Sib'e we must see the So or Seve of the Old Testament (2 Kings xvii. 4). He is there called 'king of Egypt,' but he was rather one of the subordinate princes of the Delta, who acted as the commander-in-chief of 'Pharaoh.' Pharaoh, it would seem, was still Bak-n-ran-f.

A few years later Sabako was established on the throne. He reigned at least twelve years, and was succeeded by his brother-in-law, Tirhakah, the Tarqû

The Age of the Israelitish Monarchies 115

of the Assyrian texts. Under him, Egypt once more played a part in Jewish history.

It was trust in 'Pharaoh, king of Egypt,' that made Hezekiah revolt from Assyria after Sargon's death. The result was the invasion of his kingdom by Sennacherib in B.C. 701. Tirhakah moved forward to help his ally. But his march diverted the attention of the Assyrian monarch only for a while. The armies of Sennacherib and Tirhakah met at Eltekeh, and Tirhakah the Pharaoh of Egypt was forced to retire. Both claim a victory in their inscriptions. Sennacherib tells us how 'the kings of Egypt and the bowmen, chariots, and horses of the king of northern Arabia, had collected their innumerable forces and gone to the aid' of Hezekiah and his Philistine allies, and how in sight of Eltekeh, 'in reliance on Assur,' he had 'fought with them and utterly overthrown them.' 'The charioteers and the sons of the king of Egypt, together with the charioteers of the king of northern Arabia,' he had 'taken captive in the battle.' Tirhakah, on the other hand, on a statue now in the Gizeh Museum, declares that he was the conqueror of the Bedouin, the Hittites, the Arvadites, the Assyrians, and the people of Aram-Naharaim. The battle, in fact, was a Kadmeian victory. Tirhakah was so far defeated that he was forced to retreat to his own dominions, while

Sennacherib's victory was not decisive enough to allow him to pursue it. He contented himself with marching back into Judah, burning and plundering its towns and villages, and carrying their inhabitants into captivity. Then came the catastrophe which destroyed the larger part of his army and obliged him to return ignominiously to his own capital. The spoils and captives of Judah were the only fruits of his campaign. His rebellious vassal went unpunished, and the strong fortress of Jerusalem was saved from the Assyrian. Though Sennacherib made many military expeditions during the remaining twenty years of his reign, he never came again to the south of Palestine.

Egypt lay sheltered from invasion behind Jerusalem. But with the death of Sennacherib there came a change. His son and successor, Esar-haddon, was a good general and a man of great ability. Manasseh of Judah became his vassal, and the way lay open to the Nile. With a large body of trained veterans he descended upon Egypt (B.C. 674). The sheikh of the Bedouin provided him with the camels which conveyed the water for the army across the desert. Three campaigns were needed before Egypt, under its Ethiopian ruler, could be subdued. But at last, in B.C. 670, Esar-haddon drove the Egyptian forces before him in fifteen days (from the 3rd to the

18th of Tammuz or June) all the way from the frontier to Memphis, thrice defeating them with heavy loss, and wounding Tirhakah himself. Three days later Memphis fell, and Tirhakah fled to Ethiopia, leaving Egypt to the conqueror. It was after this success that the Assyrian monarch erected the stêlê at Sinjerli, on which he is portrayed with Tirhakah of Egypt and Baal of Tyre kneeling before him, each with a ring through his lips, to which is attached a bridle held by the Assyrian king.

Egypt was reorganised under Assyrian rule, and measures taken to prevent the return of the Ethiopians. It was divided into twenty satrapies, the native princes being appointed to govern them for their Assyrian master. At their head was placed Necho, the vassal king of Sais. Esar-haddon now returned to Nineveh, and on the cliffs of the Nahr el-Kelb, near Beyrout, he engraved a record of his conquest of Egypt and Thebes by the side of the monument whereon, seven centuries previously, Ramses II. had boasted of his victories over the nations of Asia.

At first the Egyptian princes were well pleased with their change of masters. But in Thebes there was a strong party which sympathised with Ethiopia rather than with Assyria. With their help, Tirhakah returned in B.C. 668, sailed down the Nile, and took

Memphis by storm. Esar-haddon started at once to suppress the revolt. But on the way to Egypt he died on the 10th of Marchesvan or October, and his son, Assur-bani-pal, followed him on the throne.

The Ethiopian army was encountered near Karbanit, in the Delta. A complete victory was gained over it, and Tirhakah was compelled to fly, first from Memphis, then from Thebes. The tributary kings whom he had displaced were restored, and Assur-bani-pal left Egypt in the full belief that it was tranquil. But hardly had he returned to Nineveh before a fresh revolt broke out there. Tirhakah began to plot with the native satraps, and even Necho of Sais was suspected of complicity. The commanders of the Assyrian garrisons, accordingly, sent him and two other princes (from Tanis and Goshen) loaded with chains to Assyria. But Assur-bani-pal, either really convinced of Necho's innocence or pretending to be so, not only pardoned him but bestowed upon him a robe of honour, as well as a sword of gold and a chariot and horses, and sent him back to Sais, giving at the same time the government of Athribis, whose mounds lie close to Benha, to his son, Psammetikhos. Meanwhile Tirhakah had again penetrated to Thebes and Memphis, where he celebrated the festival in honour of the appearance of a new Apis. But his power was no longer what it once had been, and even before the return of Necho he found it prudent to retire to Ethiopia. There he died a few months later.

The Thebaid, however, continued in a state of revolt against the Assyrian authority. Another Ethiopian king, whom the Assyrians call Urd-Aman, had succeeded Tirhakah, and was battling for the sovereignty of Egypt. Urd-Aman is usually identified with the Pharaoh Rud-Amon, whose name has been met with on two Egyptian monuments, but about whom nothing further is known. Some scholars, however, read the name Tand-Aman, and identify it with that of Tuatan-Amon or Tuant-Amon, whose royal cartouches are engraved by the side of those of Tirhakah in the temple of Ptah-Osiris at Karnak. An inscription found built into a wall at Luxor mentions his third year, and a large stêlê erected by him at Napata was discovered among the ruins of his capital in 1862, and is now in the Museum of Gizeh. On this he states that in the first year of his reign he was excited by a dream to invade the north. Thebes opened its gates to him, and after worshipping in the temple of Amon at Karnak, he marched to Memphis, which he captured after a slight resistance. Then he proceeded against the princes of the Delta, who, however, shut themselves up in their cities or else submitted to him.

One day Paqrur of Goshen appeared at Memphis to do him homage, much to the surprise and delight of the Ethiopian king. As Paqrur was the prince of Pi-Sopd or Goshen, who had been sent to Nineveh along with Necho, the date of Tuatan-Amon is pretty clear. How he came to quit Egypt, however, he does not vouchsafe to explain.

Whether Urd-Aman were Rud-Amon or Tuatan-Amon, he gave a good deal of trouble to the Assyrians. Thebes was securely in his hands, and from thence he marched upon Memphis. The Assyrian garrison and its allies were defeated in front of the city, which was then blockaded and taken after a long siege. Necho was captured and put to death, and Psammetikhos escaped the same fate only by flight into Syria. But Assyrian revenge did not tarry long. Assur-bani-pal determined to put an end to Egyptian revolt and Ethiopian invasion once for all. A large army was despatched to the Nile, which overthrew the forces of Rud-Amon in the Delta and pursued him as far as Thebes. Thence he fled to Kipkip in Ethiopia, and a terrible punishment was inflicted on the capital of southern Egypt. The whole of its inhabitants were led away into slavery. Its temples—at once the centres of disaffection and fortresses against attack—were half-demolished, its monuments and palaces were destroyed, and all its treasures, sacred and profane, were carried away. Among the spoil were two obelisks, more than seventy tons in weight, which were removed to Nineveh as trophies of victory. The injuries which Kambyses has been accused of inflicting on the ancient monuments of Thebes were really the work of the Assyrians.

How great was the impression made upon the oriental world by the sack of Thebes may be gathered from the reference to it by the prophet Nahum (iii. 8-10). Nineveh itself is threatened with the same overthrow. 'Art thou better than No of Amon, that was situate among the rivers, that had the waters round about it, whose rampart was the sea, (the Nile), and her wall was from the sea? Ethiopia and Egypt were her strength, and it was infinite; Put and Lubim were thy helpers. Yet was she carried away, she went into captivity: her young children also were dashed in pieces at the top of all the streets: and they cast lots for her honourable men, and all her great men were bound in chains.' As the destruction of Thebes took place about B.C. 665, the date of Nahum's prophecy cannot have been much later.

In the Assyrian inscriptions Thebes is called Ni', corresponding with the No of the Old Testament. Both words represent the Egyptian Nu, 'city,'

Thebes being pre-eminently 'the city' of Upper Egypt. Its patron-deity was Amon, to whom its great temple was dedicated, and hence it is that Nahum calls it 'No of Amon.' Divided as it was into two halves by the Nile, and encircled on either side by canals, one of which—'the southern water'—still runs past the southern front of the temple of Luxor, it could truly be said that its 'rampart was the sea.' To this day the Nile is called 'the sea' by the natives of Egypt.

The Ethiopians penetrated into Egypt no more. The twenty satrapies were re-established; and Psammetikhos received his father's principality, though the precedence among the vassal-kings was given to Paqrur of Goshen. For a time the country was at peace.

Fifteen years later, however, an event occurred which shook the Assyrian empire to its foundations. A revolt broke out which spread throughout the whole of it. The revolt was headed by Assur-banipal's brother, the Viceroy of Babylonia, and for some time the result wavered in the balance. But the good generalship and disciplined forces of Assyria eventually prevailed, and she emerged from the struggle, exhausted indeed, but triumphant. The empire, however, was shrunken. Gyges of Lydia had thrown off his allegiance, and had assisted

Psammetikhos of Sais to make Egypt independent. While the Assyrian armies were battling for existence in Asia, Psammetikhos, with the Ionian and Karian mercenaries from Lydia, was driving out the Assyrian garrisons and overcoming his brother satraps. One by one they disappeared before him, and at last he had the satisfaction of seeing Egypt a united and independent monarchy, under a monarch who claimed to be of native race.

The blood of the founder of the twenty-sixth dynasty was, however, mixed. He seems to have been, partly at least, of Libyan descent, and it is even doubtful whether his name is pure Egyptian. Like his father, he surrounded himself with foreigners: the Greeks and Karians, with whose help he had gained his throne, were high in favour, and constituted the royal body-guard. The native Egyptian army, we are told, deserted the king in disgust and made their way to Ethiopia. However that may be, Greek troops were settled in 'camps' in the Delta, Greek merchants were allowed to trade and even to build in Egypt, and the Karians became dragomen, guides, and interpreters between the natives and the European tourists who began to visit the Nile.

It was during the reign of Psammetikhos I. (B.C. 664-610) that the great invasion of nomad Scyths, referred to in the earlier chapters of Jeremiah, swept over Western Asia. They sacked the towns of the Philistines and made their way to the Egyptian frontier, but there they were bought off by Psammetikhos. After their dispersion, the Egyptian Pharaoh turned his eyes towards Palestine, with the intention of restoring the Asiatic empire of Ramses II. The twenty-sixth dynasty was an age of antiquarian revival; not content with restoring Egypt to peace and prosperity, its kings aimed also at restoring the Egypt of the past. Egyptian art again puts on an antique form, temples are repaired or erected in accordance with ancient models, and literature reflects the general tendency. The revival only wanted originality to make it successful; as it is, the art of the twenty-sixth dynasty is careful and good, and under its rule Egypt enjoyed for the last time a St. Luke's summer of culture and renown.

The power of Assyria was passing away. The great rebellion, and the wars in Elam which followed, had drained it of its resources. The Scythic invasion destroyed what little strength was left. Before Psammetikhos died Nineveh was already surrounded by its foes, and four years later it perished utterly.

The provinces of the west became virtually independent. Josiah of Judah still called himself a vassal

The Age of the Israelitish Monarchies 125

of the Assyrian monarch, but he acted as if the Assyrian monarchy did not exist. The Assyrian governor of Samaria was deprived of his authority, and Jewish rule was obeyed throughout what had been the territory of the Ten Tribes.

The weakness of Assyria was the opportunity of Egypt. The earlier years of the reign of Psammetikhos were spent in reorganising his kingdom and army, in suppressing all opposition to his government, and in rebuilding the ruined cities and temples. Then he marched into Palestine and endeavoured to secure once more for Egypt the cities of the Philistines. Ashdod was taken after a prolonged siege, and an Egyptian garrison placed in it.

The successor of Psammetikhos was his son Necho, who carried out the foreign policy of his father. The old canal which ran from the Red Sea at Suez to the Nile near Zagazig, and which centuries of neglect had allowed to be choked, was again partially cleared out, and 'the tongue of the Egyptian sea was cut off' (Isa. xi. 15). Ships were also sent from Suez under Phœnician pilots to circumnavigate Africa. Three years did they spend on the voyage, and after passing the Straits of Gibraltar, finally arrived safely at the mouths of the Nile. There an incredulous people heard that as they were sailing westward the sun was on their right hand.

But long before the return of his ships, Necho had placed himself at the head of his army and entered on the invasion of Asia. The Syrians were defeated at Migdol, and Gaza was occupied. The Egyptian army then proceeded to march along the sea-coast by the ancient military road, which struck inland at the Nahr el-Kelb. But the Jewish king, pleading his duty to his Assyrian suzerain, attempted to block the way; the result was a battle in the plain of Megiddo, where the Jewish forces were totally routed, and Josiah himself carried from the field mortally wounded. Necho now overran northern Syria as far as the Euphrates, and then returned southward to punish the Jews. Jerusalem was captured by treachery, and Jehoahaz, the new king, deposed after a reign of only three months. The Pharaoh then made his brother Eliakim king in his stead, changing his name to Jehoiakim. The city was fined a talent of gold and a hundred talents of silver, and Necho sent his armour to the temple of Apollo near Miletus as a thank-offering to the god of his Greek mercenaries.

The empire of Thothmes was restored, at all events in Asia. But it lasted hardly more than three years. In B.C. 605 a decisive battle was fought at Carchemish, on the Euphrates, now Jerablûs, between Necho and the Babylonian prince

The Age of the Israelitish Monarchies 127

Nebuchadrezzar, who commanded the army of his father Nabopolassar. The Egyptians fled in confusion, and the Asiatic empire was utterly lost. The Jewish king transferred his allegiance to the conqueror, and for three years 'became his servant.' Then he rebelled, probably in consequence of a fresh attempt made by the Egyptians to recover their power in Palestine. The attempt, however, failed, and a Babylonian army was sent against Jerusalem. Jehoiakim was already dead, but his son Jehoiachin, along with the leading citizens, the military class, and the artisans—'ten thousand captives' in all—was carried into exile in Babylonia (B.C. 599). His uncle Zedekiah was placed on the throne, and for nearly nine years he remained faithful to his Babylonian master.

Then came temptation from the side of Egypt. Psammetikhos II., who had succeeded his father Necho in B.C. 594, prepared to march into Palestine, and contest the supremacy over Western Asia with the Babylonian monarch. A Babylonian army was already besieging the revolted city of Jerusalem when the forces of the Pharaoh appeared in sight. The Babylonians broke up their camp and retired, and it seemed as if the rebellion of the Jewish king had been successful (Jer. xxxvii. 5, 11; Ezek. xvii. 15).

But it was not for long. The Egyptians returned to 'their own land,' and the siege of Jerusalem was recommenced. At last, in B.C. 588, the city was taken, its king and most of its inhabitants led into captivity, and its temple and palace burned with fire. Judah was placed under a Babylonian governor, and the authority of the Babylonians acknowledged as far as Gaza.

Psammetikhos II. had died in the preceding year, and his son Uahabra, the Apries of the Greeks, the Hophra of the Old Testament, occupied his place. The army which had gone to the help of Zedekiah had doubtless been sent by him. He had recaptured Gaza, and marched along the coast to Sidon, which he captured, and Tyre, which was in rebellion against the Chaldæans, while his fleet defeated the combined forces of the Cyprians and Phœnicians, and held the sea. A hieroglyphic inscription, erected by a native of Gebal and commemorative of the invasion, has recently been found near Sidon. But the Egyptian conquests were again lost almost as quickly as they had been made.

Palestine became a Babylonian province up to the frontiers of Egypt. Many of the Jews who had been left in it fled to Egypt. Their numbers were reinforced by a band of outlaws, of whom Johanan was the leader, who had murdered the Babylonian governor and had dragged into Egypt with them the prophet Jeremiah and his scribe Baruch. Jeremiah in vain protested against their conduct, and predicted that Hophra should be slain by his enemies, and that Nebuchadrezzar should set up his throne on that very pavement 'at the entry of Pharaoh's house in Tahpanhes' where the prophet was then standing. Tahpanhes is almost certainly Tel ed-Defneh, the Daphnæ of Greek geography, which stands in the mid-desert about twelve miles to the west of Kantara on the Suez Canal, and where Professor Flinders Petrie made excavations for the Egypt Exploration Fund in 1886. There he found the remains of a great fortress and camp, which had been built by Psammetikhos I. for his Greek mercenaries. The walls of the camp were forty feet in thickness, and the ruins of the fortress still go by the name of the 'Castle of the Jew's Daughter.' In front of it is a brick pavement, just like that described by Jeremiah.

Daphnæ, in fact, was one of the chief fortresses of Egypt on the side of Asia, and it was accordingly the chief station of the Greek mercenaries. It commanded the entrance to the Delta, and was almost the first place in Egypt that the traveller from Palestine who came by the modern caravan road would approach. It was, therefore, the first settlement at which Jewish fugitives who wished to avoid the Babylonian garrison at Gaza would be likely to arrive. And it was also the first object of attack on the part of an invader from the East. Its possession opened to him the way to Memphis.

That Nebuchadrezzar actually invaded Egypt, as Jeremiah had predicted, we now know from a fragment of his annals. In his thirty-seventh year (B.C. 567) he marched into Egypt, defeating the Pharaoh Amasis, and the soldiers of 'Phut of the Ionians,' 'a distant land which is in the midst of the sea.' The enemies, therefore, into whose hands Hophra was to fall were not the Babylonians. They were, in fact, his own subjects.

He had pursued the Hellenising policy of his predecessors with greater thoroughness than they had done, and had thus aroused the jealousy and alarm of the native population. The Greek mercenaries alone had his confidence, and the Egyptians accused him of betraying the native troops whom he had sent to the help of the Libyans against the Greek colony of Kyrênê. Amasis (or Ahmes), his brother-in-law, put himself at the head of the rebels. A battle was fought near Sais between the Greek troops of Hophra on the one side and the revolted Egyptians on the other, which ended in the defeat of the Greeks and the capture of Hophra himself.

Amasis was proclaimed king (B.C. 570), and though the captive Pharaoh was at first treated with respect, he was afterwards put to death.

The change of monarch made little difference to the Greeks in Egypt. They were too valuable, both as soldiers and as traders, for the Pharaoh to dispense with their services. The mercenaries were removed from Daphnæ to Memphis, in the very heart of the kingdom, and fresh privileges were granted to the merchants of Naukratis. The Pharaoh married a Greek wife, and a demotic papyrus, now at Paris, even describes how he robbed the temples of Memphis, On and Bubastis of their endowments and handed them over to the Greek troops. 'The Council' which sat under him ordered that 'the vessels, the fuel, the linen, and the dues' hitherto enjoyed by their gods and their priests should be given instead to the foreigner. In this act of sacrilege the Egyptians of a later day saw the cause of the downfall of their country. The invasion of Nebuchadrezzar had passed over it without producing much injury; indeed, it does not seem to have extended beyond the eastern half of the Delta. But a new power, that of Cyrus, was rising in the East. Amasis had foreseen the coming storm, and had occupied Cyprus in advance. If Xenophon is to be believed, he had also sent troops to the aid of Krœsus of Lydia. But all was of no avail. The power of Cyrus steadily increased. The empires of Lydia and Babylonia went down before it, and when his son Kambyses succeeded him in July, B.C. 529, the new empire extended from the Mediterranean to India and from the Caspian to the borders of Egypt. It was clear that the fertile banks of the Nile would be the next object of attack.

Greek vanity asserted that the actual cause of the invasion was the Greek mercenary Phanês. He had deserted to Kambyses, and explained to him how Egypt could be entered. That Phanês was a name used by the Egyptian Greeks we know from its occurrence on the fragment of a large vase discovered by Professor Petrie at Naukratis. Here we read: 'Phanês the son of Glaukos dedicated me to Apollo of Naukratis.' But the invasion of Egypt by Kambyses was the necessary consequence of the policy which had laid the whole of the oriental world at his father's feet.

Amasis died while the army of Kambyses was on its march (B.C. 526), and his son Psammetikhos III. had to bear the brunt of the attack. A battle was fought near Pelusium, and though the Greek and Karian auxiliaries did their best, the invading forces gained the day. The Pharaoh fled to Memphis, which was thereupon besieged by Kambyses. The siege was a short one. The city of 'the White Wall' was taken, Psammetikhos made a .prisoner, and his son, together with two thousand youths of the leading Egyptian families, was put to death. For a while Psammetikhos himself was allowed to live, but the fears of the conqueror soon caused him to be executed, and with his death came the end of the twenty-sixth dynasty and the independence of Egypt.

CHAPTER V

THE AGE OF THE PTOLEMIES

JUDAH had profited by the revolution which had been so disastrous to the monarchy of the Nile. The overthrow of the Babylonian empire and the rise of Cyrus had brought deliverance from exile and the restoration of the temple and its services. In the Jewish colony at Jerusalem, Cyrus and his successors had, as it were, a bridle upon Egypt; gratitude to their deliverer and freedom to enjoy the theocracy which had taken the place of the Davidic monarchy made the Jewish people an outpost and garrison upon whose loyalty the Persian king could rely.

The yoke of the Zoroastrian Darius and his descendants pressed heavily, on the other hand, upon the priests and people of Egypt. Time after time they attempted to revolt. Their first rebellion, under Khabbash, saved Greece from the legions of Darius and postponed the day of Persian invasion to a time when the incapable Xerxes sat upon the throne of his energetic father. A second time they rose in insurrection in the reign of Artaxerxes I., the successor of Xerxes. But under Artaxerxes II. came a more formidable outbreak, which ended in the recovery of Egyptian independence and the establishment of the last three dynasties of native kings.

For sixty-five years (from B.C. 414 to 349) Egypt preserved its independence. More than once the Persians sought to recover it, but they were foiled by the Spartan allies of the Pharaoh or by the good fortune of the Egyptians. But civil feuds and cowardice sapped the strength of the Egyptian resistance. Greek mercenaries and sailors now fought in the ranks of the Persians as well as in those of the Egyptians, and the result of the struggle between Persia and Egypt was in great measure dependent on the amount of pay the two sides could afford to give them. The army was insubordinate, and between the Greek and Egyptian soldiers there was jealousy and feud. Nektanebo II. (B.C. 367-49), the last of the Pharaohs, had dethroned his own father, and though he had once driven the Persian king Artaxerxes Ochus back from the coasts of Egypt, he failed to do so a second time. The Greeks were left to defend themselves as best they could at Pelusium, while Nektanebo retired to Memphis with 60,000 worthless native troops. From thence he fled to Ethiopia with his treasures, leaving his country in the hands of the Persian. Ochus wreaked his vengeance on the Egyptian priests, destroying the temples, demanding a heavy ransom for the sacred records he had robbed, setting up an ass—a symbol in Egyptian eyes of all that was evil and unclean—as the patron-god of the conquered land, and slaying the sacred bull Apis in sacrifice to the new divinity. The murder of Ochus by his Egyptian eunuch Bagoas was the penalty he paid for these outrages on the national faith.

Egypt never again was free. Its rulers have been of manifold races and forms of faith, but they have never again been Egyptians. Persians, Greeks and Romans, Arabs, Kurds, Circassians, Mameluk slaves and Turks, Frenchmen and Englishmen, have all governed or misgoverned it, but throughout this long page of its history there is no sign of native political life. Religion or taxation has alone seemed able to stir the people into movement or revolt. For aspirations after national freedom we look in vain.

The Persian was not left long in the possession of his rebellious province. Egypt opened her gates to Alexander of Macedon, as in later ages she opened her gates to the Arab 'Amru. The Greeks had long been associated in the Egyptian mind with opposition to the hated Persian, and it was as a Greek that

Alexander entered the country. Memphis and Thebes welcomed him, and he did his best to prove to his subjects that he had indeed come among them as one of their ancient kings. Hardly had he reached Memphis before he went in state to the temple of Apis and offered sacrifice to the sacred bull. Then, after founding Alexandria at the spot where the native village of Rakoti stood, he made his way to the Oasis of Ammon, the modern Siwah, among the sands of the distant desert, and there was greeted by the high-priest of the temple as the son of the god. Like the Pharaohs of old, the Macedonian conqueror became the son of Amon-Ra, and in Egypt at least claimed divine honours.

Before leaving Egypt Alexander appointed the nomarchs who were to govern it, and ordered that justice should be administered according to the ancient law of the land. He also sent 7000 Samaritans into the Thebaid; some of them were settled in the Fayyûm, and in the papyri discovered by Professor Petrie at Hawâra mention is made of a village which they had named Samaria. Appointing Kleomenês prefect of Egypt and collector of the taxes, Alexander now hurried away to the Euphrates, there to overthrow the shattered relics of the Persian Empire.

It was while he was at Ekbatana that his friend

Hêphæstiôn died, and Alexander wrote to Egypt to inquire of the oracle of Ammon what honours it was lawful for him to pay to the dead man. In reply Hêphæstiôn was pronounced to be a god, and a temple was accordingly erected to him at Alexandria, and the new lighthouse on the island of Pharos was called after his name.

When Alexander died suddenly and unexpectedly, the council of his generals which assembled at Babylon declared his half-brother, Philip Arridæus, to be his successor. But they reserved to themselves all the real power in Alexander's empire. Ptolemy, the son of Lagos, chose Egypt as the seat of his government, which was accordingly handed over to him by Kleomenês on his arrival there, a year after the accession of the new king. His first act was to put Kleomenês to death.

Then came the long funeral procession bearing the corpse of Alexander from Babylon to the tomb that was to be erected for him in his new city of Alexandria. More than a year passed while it wound its way slowly from city to city, till at last it arrived at Memphis. Here the body of the great conqueror rested awhile until the gorgeous sepulchre was made ready in which it was finally to repose.

It was plain that Ptolemy was aiming at independent power. Perdikkas, the regent, accordingly attacked him, carrying in his train the young princes, Philip Arridæus, and Alexander Ægos, the infant son of Alexander. But the invading army was routed below Memphis, Perdikkas was slain, and the young princes fell into the hands of the conqueror. From this time forward, Ptolemy, though nominally a subject, acted as if he were a king.

Nikanôr was sent into Syria to annex it to Egypt. Jerusalem alone resisted the invaders, but it was assaulted on the Sabbath when the defenders withdrew from the walls, and all further opposition was at end. Palestine and Cœle-Syria were again united with the kingdom on the Nile.

The union, however, did not last long. In B.C. 315 Philip Arridæus was murdered, and Alexander was proclaimed successor to his empty dignity. The year following, Antigonus, the rival of Ptolemy in Asia Minor, made ready to invade Egypt. But Ptolemy had already conquered Kyrênê and Cyprus, and was master of the sea. Syria and Palestine, however, submitted to Antigonus, and though Ptolemy gained a decisive victory over his enemies at Gaza, he did not think it prudent to pursue it. He contented himself, therefore, with razing the fortifications of Acre and Jaffa, of Samaria and Gaza.

In B.C. 312 the generals of Alexander, who still called themselves the lieutenants of his son, came to a general agreement, each keeping that portion of the empire which he had made his own. The agreement was almost immediately followed by the murder of Alexander Ægos. Cleopatra, the sister of the great Alexander, and his niece Thessalonika alone remained of the royal family, and Cleopatra, on her way to Egypt to marry Ptolemy, was assassinated by Antigonus (in B.C. 308), and Alexander's niece soon afterwards shared the same fate. The family of 'the son of Ammon,' the annihilator of the Persian Empire, was extinct.

Two years later, in B.C. 306, an end was put to the farce so long played by the generals of Alexander, and each of them assumed the title of king. Ptolemy took that of 'king of Egypt.' To this the Greeks afterwards added the name of Sôtêr, 'Saviour,' when his supplies of corn had saved the Rhodians from destruction during their heroic defence of their city against the multitudinous war-ships of Antigonus.

Throughout his rule, Ptolemy never forgot the needs and interests of the kingdom over which he ruled. Alexandria was completed, with its unrivalled harbours, its stately public buildings, its broad quays and its spacious streets. From first to last it remained the Greek capital of Egypt. It was Greek in its origin, Greek in its architecture, Greek in its population; Greek also in its character, its manners,

The Age of the Ptolemies 141

and its faith. Cut off from the rest of Egypt by the Mareotic Lake, and enjoying a European climate, it was from its foundation what it is to-day, a city of Europe rather than of Egypt. From it, as from an impregnable watch-tower, the Ptolemies directed the fortunes of their kingdom: it was not only the key to Egypt, it was also a bridle upon it. The wealth of the world passed through its streets and harbours; the religions and philosophies of East and West met within its halls. Ptolemy had founded in it a university, a prototype of Oxford and Cambridge in modern England, of the Azhar in modern Cairo. In the Museum, as it was called, a vast library was gathered together, and its well-endowed chairs were filled with learned professors from all parts of the Greek world, who wrote books and delivered lectures and dined together at the royal charge.

But the Greeks were not the only inhabitants of the new city. The Jews also settled there in large numbers on the eastern side of the town, attracted by the offers of Ptolemy and the belief that the rising centre of trade would be better worth inhabiting than the wasted fields of Palestine. All the rights of Greek citizenship were granted to them, and they were placed on a footing almost of equality with Ptolemy's own countrymen.

The native Egyptians were far worse treated.

They had become 'the hewers of wood and carriers of water' for their new Greek masters. It was they who furnished the government with its revenue, but in return they possessed no rights, no privileges. When land was wanted for the veterans of the Macedonian army, as, for example, in the Fayyûm, it was taken from them without compensation. Taxes, ever heavier and heavier, were laid upon them; and every attempt at remonstrance or murmuring was visited with immediate punishment. The Egyptian had no rights unless he could be registered a citizen of Alexandria, and this it was next to impossible for him to be.

It is true that the Egyptians were told all this was done in order that their own laws and customs might not be interfered with. While the Greeks and Jews were governed by Greek law, the Egyptians were governed by the old law of the land. But it was forgotten that the laws were administered by Greeks, and that the higher officials were also Greeks, who, as against an Egyptian, possessed arbitrary power. It was only amongst themselves, as between Egyptian and Egyptian, that the natives of the country enjoyed any benefit from the laws under which they lived; wherever the government and the Greeks were concerned, they were like outcasts, who could be punished, but not tried.

Nevertheless the country for many years remained tranquil. Unlike the Persians, the Greeks respected the religion of the people. Ptolemy did his utmost to conciliate the priesthood; their temples were restored and decorated, their festivals were treated with honour; above all, their endowments were untouched. And with the priesthood disposed to be friendly towards him, Ptolemy had no reason to be afraid. The priests were the national leaders; they it was who had stirred up the revolts against the Persian, and the temples in which they served had been the fortresses and rallying-points of the rebel armies. The Egyptians have always been an intensely religious people; whatever may have been their form of creed, whether pagan, Christian, or Moslem, they have clung to it with tenacity and battled for it, sometimes with fanatical zeal. Religion will arouse them when nothing else can do so; by the side of it even the love of gain has but little influence.

Besides conciliating the priesthood, Ptolemy planted garrisons of Greeks in several parts of the country. Bodies of veterans colonised the Fayyûm, and Ptolemais, now Menshîyeh, in Upper Egypt, was a Greek city modelled in all respects upon Alexandria. The public accounts were kept in Greek, and though the clerks and tax-gatherers were usually natives who had received a Greek education, many of them were Greeks by birth and even Jews. 'Ostraka,' or inscribed potsherds, have been found at Thebes, which show that in the days of Ptolemy Physkôn, a Jew, Simon, the son of Eleazar, farmed the taxes there for the temple of Amon. As he did not himself know Greek, his receipts were written for him by one of his sons. After his death he was succeeded in his office by his son Philoklês. The name is noticeable, as it shows how rapidly the Jews of Egypt could become wholly Greek. The religion of his forefathers was not likely to sit heavily on the shoulders of the tax-gatherer of a heathen temple, and we need not wonder at the Hellenisation of his family. Simon was a sample of many of his brethren: in adopting Greek culture the Jews of Egypt began to forget that they were Jews. It required the shock of persecution at Jerusalem, and the Maccabean war of independence to recall them to a recollection of their past history and a sense of the mission of their race.

With the rise of the Greek kingdom in Egypt, the canonical books of the Old Testament come to an end. Jaddua, the last high-priest recorded in the Book of Nehemiah (xii. 7, 22), met Alexander the Great at Mizpeh, and if Josephus is to be trusted, obtained from him a recognition of the ancient

The Age of the Ptolemies

privileges of the Jews and their exemption from taxation every Sabbatical year. The First Book of Chronicles (iii. 23) seems to bring the genealogy of the descendants of Zorobabel down to an even later date. But where the canonical books break off, the books of the Apocrypha begin. Jesus the son of Sirach, in his prologue to the Book of Ecclesiasticus, tells us that he had translated it in Egypt from Hebrew into Greek, when Euergetês, the third Ptolemy, was king, and thirty-eight years after its compilation by his grandfather Jesus. Like most of the apocryphal books, it thus had a Palestinian origin, but its translation into Greek indicates the intercourse that was going on between the Jews of Palestine and those of Egypt, as well as the general adoption of the Greek language by the Egyptian Jews.

The translation of the Hebrew Scriptures into Greek about the same period is a yet more striking illustration of the same fact. The name of 'Septuagint,' which the translation still retains, perpetuates the legend, derived from the false Aristæas, of its having been made all at one time by seventy (or seventy-two) translators. But internal evidence shows that such could not have been the case. The various books of the Canon were translated at different times, and the translators exhibit very different degrees of

K

ability and acquaintance with the Hebrew language. The Pentateuch was the first to be rendered into Greek; the other books followed afterwards, and it would appear that the Book of Ecclesiastes never found a place in the translation at all. The Greek translation of the book which is now found in the Septuagint was probably made by Aquila.

It was under Ptolemy II., who justified his title of Philadelphus, or 'Brother-loving,' by the murder of his two brothers, that the work of translation was begun. Ptolemy Sôtêr, his father, had resigned his crown two years before his death, and the event proved that his confidence in his son's filial piety was not misplaced. The coronation of Philadelphus at Alexandria was celebrated with one of the most gorgeous pageants the world has ever seen, the details of which are preserved by Athenæus. Under the new king the internal development of the monarchy went on apace. The canal was opened which connected the Nile with the Red Sea, and at its outlet near Suez a town was built called Arsinoê, after the king's sister. The ports of Berenikê and Philotera (now Qoseir) were constructed and fortified on the coast of the Red Sea, and roads made to them from Koptos and Syênê on the Nile. In this way the ivory and gems of the Sudân could be brought to Egypt without passing through the hostile territories of the Ethiopians in Upper Nubia. In the eastern desert itself the mines of emerald and gold were worked until the royal revenue was increased to more than three millions sterling a year.

Though Ptolemy Philadelphus was fond of show, he was not extravagant, and his income was sufficient not only to maintain a large army and navy and protect efficiently the frontier of his kingdom, but also to leave a large reserve fund in the treasury. It was said to amount to as much as a hundred millions sterling. It was no wonder, therefore, that Alexandria became filled with sumptuous buildings. The Pharos or lighthouse was finished by Sôstratos, as well as the tomb of Alexander, whose body was moved from Memphis to the golden sarcophagus which had been prepared for it. The library of the Museum was stocked with books until 400,000 rolls of papyrus were collected together, and men of science and learning from all parts of the world were attracted to it by the munificence of the king. The principal librarianship, however, changed hands on the accession of the new king. Demetrius Phalereus, the ex-tyrant of Athens, who had been the first librarian, had offended Philadelphus by advising that the crown should descend to his elder brother instead of to himself, and he had accordingly to make way for Zênodotos of Ephesus, famous as a critic of Homer.

Among the books which found a place in the great library of Alexandria was doubtless the Greek translation of the Pentateuch. Philadelphus showed remarkable favour to the Jews. The Jewish captives of his soldiers were ransomed by him and given homes in various parts of Egypt. One hundred and twenty thousand slaves were thus freed, the king paying for each 120 drachmas, or 30 shekels, the price of a slave according to the Mosaic Law. It is quite possible that there may be some truth in the legend that the Greek translation of the Old Testament was made at his desire. Whether or not we believe that he sent two Greek Jews, Aristæus and Andræus, with costly gifts to Eleazar the high-priest at Jerusalem, asking him to select fit men for the purpose, he was probably not unwilling that a copy of the sacred books of his Jewish subjects, in a form intelligible to the Greeks, should be added to the library. We must not forget that it was he who employed Manetho, the priest of Sebennytos, to write in Greek the history of his country, which he compiled from the hieroglyphic monuments and hieratic papyri of the native temples.

Ptolemy III., Euergetês, the eldest son of Philadelphus, succeeded his father in B.C. 246. A war with Syria broke out at the beginning of his reign, and the march of the Egyptian army as far as

Seleucia, the capital of the Syrian kingdom on the Euphrates, was one uninterrupted triumph. On his return, Ptolemy laid his offerings on the altar at Jerusalem, and thanked the God of the Jews for his success. The Jewish community might well be pardoned for believing that in the conqueror of Syria they had a new proselyte to their faith.

The Egyptians had equal reason to be satisfied with their king. Among the spoils of his Syrian campaign were 2500 vases and statues of the Egyptian deities which Kambyses had carried to Persia nearly three centuries before. They were restored to the temples of Upper Egypt, from which they had been taken, with stately ceremonies and amid the rejoicing of the people, and Ptolemy was henceforth known among his subjects as Euergetês, their 'Benefactor.'

Euergetês, in fact, seems to have been the most Egyptian and least Greek of all the Ptolemies. Alone among them he visited Thebes and paid homage to the gods of Egypt. Their temples were rebuilt and crowded with offerings, and the priesthood naturally regarded him as a king after their own heart. He, too, like the Pharaohs of old, turned his attention to the conquest of Ethiopia, which his predecessors had been content to neglect.[1] It was

[1] Sharpe, *History of Egypt*, i. p. 346.

under Euergetês, moreover, that the so-called Decree of Canôpus was drawn up in hieroglyphics and demotic Egyptian as well as in Greek. Its occasion was the death of Berenikê, the king's daughter, to whom the Egyptian priests determined to grant divine honours. It is the first time that we find the old script and language of Egypt taking its place by the side of that of the Macedonian conqueror, and it is significant that the Greek transcript occupies the third place.

Judah had hitherto remained tranquil and at peace under the government of the Ptolemies. The high-priests had taken the place of the kings, and their authority was undisputed. At times, indeed, the coveted dignity was the cause of family feuds. Jonathan, the father of Jaddua (Neh. xii. 11, 22), had murdered his brother Joshua, whom he suspected of trying to supplant him, and the example he set was destined to have followers. But outside his own family the high-priest ruled with almost despotic power. Simon the Just (B.C. 300), with whom ends the list of 'famous men' given by Jesus the son of Sirach (iv. 1-21), repaired and fortified the temple as well as the fortress which guarded it. Jewish tradition ascribed to him the completion of the Canon of the Old Testament which had been begun by Ezra, and it was through him that the oral

Mosaic tradition of Pharisaism made its way to Antigonus Socho, the first writer of the Mishna or text of the Talmud, and the teacher of the founder of Sadduceism. The grandson of Simon, Onias II., imperilled the authority his predecessors had enjoyed. His covetousness led him to withhold the tribute of £3000, due each year from the Temple to the Jewish king, and in spite of an envoy from Ptolemy and the remonstrances of his countrymen, he refused to give it up.

Jerusalem was saved by the address and readiness of Joseph, the brother of Onias. He hastened to Egypt, ingratiated himself with Ptolemy, and succeeded in being appointed farmer of the taxes for Syria and Palestine. The Jews were saved, but a rival power to that of the high-priest was established, which led eventually to civil war. The greed of Onias was the first scene in the drama which is unfolded in the Books of the Maccabees.

Euergetês was the last of the 'good' Ptolemies. His son and successor, Ptolemy IV., was the incarnation of weakness, cruelty and vice. He began his reign with the murder of his mother and only brother, taking the title of Philopator—'Lover of his Father'—by way of compensation. Syria was reconquered by Antiochus the Great, but his Greek phalanxes were beaten at Raphia by the Egyptians, now armed and trained in the Macedonian fashion, and the gratitude of Philopator showed itself in a visit to the temple at Jerusalem, where he sacrificed to the God of the Jews and attempted to penetrate into the Holy of Holies. A tumult was the consequence, and the exasperated king on his return to Egypt deprived the Jews of their Greek citizenship, and ordered them to be tattooed with the figure of an ivy-leaf in honour of Bacchus, and to sacrifice on the altars of the Greek gods.

The Jews had hitherto been the staunch supporters of the royal house of Egypt, and had held the fortress of Jerusalem for it against the power of Syria. But Philopator had now alienated them for ever. Nor was he more successful with the native Egyptians. First the Egyptian troops mutinied; then came revolt in Upper Egypt. The Ethiopian princes, whose memorials are found in the Nubian temples of Debod and Dakkeh, were invited to Thebes, and an Ethiopian dynasty again ruled in Upper Egypt. The names of the kings who composed it have recently been found in deeds written in demotic characters.

Philopator died of his debaucheries after a reign of seventeen years (B.C. 204), leaving a child of five years of age—the future Ptolemy Epiphanês—to succeed him. The Alexandrine mob was in a state

The Age of the Ptolemies 153

of riot, the army was untrustworthy, and Antiochus was again on the march against Syria. The Egyptian forces were defeated at Banias (Cæsarea Philippi), the Jews having gone over to the invader, in return for which Antiochus remitted the taxes due from Jerusalem, and not only released all the ministers of the temple from future taxation, but sent a large sum of money for its support. By a treaty with Rome the possession of the country was assured to him (B.C. 188), and colonies of Mesopotamian Jews were settled in Lydia and Phrygia.

Meanwhile Ptolemy V., Epiphanês, was growing up, and in B.C. 196 accordingly it was determined that he should be crowned. The coronation took place at Memphis, and a decree was made lightening the burdens of the country, relieving the *fellahin* from being impressed for the navy, and granting further endowments to the priests. It is this decree which is engraved on the famous Rosetta Stone.

But the revolt of the Egyptians still continued, and had already spread northward. Reference is made in the decree to rebellion in the Busirite nome of the Delta, and to a siege of the city of Lykopolis, in which the insurgents had fortified themselves. It was at this time, too, that the city of Abydos was taken by storm and its temples finally ruined, as we gather from a Greek scrawl on the walls of the temple of Seti. But in B.C. 185 a decisive victory was gained by the Greek mercenaries over the revolted Egyptians. Their four leaders surrendered on the king's promise of a free pardon, and were brought before him at Sais. There, however, he tied them to his chariot-wheels in imitation of Achilles, and dragged them still living round the city walls, after which he returned to Alexandria and entered his capital in triumph.

The crimes of Epiphanês led to his murder in B.C. 180, and his seven-year-old son, Ptolemy VI., Philomêtor, was proclaimed king under the regency of his mother. While she lived there was peace, but after her death the Syrian king, Antiochus Epiphanês, threw himself upon Egypt, captured his nephew Philomêtor, and held his court in Memphis. Thereupon Philomêtor's younger brother, whose corpulency had given him the nickname of Physkôn, 'the Bloated,' proclaimed himself king at Alexandria, and called upon Rome for help. Antiochus withdrew, leaving Philomêtor king of the Egyptians, and Physkôn, who had taken the title of Euergetês II., king of the Greeks at Alexandria. Thanks to the brotherly forbearance of Philomêtor, the two reigned together in harmony for several years. Antiochus Epiphanês, however, had again invaded Egypt, but had been warned off its soil by the Roman ambassadors. Rome now affected to regard the kingdom of the Ptolemies as a protected state, and the successors of Alexander were in no condition to resist the orders of the haughty republic. Things had indeed changed since the days when Philadelphus in the plenitude of his glory deigned to congratulate the Italian state on its defeat of the Epirots, and the Roman senate regarded his embassy as the highest of possible honours.

The command of the Romans to leave Egypt alone was sullenly obeyed by Antiochus Epiphanês. But he had no choice in the matter. He had more than enough on his hands at home without risking a quarrel with Rome. The Jews were in full rebellion. The Hellenising party among them—'the ungodly' of the Books of Maccabees—had grown numerous and strong, and had united themselves with the civil rivals of the high-priests. Between the party of progress and the orthodox supporters of the Law there was soon open war, and in B.C. 175, Antiochus Epiphanês, tempted by the higher bribe, was induced to join in the fray, and throw the whole weight of his power on the side of innovation. Onias III. was deposed from the high-priesthood, and his brother Joshua, the leader of 'the ungodly,' was appointed in his place, with leave to change the name of the Jews to that of Antiochians. Joshua forthwith took the Greek name of Jason, established a gymnasium at Jerusalem, sent offerings to the festival of Heraklês at Tyre, and discouraged the rite of circumcision. But Jason's rule was short-lived. A Benjamite, Menelaus, succeeded in driving him out of the country and usurping the office of high-priest, while Onias was put to death.

The second Syrian invasion of Egypt took place two years later. The story of the check received by Antiochus Epiphanês came to Judæa with all the exaggerations usual in the East; Antiochus was reported to be dead, and Jason accordingly marched upon Jerusalem, massacred his opponents, and blockaded Menelaus in the citadel. But Antiochus had been wounded only in his pride, and he turned back from the Nile burning with mortification and anxious to vent his anger upon the first who came in his way. The outrage committed by Jason was a welcome pretext. The defenceless population of Jerusalem was partly massacred, partly sold into slavery, and under the guidance of Menelaus he entered the Temple and carried away the sacred vessels, as well as its other treasure. Philip the Phrygian was appointed governor of the city, while Menelaus remained high-priest.

Severer measures were to follow. In B.C. 168 there had been a rising in Jerusalem, which was thereupon captured on a Sabbath-day by the Syrian general, the greater part of it being sacked and burned, and a portion of the city wall thrown down. A garrison was established on Mount Zion, which at that time overlooked the Temple-hill, and a fierce persecution of the Jews commenced. Every effort was made to compel them to forsake their religion, to eat swine's flesh, and to worship the gods of the Greeks. It was then. that 'the abomination of desolation' was seen in the Holy of Holies, the temples of Samaria and Jerusalem being re-dedicated to Zeus Xenios and Zeus Olympios, and that at Jerusalem befouled with the rites of the Syrian Ashtoreth.

Thousands of the orthodox Jews fled to Egypt, where they found shelter and welcome. Among them was Onias, the eldest son of Onias III. Philométor granted him land in the nome of Heliopolis, and allowed him to build there a temple in which the worship of the Hebrew God should be carried on as it had been at Jerusalem. Excavation goes to show that the temple was erected at the spot now called Tel el-Yehudîyeh, 'the Mound of the Jewess,' not far from Shibîn el-Kanâtir. Here was an old deserted palace and temple of Ramses III., and here the Jews were permitted to establish themselves and found a city, which they called Onion.

158 *The Egypt of the Hebrews and Herodotos*

According to Josephus, its older name had been Leontopolis. The temple, which was destroyed by Vespasian after the Jewish war, was fortified like that at Jerusalem, and the porcelain plaques enamelled with rosettes and lotus-buds, which had been made for Ramses III., were employed once more to ornament it. Long ago the *fellahin* discovered among its ruins, and then broke up, a marble bath, such as is used to-day by the Jewish women for the purpose of purification, and in the adjoining necropolis Dr. Naville found the tombs of persons who bore Jewish names. Onias was not allowed to build his new temple without a protest from the stricter adherents of the Law that it was forbidden to raise one elsewhere than in the sacred city of David. But he was a man of ready resource, and all opposition was overcome when he pointed to the prophecy of Isaiah (xix. 19): 'In that day there shall be an altar to the Lord in the midst of the land of Egypt.' The Egyptian Jews had already secured their own version of the Scriptures; they now had their own temple, their own priesthood, and their own high-priest. True, their co-religionists in Judæa never ceased to protest against this rival centre of their religious faith, and to denounce Onias as the first schismatic; but their brethren in Egypt paid no attention to their words, and the temple

The Age of the Ptolemies

of Onion continued to exist as long as that of Jerusalem.

Onias exercised an influence not only over his own countrymen, but over the mind of the king as well. Philomêtor, like Euergetês, had Jewish leanings, and the high-priest of Onion was admitted to high offices of state. So also was Dositheus, 'the priest and Levite,' who, in 'The Rest of the Chapters of the Book of Esther' (x. 1), tells us that in the fourth year of Philomêtor, he and his son Ptolemy had brought to Egypt 'this epistle of Phurim,' which had been translated into Greek at Jerusalem by Lysimachus, the son of Ptolemy. Philomêtor even acted as a judge in the great religious controversy which raged between the Jews and the Samaritans. They called upon him to decide whether the temple should have been built on Mount Moriah or Mount Gerizim, and which of them had altered the text of Deuteronomy xxvii. 12, 13. Philomêtor decided in favour of the Jews, as his duty towards his numerous Jewish subjects perhaps compelled him to do, and his religious zeal even carried him so far as to order the two unsuccessful advocates of the Samaritan cause to be put to death.

While the king of Egypt was thus acting like a Jew, the king of Syria was engaged in a fierce struggle with the Jewish people. The national party had risen under Mattathias, the priest of Modin, and his five sons, of whom the third, Judas Maccabæus, was the ablest and best-known. One after another the Syrian armies were overthrown, and in B.C. 165 the Temple was purified and repaired, and a new altar dedicated in it to the Lord of Hosts. Two years later Antiochus Epiphanês died while on the march against Judæa, and with him died also the power of Syria. Rival claimants for the throne, internal and external discord, treachery and murder, sapped the foundations of its strength, and in spite of assassinations and religious quarrels, of Edomite hostility and the efforts of the Hellenising party among the Jews themselves, the power of the Maccabees went on increasing. The high-priesthood passed to them from the last of the sympathisers with the Greeks, and Jonathan, the brother and successor of Judas, was treated by the king of Syria with royal honours. Treaties were made with Sparta and Rome, and his successor, Simon, struck coins of his own. After his murder his son John Hyrcanus extended the Jewish dominion as far north as Damascus, annihilating Samaria and its temples and conquering the Edomites, whom he compelled to accept the Jewish faith. Aristobulus, who followed him, took the title of king, and added Ituræa to his kingdom, while his brother Alexander Jannæus

The Age of the Ptolemies 161

attacked Egypt and annexed the cities of the Phœnician coast. But with royal dignity had come royal crimes. Both Aristobulus and Alexander had murdered their brothers, and their Greek names show how the champions of Jewish orthodoxy were passing over into the camp of the foe.

Long before all this happened, many changes had fallen upon Egypt. Philomêtor died in B.C. 145. He had been weak enough to forgive his rebellious and ungrateful brother twice when he had had him in his power. Once he had been compelled to go to Rome to plead his cause before the senate, and there be indebted to an Alexandrine painter for food and lodging; on the second occasion Physkôn had endeavoured to rob him of Cyprus by a combination of mean treachery and intrigue.

The reward of his brotherly forbearance was the murder by Physkôn of Philomêtor's young son Ptolemy Philopator II. immediately after his death. Onias, the Jewish high-priest, held Alexandria for Philopator, but his uncle Physkôn was favoured by the Romans, whose word was now law. Physkôn accordingly began his long reign of vice and cruelty, interrupted only by temporary banishment to Cyprus. Then followed his widow, Cleopatra Kokkê, a woman stained with every possible and impossible crime. She held her own, however, against all opponents,

L

including her own son Ptolemy Lathyrus, thanks to her two Jewish generals, Khelkias and Ananias, the sons of the high-priest Onias. Palestine and Syria again became a battle-field where the fate of Egypt was decided, and while Cleopatra was aided by the Jews, Lathyrus found his allies among the Samaritans.

It was in the midst of these wars and rumours of wars, when men had lost faith in one another and themselves, and when the Jews after struggling for bare existence were beginning to treat on equal terms with the great monarchies of the world, that that curious Apocalypse, the Book of Enoch, seems to have been composed, at all events in its original form. It is a vision of the end of all things and the judgment of mankind, and it embodies the fully developed doctrine of the angelic hierarchy to which reference is made in the Book of Daniel.

Cleopatra was murdered by her younger and favourite son, and Lathyrus succeeded after all in obtaining the throne of Egypt, which he ascended under the title of Sôtêr II. (B.C. 87). His short reign of six years was signalised by the destruction of Thebes. Upper Egypt was still in a state of effervescing discontent, and the crimes of the last reign caused it to break into open rebellion. The government was weak and wicked; the Greeks had lost their vigour and power to rule, and their armies were now mere bodies of unruly mercenaries. But the Thebans were not wealthy or strong enough to withstand Alexandria when helped by the resources of the Mediterranean. The revolt was at last suppressed, Thebes taken by storm, and its temples, which had been used as fortresses, battered and destroyed. The population was put to the sword or carried into slavery, and the capital of the conquering Pharaohs of the past ceased to exist. Its place was taken by a few squalid villages which clustered round the ruins of its ancient shrines. Karnak and Luxor, Medinêt Habu and Qurnah, were all that remained of the former city. Under the earlier Ptolemies it had been known as Diospolis, 'the city of Zeus' Amon, the metropolis of Upper Egypt; from this time forward, in the receipts of the tax-gatherers, it is nothing more than a collection of 'villages.' Its priests were scattered, its ruined temples left to decay. What the Assyrian had failed to destroy and the Persian had spared was overthrown by a Ptolemy who called himself a king of Egypt.

After the death of Lathyrus the internal decay of the monarchy went on rapidly. A prey to civil war and usurpation, it was allowed to exist a little longer by the contemptuous forbearance of the Romans, who waited to put an end to it until they had drained it of its treasures. The kingdom of the Asmonæans at Jerusalem also had tottered to its fall. Family murders and civil feuds had become almost as common among them as among the Ptolemies, and as in Egypt, so too in Palestine, Rome was called in to mediate between the rival claimants for the crown. In B.C. 63 Jerusalem was captured by Pompey after a three months' siege, its defenders massacred, its fortifications destroyed, and its royal house abolished. The Roman victor entered the Holy of Holies, and Palestine was annexed to the Roman empire.

Among the remnant which still retained the faith of their forefathers the Roman conquest and the profanation of the temple gave new strength to the conviction that the Messiah and saviour of Israel must surely soon appear. The conviction finds expression in the so-called Psalms of Solomon, of which only a Greek copy survives. The high hopes raised by the successes of the Maccabæan family were dashed for ever, and the temporal power of Judah had vanished away. Henceforth it existed as a nation only on sufferance.

In Egypt it was not long before the Jews discovered how grievous had been the change in their fortunes. They ceased to be feared, and therefore respected: the mob and rulers of Alexandria had for them now only hatred and contempt. Their citizen-

The Age of the Ptolemies

ship was taken away, with its right to the enjoyment of their own magistrates and courts of justice, and they were degraded to the rank of the native Egyptians, whom the lowest Greek vagabond in the streets of Alexandria could maltreat with impunity. They did not recover their old privileges until Augustus had reorganised his Egyptian province, and though they were again deprived of them by Caligula, when Philo went in vain to plead for his countrymen before the emperor, they were restored by Claudius, and even Vespasian after the Jewish war did not interfere with them.

The house of Ptolemy fell ignobly. But it fell amid the convulsions of a civil war which rent the empire of its conquerors to the foundation, and among the ruins of the Roman republic. Cleopatra, its last representative, bewitched not only the coarser Mark Antony but even the master mind of Julius Cæsar. Her charms were fatal to the life and reputation of the one; they nearly proved equally fatal to the life of the other. Besieged with her in the palace of the Ptolemies by the Alexandrine mob, Cæsar's life trembled for a while in the balance. But the Library of Alexandria was given in its stead; he saved himself by firing the docks and shipping, and the flames spread from the harbour to the halls of the Museum. The precious papyri perished in the flames, and the rooms in which the learning and talent of the Greek world had been gathered together were a heap of blackened ruins. It is true that Cleopatra subsequently obtained from Mark Antony the library of Pergamos, with its 200,000 volumes, which she placed in the temple of Serapis, but the new library never equalled the old, either in its extent or in the value of its books.

Cleopatra and Mark Antony died by their own hands, and Augustus was left master of Egypt and the Roman world (B.C. 30). Cæsarion, the son of Cleopatra and Julius Cæsar, was put to death, and Egypt was annexed to the emperor's privy purse. It never, therefore, became a province of the Roman empire: unhappily for its inhabitants, it remained the emperor's private domain. Its prefect was never allowed to be of higher rank than the equestrian order, and a senator was forbidden to set foot in it. Its cities could not govern themselves, and the old Greek law, which restricted the rights of citizenship to the Greeks and Jews and prevented any native Egyptians from sharing them, was left in force. Egypt was the granary of Rome, and the riches of its soil and the industry of its inhabitants made it needful that no rival to the reigning sovereign should establish himself in it. History had shown with what ease the country could be invaded and occupied and with what difficulty the occupier could be driven out. And the master of Egypt commanded the trade between East and West; he commanded also the Roman mob whose mouths were filled with Egyptian corn. It was dangerous to allow a possible rival even to visit the valley of the Nile.

The history of Alexandria under the Romans is the history of Alexandria rather than of the Egyptians. The *fellahin* laboured for others, not for themselves, and the burdens which weighed upon them became ever greater and more intolerable. Now and again there were outbreaks in Upper Egypt, which were, however, quickly repressed, and in the third century the barbarian Blemmyes made Coptos and Ptolemais their capitals. The reconquest of the Thebaid by Probus (A.D. 280) was judged worthy of a triumph. About eight years later the whole country was once more in rebellion, and proclaimed their leader Akhilleus emperor. The war lasted for nine years, and the whole force of the empire was required to finish it. The emperor Diocletian marched in person into Upper Egypt and besieged Coptos, the centre of the revolt. After a long siege the city was taken and razed to the ground. But the war had ruined the people. The embankments were broken, the canals choked up, the fields untilled and overrun by the barbarians from the Sûdan or the Bedouin of the eastern desert. Diocletian, when the struggle was over, found himself obliged to withdraw the Roman garrisons south of the First Cataract, and to fix the frontier of the empire at Assuan.

The war was followed by the great persecution of the Christians, the last expiring effort of Roman paganism against the invasion of the new faith. Christianity had become a mighty power in the Roman world, which threatened soon to absorb all that was left of the Rome of the past, with its patriotism, its devotion to the emperor, its law and its administration. The struggle between it and the empire of Augustus could no longer be delayed. The edict of Diocletian was signed, and the empire put forth its whole strength to crush its rival and root Christianity out of its midst.

But the attempt came too late. The new power was stronger than the old one, and the persecution only proved how utterly the old Rome had passed away. The empire bowed its head and became Christian; the bishops took the place of the prefects and senators of the past, and theological disputations raged in the halls of philosophy. Nowhere had the persecution been fiercer than in Egypt; nowhere had the martyrs and confessors of the Church been more heroic or more numerous.

The result was one which we should hardly have

The Age of the Ptolemies

expected. Hitherto Christianity in Egypt had been Greek. It was associated with Alexandria and the Greek language, not with the villages and tongue of the people. Its bishops and theologians were Greeks, and the school of Christian Platonism which flourished in Alexandria had little in common with Egyptian ideas. With the Diocletian persecution, however, came a change. Even while it was still at its height, martyrs and confessors come forward who bear Egyptian and not Greek names. Hardly is it over before the native population joins in one great body the new religion. Osiris and Isis make way for Christ and the Blessed Virgin, the Coptic alphabet replaces the demotic script of heathenism, and the bodies of the dead cease to be embalmed. It is difficult to account for the suddenness and completeness of the change. The decay of the Roman power, and therewith the barriers between Greek and Egyptian, may have had something to do with it. So too may the revolt in Upper Egypt, which united in one common feeling of nationality all the elements of the population. Perhaps a still more potent cause was the spectacle of the heroism and constancy of those who suffered for the Christian faith. The Egyptian has always been deeply religious, and his very enjoyment of life makes him admire and revere the ascetic. But whatever may have been the reason, the fact remains: before the persecution of Diocletian Egyptian Christianity had been Greek; when the persecution was over it had become Copt. The pagans who still survived were not Egyptians but the rich and highly-educated Greeks, like the poet Nonnus, who was tortured to death by St. Shnûdi, or the gifted Hypatia, whose flesh was torn from her bones with oyster-shells by the monks of St. Cyril.

The literature of Coptic Christianity was almost wholly religious. Little else had an interest for the devoted adherents of the new faith. The romances which had delighted their forefathers were replaced by legends of the saints and martyrs, and Christian hymns succeeded to the poems of the past. We owe to this passion for theology the preservation of productions of the Jewish and Christian Churches which would otherwise have been lost. The Book of Enoch, quoted though it is by St. Jude, would have perished irrevocably had it not been for Coptic Christianity. The Church of Abyssinia, a daughter of that of Egypt, has preserved it in an Ethiopic translation, and portions of the Greek original from which the translation was made have been found in a tomb at Ekhmîm, which was excavated in 1886. It has long been known that the text used by the Abyssinian translator must have differed considerably from that of which extracts have been preserved for us in the Epistle of St. Jude and the writings of the Byzantine historians Kedrenos and George the Syncellus; the newly-discovered fragments now enable us to see what this text actually was like. If the original book was written in Aramaic it would seem that at least two authorised Greek versions of it existed, one of which was used in Europe and Syria, the other in Egypt. Which was the older and more faithful we have yet to learn.

The excavations at Ekhmîm have brought to light fragments of two other works, both belonging to the early days of Christianity and long since lost. One of these is supposed by its first editor, M. Bouriant, to be the Apocalypse of St. Peter; it opens with an account of the Transfiguration, which is followed by a vision of heaven and hell. The book appears to have been composed or interpolated by a Gnostic, as there is a reference in it to 'the Æon' in which Moses and Elias dwelt in glory. The other work is of more importance. It is the Gospel known to the early Church as that of St. Peter, and the portion which is preserved contains the narrative of the Passion and Resurrection of Christ. Throughout the narrative the responsibility for the death of our Lord is transferred from Pilate to the Jews; when the guard who watched the tomb under the centurion Petronius ran to tell Pilate of the resurrection they had witnessed, 'grieving greatly and saying: Truly he was the son of God': he answered: 'I am clean of the blood of the son of God: I too thought he was so.' Docetic tendencies, however, are observable in the Gospel: at all events the cry of Christ on the cross is rendered, 'My power, (my) power, thou hast forsaken me!'

What further discoveries of the lost documents of early Christianity still await us in Egypt it is impossible to say. It is only during the last few years that attention has been turned towards monuments which, to the students of Egyptian antiquity, seemed of too recent a date. Countless manuscripts of priceless value have already perished through the ignorance of the *fellahin* and the neglect of the tourist and *savan*, to whom the term 'Coptic' has been synonymous with 'worthless.' But the soil of Egypt is archæologically almost inexhaustible, and the land of the Septuagint, of the Christian school of Alexandria, and of the passionate theology of a later epoch, cannot fail to yield up other documents that will throw a flood of light on the early history of our faith. It is only the other day that, among the Fayyûm papyri now in the British Museum, there was found a fragment of the Septuagint version of the Psalms older than the oldest MS. of the Bible hitherto known. And the traveller who still wishes to see the Nile at leisure and in his own way will find in the old Egyptian quarries behind Dêr Abu Hannes, but a little to the south of the city which Hadrian raised to the memory of Antinous, abundant illustrations of the doctrine and worship of the primitive Coptic Church. He can there study all the details of its ancient ecclesiastical architecture cut out of the living rock, and can trace how the home of a hermit became first a place of pilgrimage and then a chapel with its altar to the saints. The tombs themselves, inscribed with the Greek epitaphs of the sainted fugitives from persecution, still exist outside the caves in which they had dwelt. We can even see the change taking place which transformed the Greek Church of Alexandria into the Coptic Church of Egypt. On either side of a richly-carved cross is the record of ' Papias, son of Melito the Isaurian,' buried in the spot made holy by the body of St. Macarius, which is written on the one side in Greek, on the other side in Coptic. Henceforward Greek is superseded by Coptic, and the numerous pilgrims who ask St. Victor or St. Phœbammon to pray for them write their names and prayers in the native language and the native alphabet. With the betrayal of Egypt to the Mohammedans by George the Makaukas the doom of the Greek language and Bible was sealed. Coptic had already become the language of the Egyptian Church, and though we still find quotations from the Greek New Testament painted here and there on the walls of rock-cut shrines they are little more than ornamental designs. Christian Egypt is native, not Greek.

HERODOTOS IN EGYPT

FROM Coptic Christianity, just preparing to confront twelve centuries of Mohammedan persecution, we must now turn back to Pagan Greece. The Persian wars have breathed a new life into Greece and its colonies, and given them a feeling of unity such as they never possessed before. Athens has taken its place as leader not only in art and literature, but also in war, and under the shelter of her name the Ionians of Asia Minor have ventured to defy their Persian lord, and the Ionic dialect has ceased to be an object of contempt. The Greek, always restless and curious to see and hear 'some new thing,' is now beginning to indulge his tastes at leisure, and to visit as a tourist the foreign shores of the Mediterranean. Art has leaped at a single bound to its perfection in the sculptures of Pheidias; poetry has become divine in the tragedies of Æschylus and Sophocles, and history is preparing to take part in the general development. The modern world of Europe is already born.

The founder of literary history—of history, that is to say, which aims at literary form and interest—was Herodotos of Halikarnassos. If Greek tradition may be trusted, his uncle had been put to death by Lygdamis, the despot of the city, and the subsequent expulsion of the tyrant was in some measure due to the political zeal of the future historian. Herodotos was wealthy and well educated, as fond of travel as the majority of his countrymen, and not behind them in curiosity and vanity. He had cultivated the literary dialect of Ionia, perhaps during his stay in Samos, and had made good use there of the library of Polykratês, the friend and correspondent of Amasis. What other libraries he may have consulted we do not know, but his history shows that he had a considerable acquaintance with the works of his predecessors, whom he desired to eclipse and supersede. Hekatæus of Miletus, who had travelled in Egypt as far south as Thebes, if not Assuan, and had written a full account of the country, its people and its history, Xanthus, the Lydian, who had compiled the annals of his native land, beside numberless other authors, historians and geographers, poets and dramatists, philosophers and physicists, had been made to contribute to his work. Now and again he refers to the older historians when he wishes to correct or contradict them; more frequently he silently incorporates their statements and words without mentioning them by name. It was thus, we are told by Porphyry, that he 'stole' the accounts given by Hekatæus of the crocodile, the hippopotamus and the phœnix, and the incorrectness of his description of that marvellous bird, which, like Hekatæus, he likens to an eagle, proves that the charge is correct. Reviewers did not exist in his days, nor were marks of quotation or even footnotes as yet invented, and Herodotos might therefore plead that, although he quoted freely without acknowledgment, he was not in any real sense a plagiarist. He only acted like other Greek writers of his time, and if his plagiarisms exceeded theirs it was only because he had read more and made a more diligent use of his notebook.

It is we, and not the Greek world for which he wrote, who are the sufferers. It is frequently difficult, if not impossible, for us to tell whether Herodotos is speaking from his own experience or quoting from others, whose trustworthiness is doubtful or whose statements may have been misunderstood. From time to time internal evidence assures us that we are dealing, not with Herodotos himself, but with some other writer whose remarks he has embodied. His commentators have continually argued on the supposition that, wherever the first person is used, it is

Herodotos himself who is speaking. Statements of his accordingly have been declared to be true, in spite of the contrary evidence of oriental research, because, it is urged, he is a trustworthy witness and has reported honestly what he heard and saw. But if he did not hear and see the supposed facts, the case is altered and the argument falls to the ground.

Herodotos took part in the foundation of the colony of Thurii in southern Italy in B.C. 445, and there, rather than at the Olympic festival, as later legend believed, he read to the assembled Greeks the whole or a part of his history. His travels in Egypt, therefore, must have already taken place. Their approximate date, indeed, is fixed by what he tells us about the battlefield of Paprêmis (iii. 12).

At Paprêmis, for the first time, an Egyptian army defeated the Persian forces. Its leader was Inarôs the Libyan, and doubtless a large body of Libyans was enrolled in it. Along with Amyrtæos he had led the Egyptians to revolt in the fifth year of the reign of Artaxerxes I. (B.C. 460). Akhæmenes, the satrap of Egypt, was routed and slain, and for six years Egypt maintained a precarious freedom. The fortresses at Memphis and Pelusium, however, remained in the hands of the Persians, and in spite of all the efforts of the Egyptians, they could not be dislodged. Greek aid accordingly was sought, and the Athenians, still at war with Persia, sent two hundred ships from Cyprus to the help of the insurgents. The ships sailed up the Nile as far as Memphis, where the Persian garrison still held out.

All attempts to oust it proved unavailing, and the approach of a great Persian army under Megabyzos obliged the Greeks to retreat to the island of Prosopites. Here they were blockaded for a year and a half; then the besiegers turned the river aside and marched over its dry bed against the camp of the allies, which they took by storm. The Greek expedition was annihilated, and Inarôs fell into the hands of his enemies, who sent him to Persia and there impaled him. Amyrtæos, however, still maintained himself in the marshes of the Delta, and in B.C. 449 Kimon sent sixty ships of the Athenian fleet to assist him in the struggle. But before they could reach the coast of Egypt news arrived of the death of Kimon, and the ships returned home. Four years later, if we may trust Philokhorus, another Egyptian prince, Psammetikhos, who seems to have succeeded Amyrtæos, sent 72,000 bushels of wheat to Athens in the hope of buying therewith Athenian help. But it does not appear to have been given, and Egypt once more sullenly obeyed the Persian rule. We learn from Herodotos (iii. 15) that 'the great king' even allowed Thannyras and Pausiris, the sons of his inveterate enemies Inarôs and Amyrtæos, to succeed to the principalities of their fathers.

Paprêmis was visited by Herodotos, and he saw there the sham fight between the priests at the door of the temple on the occasion of their chief festival. He also went to the site of the battle-field, and there beheld 'a great marvel.' The skeletons of the combatants lay on separate sides of the field just as they had fallen, and whereas the skulls of the Persians were so thin that they could be shattered by a pebble, those of the Egyptians were thick and strong enough to resist being battered with a stone. The cause of this difference was explained to him by the dragoman: the Egyptians shaved their heads from childhood and so hardened the bones of it against the sun, while the Persians shaded their heads by constantly wearing caps of thick felt.

Not many years could have elapsed since the battle had occurred. The visit of the Greek traveller to the scene of it may therefore be laid between B.C. 455 and 450. The patriots of Egypt must have been still struggling for their liberty among the marshes of the northern Delta.

But the rebellion must have been practically crushed. No Greek could have ventured into Persian territory while his countrymen were fighting against its Persian masters. The army of Megabyzos must have done its work, and the Athenian fleet been utterly destroyed. Moreover, it is evident that when Herodotos entered the valley of the Nile the country was at peace. His references to the war are to a past event, and when he speaks of Inarôs and Amyrtæos it is of men who have ceased to be a danger to the foreign government. The passage, indeed, in which he notices the peaceable appointment of their sons to the principalities of their fathers may have been inserted after his return to Greek lands, but this makes no difference as to the main fact. When he came to Egypt it had again lapsed into tranquil submission to the Persian power.

In B.C. 450, Kimon, the son of Miltiades, had destroyed the naval power of Persia, and in the following year Megabyzos was overthrown at Salamis. It was then that the 'peace of Kimon' is said to have been concluded between Athens and the Persian king, which put an end to the long Persian war, freed the Greek cities of Asia, and made the Mediterranean a Greek sea. The reality of the peace has been doubted, because there is no allusion to it in the pages of Thucydides, and it may be that it was never formally drawn up. But the fact embodied by the story remains: for many years to come there was truce between Greece and Persia, and the independence of the Greek colonies in Asia Minor was acknowledged at the Persian court. The year 449 marks the final triumph of Athens and the beginning of Persian decline.

Had Herodotos travelled in Egypt a year or two later, the ease and security with which he did so would be readily explained. But in this case we should be brought too near the time when his history was finished and he himself was a resident in Italy. We must therefore believe that he was there before the final blow had been struck at Persian supremacy in the Mediterranean, but when the Athenian invasion of Egypt was already a thing of the past, and the unarmed trader and tourist were once more able to move freely about.

For more than half a century Egypt had been closed to Greek curiosity. There had been an earlier period, when the Delta at least had been well-known to the Hellenic world. The Pharos of the future Alexandria is already mentioned by Homer (*Od.* iv. 355); it was there, 'in front of Egypt,' that Menelaos moored his ships and forced 'Egyptian Prôteus' to declare to him his homeward road. Even 'Egyptian Thebes,' with its hundred temple-gates, is known both to the *Iliad* (ix. 381) and to the *Odyssey* (iv. 126), and the Pharaoh Polybos dwelt there when Alkandra, his wife, loaded Menelaos with gifts. Greek mercenaries

Herodotos in Egypt

enabled Psammetikhos to shake off the yoke of Assyria, and Greek traders made Naukratis and Daphnæ wealthy centres of commerce. Solon visited Egypt while Athens was putting into practice the laws he had promulgated, and there he heard from the priest of Sais that, by the side of the unnumbered centuries of Egyptian culture, the Greeks were but children and their wisdom but the growth of to-day. Before the Ionic revolt had broken out, while Ionia and Egypt were still sister provinces of the same Persian empire, Hekatæos of Miletus had travelled through the valley of the Nile, enjoying advantages for information which no Greek could possess again till Egypt had become a Macedonian conquest, and embodying his knowledge and experiences in a lengthy book.

But the Persian wars had put an end to all this peaceful intercourse between Greece and the old land of the Pharaohs, and the Karian dragomen who had made their living by acting as interpreters between the Greeks and the Egyptians were forced to turn to other work. At length, however, Egypt was once more open to visitors, and once more, therefore, visitors came from Greece. Anaxagoras, the philosopher and friend of Periklês, was among the first to arrive and to investigate the causes of the rise and fall of the Nile. Hellanikos the historian, too, the older contemporary of Herodotos, seems to have travelled in Egypt, though doubt has been cast on the authenticity of the works in which he is supposed to have recorded his experiences of Egyptian travel. At any rate, Herodotos found a public fresh and eager to hear what he had to tell them about the dwellers on the Nile.

Herodotos must have reached Egypt in the summer. When he arrived, the whole of the Delta was under water. He describes with the vividness of an eye-witness how its towns appeared above the surface of the water, like the islands in the Ægean, and how the traveller could sail, not along the river, but across the plain. At the time of the inundation, he says, all Egypt 'becomes a sea, above which the villages alone show themselves.' The voyage from Naukratis to Memphis was direct and rapid, and the tourists in making it passed by the pyramids instead of the apex of the Delta.

In northern Egypt the rise of the Nile begins to be perceptible during the first few days of July. Criers go about the streets of Cairo announcing each day how high it has risen, and in the first or second week of August the ceremony of cutting the Khalîg or Canal of Cairo, and therewith declaring that the Nile was once more flooding its banks, used to be observed with great rejoicings. It is, in fact, in

August that the land is first covered with the flood. For another month the height of the water continues to increase, and then for a short while to remain stationary. But towards the end of October, when the canals of Upper Egypt are emptied, there is again another rise, soon followed by a rapid fall. If the Delta was like a sea when Herodotos saw it, he must have been there between the beginning of July and the end of October.

These are the limits of the time which he could have spent in the country. That he did not remain till after the fall of the river and the drying up of the land is evident from incidental statements in his work. Thus when he visited the Fayyûm it was like the Delta, a sea of waters, and the pyramids of Biahmu, which Professor Petrie's excavations have shown to have always stood on dry land, as they still do to-day, were seen by him in the middle of a vast lake. Nowhere, indeed, is there any hint of his having seen the country in its normal condition. Even his reference to Kerkosôros, at the apex of the Delta, which every traveller to Memphis had to pass except at the period of high Nile, is derived from 'the Ionian' writers of a previous generation, not from his own experience. Neither in going nor in returning was his boat obliged to pass that way. We need not be surprised, therefore, at finding that the festivals he witnessed in the Egyptian towns were those which took place in the summer.

Herodotos had not the time to imitate the example of his predecessor Hekatæos and visit Upper Egypt, nor, indeed, was the summer a fitting season for doing so. Consequently, while he lavishes his admiration on the temples and pyramids of the Delta, of Memphis and of the Fayyûm, he has nothing to say about the still more striking temples of the south. 'Hundred-gated Thebes,' whose fame had already penetrated to the Homeric Greeks, and whose tombs and colossi led the Greek tourists of the Macedonian age to scribble upon them their expressions of admiration and awe, is known to him only by name. The extravagance of his praise is reserved for the Labyrinth; about the nobler and more majestic buildings of the capital of Upper Egypt he is absolutely silent. Against the statues of the Egyptian kings which Hekatæos saw at Thebes, Herodotos can bring only a smaller number which he saw at Memphis.

The monuments even now contain evidence that, after the age of Hekatæos, Greek sightseers did not make their way into southern Egypt until the Macedonian conquest had made travel there easy and safe. At Abu-Simbel in Nubia and Abydos in Upper Egypt are the records of the Greek mercenaries of Psammetikhos and their Greek and Karian contemporaries who visited the oracle of Abydos. But then comes a long blank in the history of Greek writing in Egypt. With the foundation of Alexander's empire a new epoch in it begins. From that time forward the walls of the tombs and temples were covered with the scrawls of innumerable Greek visitors. At Thebes the royal tombs were especial objects of attention, and ciceroni led the inquisitive stranger round them just as they do to-day.

But among all the mass of Greek names that have been collected from the monuments of Upper Egypt we find neither that of Herodotos nor of any other of his countrymen of the same age. In fact, it was not a time for sightseeing in the southern valley of the Nile. The population were in only half-repressed rebellion against their Persian rulers, and the whole country swarmed with bandits. Persian authority was necessarily weaker than in the north, and the people were more combative and had near allies in the desert, the Bedouin and the Ethiopians. A voyage up the river was even more dangerous than in the anarchical days of the last century: pirates abounded, and out of reach of the Persian garrison at Memphis the traveller carried his life in his hand. As in the time of Norden no Egyptian bey could or would allow the traveller in Nubia to go south of Dirr, so in the time of Herodotos the southern limit of the foreigner's travels was the Fayyûm. The 'Egypt into which Greeks sail' was, as he himself declares, the Egypt which lay north of the Theban nome and Lake Mœris.

Even a visit to the Fayyûm was doubtless a bold and unusual undertaking, and on this account Herodotos describes what he saw there at more than ordinary length, and extols the wonders of the district at the expense of the better-known monuments of Memphis and the Delta. But the Oasis had suffered much from the civil troubles which had afflicted Egypt. The dykes which kept out the inundation had been neglected, and the fertile nome was transformed into a stagnant lake. Herodotos saw it as the French *savans* saw it at the beginning of the present century; the embankments were broken, and fields and roads were alike submerged.

From the walls of the capital of the province, whose mounds now lie outside Medînet el-Fayyûm, Herodotos looked northward over a vast expanse of water. 'Nearly in the middle of it,' he tells us, 'stand two pyramids, each of them rising 304 feet above the water . . . and both surmounted by colossal stone figures seated upon a throne.' The shattered fragments of the colossi were found by Professor Petrie in 1888, scattered round the pyramidal pedestals, twenty-one feet high, on which they had been placed. Cut out of hard quartzite sandstone, they represented Amon-em-hat III., the creator of the Fayyûm, and their discoverer calculates that they were each thirty-five feet in height. The fragments are now at Oxford in the Ashmolean Museum. The statues faced northward, and the court within which they stood was surrounded by a wall with a gateway of red granite. The pedestals still remain fairly intact, and the road by the side of which they had been erected is still used to-day. The monuments, in fact, were erected high above the inundation, and that Herodotos should have seen them in the midst of the water is but a further proof of the condition of the country at the time. The Lake Mœris he describes was not the true Mœris of Egyptian geography; it was the Fayyûm itself buried beneath the flood.

The total height of the colossi from the ground, according to Professor Petrie, was about sixty feet. Between this and the 304 feet assigned to them by the Greek traveller there is indeed a wide difference. But Herodotos could not have seen them close at hand, and the measurement he gives must have been a mere guess. It warns us, however, not to put overmuch faith in his statements, even when they are the results of personal observation. He was but a tourist, not a man of science, and he cared more for the tales of his dragoman and novel sights than for scientific surveying and exactitude.

Hence comes the assertion that before the time of Menes the whole country between the sea and Lake Mœris was a marsh. Such a statement is intelligible only if we remember that, when Herodotos sailed· up the Nile, its banks were inundated on either side. Had he seen the country south of Memphis as the modern traveller sees it when the water is subsiding and green fields begin to line the course of the river, he could never have entertained the belief. But all distinction between the Delta and the rest of Egypt was hidden from him by the waters of the inundation. That he should have made the Fayyûm the limit of the marsh is indeed natural ; it was the limit of his exploration of Upper Egypt, and consequently he did not know that from Memphis southward to Edfu the valley of the Nile presents the same features.

The strange error he twice commits in imagining that there were vaults under the pyramid of Kheops in an island formed by a canal which the builder had introduced from the Nile is due to the same cause. Doubtless his dragoman had told him something of the kind. A subterraneous chamber in the rock actually exists under the great pyramid, as was discovered by Caviglia, and there are pyramids into whose lower chambers the Nile has long since infiltrated. Professor Maspero found his exploration of the pyramids of Lisht, south of Dahshûr, stopped by the water which had filled them, and Professor Petrie had the same experience in the brick pryamid of Howâra, though here the infiltration of the water seems to have been caused by a canal dug in Arab times. But the pyramids of Gizeh stand on a plateau of limestone rock secure against the approach of water, and the story reported by Herodotos is more probably the result of misapprehension on his own part than of intentional falsehood on the part of his guides. His ready credence of it, however, can be explained only by the condition of the country at the time of his visit. The whole land was covered with water, and in going to Memphis he had to sail by the pyramids themselves. It was in a boat that his visit to them must have been made; and it was easy, therefore, to believe that a canal ran from the water on which he sailed through the tunnelled rock whereon they stood. He did not know that the lowest chamber of the pyramid was high above the utmost level of the flood.

Surprise has often been expressed that Herodotos should make no mention of the Sphinx, which to Arabs and modern Europeans alike has appeared one of most noteworthy monuments of Gizeh. But in sailing along the canal which led from Memphis to the pyramids he would have passed by it without notice. As his boat made its way to the rocky edge on which the huge sepulchres of Kheops and Khephren are built, it would have been concealed from his view; and buried as it was in sand his guides did not think it an object of such surpassing importance as to lead him to it over the burning sand. In the immediate neighbourhood of the great pyramid he was surrounded by monuments more interesting and more striking, which were quite enough to occupy his day and satisfy his curiosity.

South of the Fayyûm and the adjoining city of Herakleopolis, whose ruins are now known as Ahnas el-Medîneh, all that Herodotos has to tell us is derived from older authors. Now and then, it is true, the first person is used, and we think for a moment that he is describing his own adventures. But he is merely quoting from others, and there are no marks of quotation in the manuscript to show us that such is the case. His book is thus like that of another and later Egyptian traveller, Mr. J. A. St. John, whose *Egypt and Nubia* was published in English only fifty years ago. He too embodies the narratives of his predecessors in the record of his own journey up the Nile without any notice or signs that he is doing so, and it is not until we suddenly light on the name of an earlier writer at the bottom of the page that we become aware of the fact. Herodotos has not given us even this help; and we need not wonder, therefore, that commentators who have never been in Egypt have been deceived by his method of work. But he has preserved fragments of older writers which would otherwise have been lost, and if he has mingled them with the stories he heard from the dragomen of Memphis and Sais, or the answers he received to his questions about Greek legends, we must not feel ungrateful.

Upper Egypt is mentioned only incidentally in his narrative, and, as might be expected in a writer who had to depend upon others for his information, what he tells us about it is very frequently incorrect. Thus he asserts that the hippopotamus was 'sacred in the nome of Paprêmis, but nowhere else in Egypt,' although it was also worshipped in Thebes, and he fancies that all the cats in the country were embalmed and buried at Bubastis, all the hawks and mice at Buto, and all the ibises at Hermopolis or Damanhur. But this was because he had visited these places and had not travelled in the south. Had he done so, he would never have imagined that the body of every cat or hawk that died was carried to a distant place in the Delta. Indeed, in the hot weather of the summer months, anything of the kind would have been impossible. Cemeteries, however, of these sacred animals are found all up and down the Nile. The mummies of the sacred cats are to be met with in the cliffs of Gebel Abu Foda, at Thebes, and above all at Beni Hassan, where a little to the south of the Speos Artemidos such quantities of them were recently discovered as to suggest that a commercial profit might be made out of their bones. Tons of them were accordingly shipped to Liverpool, there to be converted into manure; but as it was found that the mummified bones refused to yield to the process, the exportation ceased. Mummies of the sacred hawks were disinterred in equal numbers when the ancient cemeteries of Ekhmîm were excavated a few years ago, and the construction of the canal on the eastern bank opposite Abutîg has lately brought to light another of their burial-places, thus fixing the site of Hierakon, 'the city of the Hawk,' the capital of the twelfth nome.

In his geography of the river above the Fayyûm Herodotos was similarly misinformed. Thus, he avers that 'the country above the Fayyûm for the distance of a three days' voyage resembles the country below it.' A three days' voyage would mean about eighty miles, since he reckons it a voyage of seven days from the sea to the Fayyûm, a distance of about 190 miles. Dahabîyeh travellers will willingly assent to the calculation. With a fair wind, a day's voyage is about thirty miles, more or less, so that 190 miles could be easily traversed in seven days. Now eighty miles would bring the visitor from the Fayyûm to Qolosaneh and the Gebel et-Têr. For many miles before reaching the Gebel the banks of the Nile wear a very different aspect from that which they present lower down. In place of a dull monotony of sand-banks and level plains, there are picturesque lines of cliff, amphitheatres of desert and rugged headlands. It is only as far as Feshn, twenty miles to the south of Herakleopolis, that the description of Herodotos is correct. It is, in fact, merely based on what he could see from the southernmost point to which he attained.

The view which he had from thence over the flat desert reaches of Libya led him to make another statement equally wide of the truth. It is that for four days after leaving Heliopolis the valley of the Nile is narrow, but that then it once more becomes broad. But such was the case only where the Fayyûm and the province of Beni-Suef spread towards the west, and there too only when they are covered with the waters of the inundation. Elsewhere the cultivated valley is for the most part narrower even than in the neighbourhood of Memphis, where it seemed to the Greek traveller to be so confined; here and there, indeed, as at Abydos and

Thebes, it broadens out for a space, but otherwise the wilderness encroaches upon it ever more and more until at Silsilis the barren rocks obliterate it altogether.

Herodotos knows nothing of the great monuments of Thebes, and the Pharaohs accordingly whose names he records have no connection with the ancient capital of the empire. They belong to Memphis, to the Fayyûm, and to the Delta—none of them to Thebes. Even Sesostris, in whom some of the features of Ramses II. may be detected, reigns in the north rather than in the south. Of all the multitudinous monuments that he has left, two only are known to the Greek traveller, and these are the two statues of himself which stood before the temple of Ptah in Memphis.

Of Thothmes and Amenôphis and the other great monarchs of the eighteenth dynasty whose memorials were to be found chiefly in the south, Herodotos had never heard. All that he knew of the kings of Egypt before the age of Psammetikhos was derived from the stories which his guides attached to the monuments which he actually saw. Had he visited the temples and tombs of Thebes and Abydos and Assuan we should have been told how Memnon led his troops to Troy or how Osymandyas conquered the world. But we have to turn to others for the dragoman's tales of Upper Egypt; Herodotos could not record them, for he was never there. The Fayyûm is the southernmost limit of his historical knowledge, because it is also the southernmost limit of his geographical knowledge.

And yet here and there we come across notices of Upper Egypt, some of which have been written by an eye-witness. But the eye-witness was not Herodotos himself, and in giving them he generally gives an indication of the fact. Thus he describes Khemmis or Ekhmîm as 'near Neapolis,' the modern Qeneh, although the distance between the two towns is really ninety-five miles, a voyage of at least three days, and Neapolis was but an insignificant city by the side of Khemmis itself, or of other towns like This and Abydos that were nearer to it. Even Tentyris or Denderah, with its ancient temple of Hathor opposite Neapolis, was more important and better-known, while Thebes itself was only forty-five miles higher up the river.

But the account given by Herodotos of Khemmis and its temple is a mere product of the imagination. Indeed, he implies that he received it from certain 'people of Khemmis' whom he had questioned, probably through his interpreter. They told him that the temple, of which a few remains are still visible, and which was really dedicated to Min or Amon-Khem, was that of the Greek hero Perseus—a name suggested, it may be, by its likeness to that of the sacred persea tree. Each year, it was further alleged, gymnastic games in the Greek fashion were celebrated in honour of the foreign deity, who at times appeared to his worshippers, leaving behind him his sandal famous in Greek mythology. But the inventive powers of the informants of the Greek traveller did not stop here. He further assures us that the pylon of the temple bore on the summits of its two towers two images of the deity. The statement is of itself sufficient to discredit the whole story and to prove that Herodotos could never have seen the temple with his own eyes. The watch-towers that guarded the entrance of an Egyptian temple never had, and never could·have, images on their roofs. They were needed for other purposes, and the very idea of their supporting statues was contrary to the first principles of Egyptian architecture and religion. It was a conception wholly Greek.

Equally wide of the truth is what Herodotos has to tell us about the First Cataract. Like other travellers to Egypt before and since he was anxious to learn something about the sources of the Nile. But neither 'the Egyptians nor the Libyans nor the Greeks' whom he met could give him any information. Perhaps had he sailed as far as Assuan some of the

Ethiopians who lived there might have been more communicative. At last, however, he was introduced to one of the sacred scribes in the temple of Neit at Sais—the only Egyptian priest, in fact, of higher rank, whom he seems to have conversed with—and the scribe humoured the curiosity of the traveller to the utmost of his desires, though even Herodotos suspected that he was being made fun of. However, as in duty bound, he gravely writes down what he was told. 'Two mountains are there with pointed tops, between Syênê, a city of the Thebais, and Elephantinê, which are called Krôphi and Môphi. Out of the heart of these mountains flow the sources of the Nile, which are bottomless, half the water running towards Egypt and the north, while the other half goes to Ethiopia and the south. That the sources are bottomless was proved by Psammetikhos, the king of Egypt, for after letting down into them a rope several hundred thousand fathoms in length, he did not find the bottom.' Herodotos adds that this was probably because there were violent eddies in the water which carried the rope away.

Egyptian priests did not, as a rule, know Greek, and they avoided any kind of intercourse with the 'unclean' foreigner. Even to have conversed with him would have caused pollution. Consequently 'the priests' to whom Herodotos so frequently alludes were merely the 'beadles' of the day, who took the tourist over the temples and showed him the principal objects of interest. The sacred scribe of Sais was an exception to the general rule. Since the days of Psammetikhos, Sais had been accustomed to Greek visitors, and the prejudices against them were less strong there than in other Egyptian towns. It is quite possible, therefore, that the scribe whom Herodotos met was acquainted with the Greek language, and that no dragoman was required to interpret his words.

There is a reason for thinking that such was the case. The story of Krôphi and Môphi, in spite of the suspicions of Herodotos, is remarkably correct; even the name of Krôphi has not undergone a greater amount of transformation than it might have done if Herodotos had written it down himself from the scribe's mouth. It is the Egyptian Qerti or Qoriti, 'the two holes' out of which Egyptian mythology supposed Hâpi, the Nile-god, to emerge at the period of the inundation. The Qerti were at the foot of the granite peaks of Senem, the island of Bigeh, and of the opposite cliff on the southern side of the First Cataract. We can almost fix the exact spot where one of these Qerti was believed to have been. On the western bank of Philæ, immediately facing Bigeh, is a portal built in the reign of Hadrian, on the inner north wall of which is a picture of it. We see the granite blocks of Bigeh piled one upon the other up to the summit of the island where Mut the divine mother, and Horus the saviour, sit and keep watch over the waters of the southern Nile. Below is the cavern, encircled by a guardian serpent, within which the Nile-god is crouched, pouring from a vase in either hand the waters of the river. Though in certain points Herodotos has misunderstood his informant, on the whole the story of Krôphi and Môphi is a fairly accurate page from the volume of Egyptian mythology. Even the jingling Môphi may be derived from the Egyptian *moniti* or 'mountains' between which the river ran, though Lauth may be right in holding that Krôphi is Qer-Hâpi, 'the hollow of the Nile,' and Môphi Mu-Hâpi, 'the waters of the Nile.'

But in one point the Greek historian has made a serious mistake. It was not between Assuan and Elephantinê that the sources of the Nile were placed, but between Bigeh and the mainland, on the other side of the Cataract. Between Assuan and Elephantinê there are no 'mountains,' only the channel of the river. In saying therefore that Krôphi and Môphi were mountains and that they rose between Syênê and Elephantinê, Herodotos proves beyond all possibility of doubt that he had never been at the spot. Had he actually visited Assuan the words of the sacred scribe would have been reported more correctly.

At Elephantinê honours were paid to 'the great' god of the Nile, who rose from his caverns in the neighbourhood. Of this we have been assured by a mutilated Greek inscription on a large slab of granite which was discovered by English sappers at Assuan in 1885. It records the endowments and privileges which were granted to the priests of Elephantinê by the earlier Ptolemies, and one line of it refers to the places 'wherein is the fountain of the Nile.' But long before the days of the Ptolemies and of Greek visitors to Egypt, when the First Cataract was the boundary of Egyptian rule and knowledge, the fountain of the Nile was already placed immediately beyond it. This infantile belief of Egyptian mythology was preserved, like so much else of prehistoric antiquity, in the mythology of later days. In the temple of Redesîyeh, on the road from Edfu to Berenikê, an inscription relates how Seti I. dug a well in the desert and how the water gushed up, 'as from the depth of the two Qerti of Elephantinê.' Here the bottomless springs are transferred from Bigeh to Elephantinê, thus explaining how Herodotos could have been led into his error of supposing them to be two mountains between Elephantinê and Assuan. Doubtless the sacred scribe had marked the position of the island of Bigeh by its relation to the better known island of Elephantinê.

The very name of the city which stood on the southern extremity of Elephantinê implied that here, in the days of its foundation, was placed the source of the Egyptian Nile. It was called Qebhu, the city of 'fresh water,' a word represented by the picture of a vase from which water is flowing. At times the city was also called Abu, but Abu was more correctly the name of the island on which it stood. Abu, in fact, signified the island 'of elephants,' of which the Greek Elephantinê was but a translation. In that early age, when it first became known to the Egyptians, the African elephant must still have existed there.

Herodotos does not seem to have been aware that Elephantinê was an island as well as a city. Except where he is reporting the words of the sacred scribe, he always speaks of it as 'a city,' sometimes to the exclusion of the more important Syênê. It is another sign that his voyage up the Nile did not extend so far.

We need not point out other instances of his ignorance of the country above the Fayyûm. Those which have been already quoted are enough. The summer months which he spent in Egypt were more than fully employed in visiting the wonders of

Memphis and the chief cities of the Delta, and in exploring the Fayyûm. Upper Egypt was closed to him, as it was to the rest of his countrymen for many a long day. But we are now able to trace his journey with some degree of exactness. He must have arrived about the beginning of July at the mouth of the Kanôpic arm of the Nile—the usual destination of Greek ships—and thus have made his way by Hermopolis or Damanhur to the Greek capital Naukratis. There he doubtless hired his Karian dragoman, with whom he sailed away over the inundated land to Sais. But his expedition to Sais was only an excursion, from which he returned to continue his voyage in a direct line past Prosôpitis and the pyramids of Gizeh to Memphis. There he inspected the great temple of Ptah, whom his countrymen identified with their Hephæstos, and from thence he went by water to see the pyramids. It was while he was at Memphis, moreover, that he paid a visit to Heliopolis, with its university and its temple, of which all that is left to-day is the obelisk of Usertesen. Next he made his voyage up the Nile, past the brick pyramids of Dahshûr, to Anysis or Herakleopolis, and from thence to the Fayyûm. Then he returned to Memphis, and then again passing Heliopolis sailed northward to Bubastis and Buto. It was now probably that he made excursions to Paprêmis and Busiris, though our ignorance of the precise situation of these places unfortunately prevents us from being certain of the fact. Eventually he found himself at Daphnæ, on the Pelusiac branch of the Nile. This brought him to Pelusium, where he took ship for Tyre.

CHAPTER VII

IN THE STEPS OF HERODOTOS

LET us follow Herodotos in his Egyptian journey and meet him where he landed at the Kanôpic mouth of the Nile. The place had been known to Greek sailors in days of which tradition alone had preserved a memory. It was here that pirates and traders had raided the fields of the *fellahin* or exchanged slaves and Ægean vases for the precious wares of Egypt in the age when Achæan princes ruled at Mykenæ and Tiryns. Guided by the island of Pharos, they had made their way a few miles eastward to the mouth of the great river which is called Aigyptos in the *Odyssey*.

When Egypt was at last opened to Greek trade and enterprise in the time of the twenty-sixth dynasty it was still the Kanôpic arm of the Nile towards which their vessels had to steer. Nowhere else were they allowed to land their goods or sail up the sacred stream of the Nile. If stress of weather drove them to some other part of the coast, they were forced to remain there till the wind permitted them to sail to Kanôpos or to send their goods in native boats by the same route. From time immemorial the coast of the Delta had been carefully guarded against the piratical attacks of the barbarians of the north. Watch-towers and garrisons were established at fitting intervals along it, which were under the charge of a special officer. The mouth of the Kanôpic branch of the river was guarded with more than usual care, and here was the custom-house through which all foreign goods had to pass.

Kanôpos, from which the arm of the river took its name, was a small but wealthy city. It was called in Egyptian Peguath, sometimes also Kah-n-Nub, 'the soil of gold' from the yellow sand on which it was built, though Greek vanity believed that this name had been given to it from Kanôbos, the pilot of Menelaos, whose tomb was of course discovered there. In later days, when Alexandria had absorbed its commerce and industry, it became, along with the outlying Zephyrion, a fashionable Alexandrine suburb. It was filled with drinking-shops and chapels, to which the pleasure-loving crowds of Alexandria used to make their way by the canal that united the two cities. The sick came also to seek healing in the temple of Serapis, or to ask the god to tell them the means of cure. The rich, too, had their villas close to the shrine of Aphroditê Arsinoê, on the breezy promontory of Zephyrion, while the rocks on the shore were cut into luxuriously-fitted baths for those who wished to bathe in the sea.

The site of Zephyrion is now occupied by the little village of Abukîr, memorable in the annals of England and France. In 1891 Daninos Pasha made some excavations there which brought to light a few scanty remains of the temple of Aphroditê. The foundations of its walls were found, as well as two limestone sphinxes inscribed with the name of Amon-em-hat IV., and three great statues of red granite, one of them upright, the others seated. The upright figure was that of Ramses II. with a roll of papyrus in his hand; while the other two were female, one of them being a representation of Hont-mâ-Ra, the Pharaoh's wife. The sphinxes and statues must have been brought from some older building to decorate the shrine of the Alexandrine goddess, and their discoverer believes that the figure of Ramses II. is older even than the age of that monarch, who has usurped it, and that it goes back to the epoch of the twelfth dynasty. Other relics of the temple—fragments of red granite from some gigantic naos, portions of statues, broken sphinxes, and a colossal human foot—strew the rocks at the foot of the promontory whereon Zephyrion stood and bear witness to the intensity of Christian zeal when paganism was abolished in Egypt.

The Kanôpic arm of the Nile has long since been filled up, and the *fellah* ploughs his field or the water-fowl congregate in the stagnant marsh where Greek trading ships once sailed. But a large part of the marsh is now in process of being reclaimed, and the engineers who have been draining and washing it have come across many traces of the ancient Kanôpos. It lay to the east of Zephyrion, between the shore and the marshy lake.

Though the journey from Alexandria to Abukîr must now be undertaken in a railway carriage and not in a barge, it is still pleasant in the early autumn. We pass through fertile gardens and forests of fig-trees, past groves of palm with rich clusters of red dates hanging from them, while the cool sea-breeze blows in at the window, and the clear blue sky shines overhead. But instead of temples and taverns we find at the end of our journey nothing but sand and seashells, broken monuments, and a deserted shore.

The vessel in which Herodotos must have gone from Kanôpos to Naukratis was probably native rather than Greek. It would have differed in one important respect from the Nile-boats of to-day. Its sail was square, not triangular like the modern lateen sails which have been introduced from the Levant.

But in other respects it resembled the vessels which are still used on the Nile. Part of the deck was covered with the house in which the traveller lived, and which was divided into rooms, and fitted up in accordance with the ideas of the day. Awnings protected it from the sun, and the sides of the boat as well as the rudder were brilliantly painted.

On the way to Naukratis the voyager passed Hermopolis, the modern Damanhur, a name which is merely the old Egytian *Dema n Hor*, or 'City of Horus.' It is not surprising, therefore, that Herodotos refers to the city, though the statement he makes in regard to it is not altogether correct. All the dead ibises of Egypt, he says, were carried to Hermopolis to be embalmed and buried. Such might have been the case on the western side of the Delta, but it was true only of that limited district. There was another Hermopolis in the east of the Delta, called Bah in ancient Egyptian, Tel el-Baqlîyeh in modern times, where a large burial-place of the sacred ibises was discovered by the *fellahin* six or seven years ago. Tel el-Baqlîyeh is the second station on the line of railway from Mansurah to Abu Kebîr, and from it have come the bronze ibises and ibis-heads which have filled the shops of the Cairene dealers in antiquities. The bronzes were found among the multitudinous mummies of the sacred bird, like the bronze cats in the cemetery of the sacred cat at Bubastis. Bah was, in fact, the holy city of the 'nome of the Ibis.' The mound of the old city has now been almost demolished by the hunter for *antikas*, but Dr. Naville noticed some fragments of inscribed stone in the neighbouring village which led him to believe that Nektanebo II. once intended to erect a temple here to Thoth.

From Hermopolis to Naukratis was a short distance. Naukratis was the capital of the Egyptian Greeks, and its site, which had been lost for centuries, was discovered by Professor Flinders Petrie in 1884, when he was working for the Egypt Exploration Fund. The Fund had been formed with the primary intention of finding the sites of Pithom and Naukratis, and it had been hardly two years in existence before that intention was fulfilled.

If we leave the train at Teh el-Barûd, the junction of the Upper Egyptian line of railway with that from Alexandria to Cairo, and turn our faces westward, we shall have a pleasant walk of about five miles, part of it under an avenue of trees, to a mound of potsherds which covers several acres in extent and is known to the natives as Kôm Qa'if. This mound represents all that is left of Naukratis. To the west of it runs a canal, the modern successor of the ancient Kanôpic branch of the Nile.

When Professor Petrie first visited the spot, the diggers for *sebah* had already been busily at work. *Sebah* is the nitrous earth from the sites of old cities, which is used as manure, and to the search for it we owe the discovery of many memorials of the past. At Kôm Qa'if the larger part of the earth had been removed, and all that remained were the fragments of pottery which had been sifted from it. But the fragments were sufficient to reveal the history of the place. Most of them belonged to the archaic period of the Greek vase-maker's art, and were such as had never before been found in the land of Egypt. It was evident that the great city whose site they covered must have been the Naukratis of the Greeks.

As soon as Professor Petrie had settled down to the excavation of the mound, a few months after his discovery, the evidence of inscriptions was added to the evidence of potsherds. An inscribed stone from the mound was standing at the entrance of the country-house in which he lived, and on turning it over he found it was engraved with Greek letters which recorded the honours paid by 'the city of the Naukratians' to Heliodôros the priest of Athêna and the keeper of its archives. For two winters first Mr. Petrie and then Mr. Ernest Gardner worked at the ruins, and though more excavations are needed before they can be exhaustively explored,

In the Steps of Herodotos 213

the plan of the old city has been mapped out, the history of its growth and decline has been traced, and a vast number of archaic Greek inscriptions from the dedicated vases of its temples have been secured.

To the south of the town were the fortress and camp of the Greek mercenaries, who were probably settled there by Psammetikhos. The camp was surrounded by a wall, and within it stood the Hellênion, the common altar of the Ionians from Khios, Teos, Phokæa and Klazomenæ, of the Dorians from Rhodes, Knidos, Halikarnassos and Phasêlis, and of the Æolians of Mytilênê. The great enclosure still remains, as well as the lower chambers of the fort, and Mr. Petrie found that in the time of Ptolemy Philadelphos, when it was no longer needed for purposes of defence, it was provided with a stately entrance, to which an avenue of ruins led from the west.

The traders and settlers built their houses north of the camp. Here too the Greek sailors and merchants, who had taken no part in the erection of the great altar, and who perhaps had no relations among the soldiers of the fort, built special temples for themselves. If we walk across the level ground which separates the fort from the old city, the first heap of rubbish we come to marks the site of the temple and sacred enclosure of Castor and Pollux. A little to the north was the still larger temple and *temenos* or sacred enclosure of Apollo, and adjoining it, still on the north side, was the temple of Hêrê, whose *temenos* was the largest of all. The temple of Apollo had been erected by the Milesians, and that it was the oldest in the city may be gathered from the archaic character of the inscriptions on the potsherds discovered in the trench into which the broken vases of the temple were thrown. The Samians were the builders of the temple of Hêrê, and Herodotos tells us that there was another dedicated to Zeus by the Æginetans. The ruins of this, however, have not yet been found, but far away towards the northern end of the ruin a small temple and *temenos* of Aphroditê have been brought to light. Here Rhodôpis worshipped, who had been freed from slavery by the brother of Sappho, and whose charms were still celebrated at Naukratis in the days of Herodotos.

Among the potsherds disinterred from the rubbish-trench of the temple of Apollo were portions of a large and beautiful bowl dedicated to 'Phanês, the son of Glaukos.' Mr. Gardner is probably right in believing that this is the very Phanês who deserted to Kambyses, and, according to the Greek story, instructed him how to march across the desert into Egypt. It may be that Herodotos saw the bowl when it was still intact, and that the story of the deserter was told him over it; in any case, it was doubtless at Naukratis, and possibly from the priests of Apollo, that he heard it.

To the west of the temple of Apollo and divided from it only by a street, Mr. Petrie found what had been a manufactory of scarabs. They were of the blue and white kind that was fashionable in the Greek world in the sixth century before our era, and the earliest of them bear the name of Amasis. From Naukratis they were exported to the shores of Europe and Asia along with the pottery for which the Greek city was famous.

On his way to Naukratis Herodotos had passed two other Greek settlements, Anthylla and Arkhandropolis. But we do not yet know where they stood. Nor do we know the position of that 'Fort of the Milesians' which, according to Strabo, was occupied by Milesian soldiers near Rosetta in the time of Psammetikhos, before they sailed upon the river into 'the nome of Sais' and there founded Naukratis.

The city of Sais was one of the objects of Herodotos's journey. In the period of the inundation it was within an easy distance of Naukratis, so that an excursion to it did not require much time. Sais was the birthplace and capital of the Pharaohs of the twenty-sixth dynasty; it was here that Psammetikhos raised the standard of rebellion against his Assyrian suzerain with the help of the Greek mercenaries, and his successors adorned it with splendid and costly buildings. When Herodotos visited it, it had lost none of its architectural magnificence. He saw there the palace from which Apries had gone forth to attack Amasis, and to which he returned a prisoner; the great temple of Neit, with its rows of sphinxes and its sacred lake; and the huge naos of granite which two thousand men spent three whole years in bringing from Assuan. It had been left just outside the enclosure within which the temple stood, as well as the tombs of Apries and Amasis, and even of the god Osiris himself. True, there was a rival sepulchre of Osiris at Abydos, venerated by the inhabitants of Upper Egypt since the days of the Old Empire, but Abydos was far distant from Sais, and when the latter city became the capital of the kingdom there was none bold enough to deny its claim. Herodotos, at all events, who never reached Abydos, was naturally never informed of the rival tomb.

He was told, however, of the mystery-play acted at night on the sacred lake of Sais in memory of the death and resurrection of Osiris, and he was told also of the shameful insult inflicted by Kambyses on the dead Amasis. It was said that the Pharaoh's mummy had been dragged from its resting-place, and after being scourged was burnt to ashes. The Egyptian priests bore no good-will to Kambyses, and it may be, therefore, that the story is not true.

Sais was under the protection of the goddess Neit, the unbegotten mother of the sun. When the Greeks first came there, they identified the goddess with their own Athêna, led thereto by the similarity of the names. But this identification led to further results. As Athêna was the patron goddess of Athens, so it was supposed that there was a special connection between Sais and Athens. While Athêna was fabled to have come from Libya, Kekrops, the mythic founder of Athens, was transformed into an Egyptian of Sais. It was from a priest of Sais, moreover, that Solon, the Athenian legislator, learned the wisdom of the Egyptians.

The squalid village of Sa el-Hagar, 'Sais of the stone,' is the modern representative of the capital of Psammetikhos. In these days of railways it is difficult of access, as there is no station in its neighbourhood. In the earlier part of the century, however, when the traveller had to go from Alexandria to Cairo in a dahabîyeh, he was compelled to pass it, and it was consequently well-known to the tourist. But little is left of the populous city and its stately monuments except mounds of disintegrated brick, a large enclosure surrounded by a crude brick wall seventy feet thick, and the sacred lake. The lake, however, is sacred no longer; shrunken in size and choked with rubbish, it is a stagnant pool in the winter, and an expanse of half-dried mud in the late spring. It is situated within the great wall, which is that of the *temenos* of Neit. Stone is valuable in the Delta, and hardly a fragment of granite or limestone survives from all the buildings and colossal monuments that Herodotos saw. But in 1891 a great number of bronze figures of Neit, some of them inlaid with silver, were found there by the *fellahin*. They are of the careful and finished workmanship that marks the age of the twenty-sixth dynasty, and on one of the largest of them is a two-fold inscription in Egyptian hieroglyphs and the letters and language of the Karians. It was dedicated to the goddess of Sais in the reign of Psammetikhos by a son of a Karian mother and an Egyptian father who bore both an Egyptian and a Karian name. It is an interesting proof of the readiness of some at least among the natives of Sais to mingle with the foreigner, and it shows further that the Karian mercenaries, like the Greeks, brought their wives and daughters along with them.

Herodotos seems to have been at Sais when the

festival of 'burning lamps' was celebrated there. On the night of the festival lamps were lighted round about the houses in the open air, the lamps being cups filled with salt and oil, on the surface of which a wick floated. All who could thronged to Sais to take part in the ceremonies; those who could not be there lighted their lamps at home and so observed the rites due to Neit. The festival took place in the summer, probably at the time of the summer solstice, and the illuminations characteristic of it are still perpetuated in some of the numerous festivals of modern Egypt. The annual festival in honour of Isis was observed all over Egypt in the same way.

As the Greek traveller approached Memphis the pyramids of Gizeh were shown to him towering over the water on his right. His visit to them was reserved to another day, and he continued to sail on to the ancient capital of the country. Memphis was still in all its glory. Its lofty walls of crude brick, painted white, shone in the sun, and its great temple of Ptah still preserved the monuments and records of the early dynasties of Egypt. Built on an embankment rescued from the Nile, it was said, by Menes, the first monarch of the united kingdom, Memphis, though of no great width, extended along the banks of the river for a distance of half-a-day's journey. To the west, in the desert, lay its necropolis, the city of the dead, reaching from Abu Roâsh on the north to Dahshûr on the south. On the opposite side of· the Nile, a little to the north, was the fortress of Khri-Ahu, which guarded the approach to the river. Where Cairo now stands Herodotos saw only sand and water. Even Khri-Ahu was merely an insignificant village at the foot of a fortress of mud brick; the strong walls and towers of hewn stone in which the Roman legion afterwards kept ward over Egypt were as yet unbuilt. All who could afford it lived in Memphis and its suburbs, and the rock-hewn tombs above the citadel of modern Cairo are of the Roman age.

From Memphis to Heliopolis was rather more than twenty miles, or a morning's row on the river. Herodotos, therefore, after having been told at Memphis of the experiment made by Psammetikhos to discover the origin of language, speaks of having 'turned into' Heliopolis in order to make further inquiries about the matter, 'for the Heliopolitans are said to be the best informed of the Egyptians.' We may gather from his words that he made an excursion to Heliopolis while he was staying in Memphis. But he would have passed it again on his homeward voyage.

The site of Heliopolis is well-known to every tourist who has been to Cairo. The drive to the garden and ostrich-farm of Matarîyeh and the obelisk of Usertesen I. is a pleasant way of filling up an afternoon. But of the ancient city of Heliopolis or On, with its famous temple of Ra, the Sun-god, its university of learned priests, and its innumerable monuments of the past, there is little now to be seen. The obelisk reared in front of its temple a thousand years before Joseph married the daughter of its highpriest still stands where it stood in his day; but the temple has vanished utterly. So, too, has the sister obelisk which was erected by its side, and of which Arabic historians still have something to say. Nothing is left but the mud-brick wall of the sacred enclosure, and a thick layer of lime-stone chippings which tell how the last relics of the temple of the Sun-god were burnt into lime for the Cairo of Ismail Pasha. One or two fragments were rescued from destruction by Dr. Grant Bey, the most noticeable of which is a portion of a cornice, originally 30 feet 4 inches in length, which had been erected by Nektanebo II., the last of the native Pharaohs. Blocks with the names of the second and third Ramses are also lying near the western gate of the enclosure, and in the eastern desert are the tombs of the dead. Nothing more remains of the old capital of Egyptian religion and learning. The destruction is indeed complete; the spoiler whom Jeremiah saw in prophetic vision has broken 'the images of Beth-Shemesh,' and burnt with fire 'the houses of the gods of the Egyptians.' If we would see the obelisks and images of On we must now go to the cities and museums of Europe or America. It was from Heliopolis that the huge scarab of stone now in the British Museum was originally brought to Alexandria, and at Heliopolis Cleopatra's Needle was first set up by Thothmes III. in front of the temple of Amon.

Heliopolis was the centre and source of the worship of the Sun-god in ancient Egypt, in so far, at all events, as he was adored under the name of Ra. The worship goes back to prehistoric days. Menes was already a 'son of Ra,' inheriting his right to rule from the Sun-god of On. The theology of Heliopolis is incorporated in the earliest chapters of the Book of the Dead, that Ritual of the Departed, a knowledge of which ensured the safe passage of the dead man into the world to come. It was in the great hall of its first temple that Egyptian mythology believed Horus to have been cured of his wounds after the battle with Set. The origin of the temple, in fact, like the origin of the school of priests which gathered round it, was too far lost in the mists of antiquity for authentic history to remember.

As befitted its theological character, Heliopolis was rich in sacred animals. The bull Mnêvis, in which the Sun-god was incarnated, was a rival of the bull Apis of Memphis, the incarnation of Ptah. The two bulls point to a community of worship between the two localities in that primeval age when neither Ra of Heliopolis nor Ptah of Memphis was known, and when the primitive Egyptian population—whoever they may have been—were plunged in the grossest superstitions of African fetichism. Herodotos did not hear of the bull Mnêvis. But he was acquainted with the story of another sacred animal of Heliopolis, the *bennu* or Phœnix, the sacred bird of Ra. Indeed, the fame of the phœnix had long before penetrated to Greece. Hesiod alludes to it, and the account of the marvellous bird given by Herodotos was 'stolen,' we are told by Porphyry, from his predecessor Hekatæos. Hekatæos says that it was like an eagle, whereas the monuments show that it was a heron, and Herodotos follows him in the blunder. We may argue from this, as Professor Wiedemann does, that Herodotos himself never saw its picture. But otherwise his account is correct. Its wings were red and gold, and it represented the solar cycle of five hundred years.

When Strabo visited Heliopolis in the age of Augustus he found it already half deserted. Its schools and library had been superseded by those of Alexandria, and although the houses in which the priestly philosophers had once lived were still standing, they were now empty. Among them was the house in which Plato and Eudoxos had studied not long after the time when Herodotos was there. In spite, therefore, of the Persian wars Herodotos must have found the ancient university still famous and flourishing. Just as in the Cairo of to-day the whole circle of Mohammedan science is taught in the University of El-Azhar on the basis of the Qorân, so in the Heliopolis which Herodotos visited all the circle of Egyptian knowledge was still taught and learned on the basis of the doctrines of the Heliopolitan school. The feelings with which the Greek traveller viewed the professors and their pupils —if, indeed, he was allowed to do so—must have been similar to those with which an English tourist now passes through the Azhar mosque.

From Heliopolis Herodotos continued his voyage down the Pelusiac arm of the Nile to Bubastis, thus following nearly the same line of travel as the modern tourist who goes by train from Cairo to Zagazig. The rubbish heaps of Tel Basta, just beyond the station of Zagazig, mark the site of Bubastis, called Pi-beseth in the Old Testament (Ezek. xxx. 17), Pi-Bast, 'the Temple of Bast,' by the Egyptians. The cat-headed goddess Bast presided over the fortunes of the nome and city, where she was identified

In the Steps of Herodotos 225

with Sekhet, the lion-headed goddess of Memphis. But the cat and the lion never lay down in peace together. As a hieroglyphic text at Philæ puts it, Sekhet was cruel and Bast was kindly.

The exclusive worship of Bast at Bubastis, however, dated from the time of Osorkon II. of the twenty-second dynasty, as Dr. Naville's excavations have made plain. Before that period other deities, more especially Butô and Amon-Ra, reigned there. Bast, in fact, was of foreign origin. She was the feminine form of Bes, the warrior god who came from the coasts of Arabia, and her association with the cat perhaps originated far away in the south.

The description given by Herodotos of Bubastis and its festival is clearly that of an eye-witness. He tells us how the temple stands in the middle of the town surrounded by a canal which is shaded with trees, and how the visitor looks down upon it from the streets of the city, which had grown in height while the level of the temple had remained unaltered. He tells us further how a broad street runs from it to the market-place, and thence to a chapel dedicated to Hermês, and how at the great annual festival crowds of men and women flocked to it in boats, piping and singing, clapping the hands and dancing, offering sacrifices when they arrived at the shrine, and drinking wine to excess. A similar sight can be

P

seen even now in the month of August at Tantah, where the religious fair is thronged by men and women indulging in all the amusements recounted by the old Greek traveller, sometimes beyond the verge of decency. Wine alone is absent from the modern feast, its place being taken by *hashish* and *raki*.

As the festival was held in honour of Bast, it was probably an annual commemoration of the great 'Shed-festival' of thirty years celebrated by Osorkon II. in his twenty-second year, and depicted on the walls of the hall which Dr. Naville has discovered. The 'Shed-festival' took place during the month of August—in the time of the sixth dynasty on the 27th of Epiphi. It was probably, therefore, at the end of August or the beginning of September that Herodotos found himself in the city of Bast.

The description Herodotos gives of the position of the temple is still true to-day. The temple, which he pronounced to be the prettiest in Egypt, is now in ruins, like the houses and streets that encircled it. But the visitor to Tel-Bast still looks down upon its site from the rubbish-mounds of the ruined habitations, and can still trace the beds of the canals which were carried round it. Even the street which led to the market-place is still visible, and Dr. Naville has found the remains of the little temple which

Herodotos supposed to be that of Hermês, the Egyptian Thoth. In this, however, he was wrong. Like the larger edifice, it was dedicated to Bast, and seems to have been used as a treasury. It was, therefore, under the protection of Thoth, whose figure decorated its walls, and Dr. Naville is doubtless right in believing that this has led to the mistake of Herodotos or his guides. Osorkon I. consecrated in it large quantities of precious things, including about £130,300 in gold and £13,000 in silver—an evident proof that the internal condition of his kingdom was flourishing.

Dr. Naville's excavations were undertaken for the Egypt Exploration Fund in 1887-89, and were chiefly made among the broken columns and dislocated stones of the larger temple. They have given us the outlines of its history. Like most of the great temples of Egypt, its foundation went back to the very beginning of Egyptian civilisation. The Pharaohs of the Old Empire repaired or enlarged it, and the names of Kheops and Khephren, as well as of Pepi I., have been found upon its blocks. The kings of the twelfth and thirteenth dynasties embellished it, and even the Hyksos princes did the same. In the days when they had adopted the culture and customs of Egypt and were holding royal state at Zoan, two of them at least restored and beautified the temple of

Bubastis and called themselves the sons of Ra. One of them, Apophis, may have been the Apophis whose demand that the vassal-king of Thebes should worship Sutekh instead of Amon brought about the war of independence; the other, Khian User-n-Set-Ra, the Iannas of Manetho, has engraved his name on a colossal lion which was carried to Babylon by some Chaldæan conqueror.

The monarchs of the eighteenth dynasty continued the pious work of the Hyksos whom they had expelled. But the civil disturbances which attended the fall of the dynasty caused injury to the temple, and we find Seti I. and Ramses II. once more restoring it. The kings of the twentieth dynasty have also left memorials in it, but it was under the twenty-second dynasty—the successors of Shishak —that Bubastis reached the highest point of its prosperity. The princes who followed Shishak made the city their capital and its temple their royal chapel. The great festival hall was built by Osorkon II. between the entrance hall and the main court, and the worship of Bast was exclusively installed in it. Temple and city alike underwent but little change down to the days of Herodotos. It was after his visit that the last addition was made to the sacred buildings. With the recovery of Egyptian independence after the successful revolt from Persia

In the Steps of Herodotos 229

came a new era of architectural activity, and Nektanebo I., the first king of the thirtieth dynasty, erected a great hall in the rear of the shrine. After this the history of the temple fades out of view.

Herodotos was told that the height of the mound on which the city of Bubastis stood was an indication of the evil deeds of its inhabitants. Sabako, the Ethiopian conqueror, it was said, had caused the sites of the Egyptian cities to be raised by convict labour, just as they had been previously raised by those who cut the canals under Sesostris. But the whole story was an invention of the dragomen. The disintegration of the crude brick of which the houses of Egypt are built makes them quickly decay and give place to other buildings, which are erected on the mound they have formed. As the city grows in age, so does the *tel* or mound whereon it stands grow in height, and had Herodotos travelled in Upper Egypt he would have seen the process going on under his eyes. In the Delta, moreover, there was a special cause for the great height of the city-mounds. The water of the inundation percolated through the ground, and in order that the lower floor of a house should be dry, it was necessary to build it on a series of vaults or cellars. A few years ago these vaults were very visible in some of the old houses of Tel-Bast. They had no outlet, either by door or window, and were consequently never employed as store-rooms. Their sole use was to keep the rest of the house dry.

The cemetery of the sacred cats was on the western side of the town. But the cats do not appear to have been embalmed, as elsewhere in Egypt; they were either buried or burned. Among the bones which have been sent to England naturalists have found none of our modern domestic cat. Several, however, of the bronze cats of the Ptolemaic age which have been discovered with the bones unmistakably represent the domestic animal. Generally they have the small head of the modern Egyptian puss.

'A little below Bubastis' Herodotos passed the deserted 'camp' and fortress of the Ionian and Karian mercenaries of Psammetikhos, and saw the slips for their vessels and the ruins of their houses still standing on the shore. Amasis had transferred them to Memphis, in the belief that it was rather from his Egyptian subjects that he needed protection than from his neighbours in Asia. The site of the camp was discovered and partially excavated by Professor Petrie for the Egypt Exploration Fund in 1886, and one of the results of his discoveries was to show that it was also the site of the frontier fortress called by the Greeks Daphnæ. What its

Egyptian name was we do not know with certainty, though it is probable that Professor Petrie is right in holding it to be the Tahpanhes of the prophet Jeremiah. It is now known as Tel ed-Deffeneh.

The drying up of the Pelusiac arm of the Nile has brought the desolation of the desert to Tel ed-Deffeneh. The canal which has replaced it is brackish; Lake Menzaleh, which bounds the Tel to the east, is more brackish still. The land is impregnated with salt, and covered in places with drifts of sand. There is no cultivated soil nearer than Salahîyeh, twelve miles away; no water-way less distant than Kantara on the Suez Canal.

The greater part of the ancient site lies between Lake Menzaleh on the east and a swamp out of which the canal flows on the west, and it covers a large acreage of ground. Northward are the canal, a marsh, and mounds of sand, and beyond the canal lies the cemetery of the ancient fortress, as well as a suburb which was probably the Karian quarter. In the centre of the site rises the Tel proper, a great mound of disintegrated brickwork called 'the palace of the Jew's daughter.' Excavation soon made it clear that it represented the fortress of Daphnæ, and that it was built by Psammetikhos when he settled his Greek garrison there. For a frontier fortress no place could have been better chosen. It guarded the eastern branch of the Nile, while from its summit we look across the desert, on one side along the highroad which once led to Syria, and on the other as far as the mounds of Tanis. The fort itself has crumbled into dust, but the vaulted chambers on which it was erected still exist, as well as the 'pavement' at its entrance.

The pottery found at Tel ed-Deffeneh is early Greek, but of a different type from that of Naukratis. Like the latter, it would seem to have been manufactured on the spot and exported from thence to all parts of the Greek world. Jewellery, too, appears to have been made there by the Greek or Karian artisans who lived under the protection of their military kinsmen. But the manufacture of both pottery and jewellery came to a sudden end. When Amasis removed the mercenaries to Memphis in the middle of the sixth century before Christ the civilian population departed with them. Between that date and a new and unimportant settlement in the Ptolemaic period the site seems to have been deserted. When Herodotos passed it by, it had no inhabitants.

From Daphnæ to Pelusium the voyage was short. Pelusium, once the key of Egypt, has shared the fate of Daphnæ. The channel of the river that flowed by it has become a dreary reach of black salt mud, and the fields which once supplied the city with food are wastes of sterile soil or mountains of yellow sand. Not even a solitary Bedoui disturbs the solitude of the spot at most seasons of the year. All that reminds the traveller of human life as he encamps on the edge of the sand-dunes is the electric light which flashes through the night from Port Said far away on the horizon.

In the midst of the desolate waste of poisonous mud rise the two large mounds which alone are left of Pelusium. On the larger of these, to the westward, lie the granite columns and other relics of the Roman temple, beneath which, and below the present level of the water, are the ruins of the temple of the Pharaonic age. The ground is strewn with broken glass and pottery, some Roman, some Saracenic.

The Egyptian name of Pelusium is still unknown, and before we can discover it excavations upon its site will be necessary. Ezekiel calls it Sin (xxx. 15, 16)—at least, if the commentators are to be trusted —and when the Greeks sought an etymology for the name they gave it in their own word for 'mud.' But it was a famous spot in the records of Egyptian history. Avaris, the Hyksos stronghold, must have been in its neighbourhood, and it was outside its walls that the Persian conquest of Egypt was decided. The battle-field where the army of Kambyses, led by the Greek deserter Phanês, overthrew the Greek mercenaries of the Pharaoh, was near enough for Herodotos to walk over it and compare the skulls of the Egyptian and Persian combatants, as he had already done at Paprêmis. Here, too, he was shown the spot where the Greek and Karian soldiers of Psammetikhos III. had slaughtered the sons of Phanês over a huge bowl in the sight of their father, and after mixing the blood of the boys with wine and water, had savagely drunk it and then rushed to the battle.

Not far from Pelusium another tragedy took place four centuries after Herodotos had been there. The fugitive Pompey was welcomed to the shore by Septimius, the general of the Roman forces in Egypt, and Akhillas, the commander of the Egyptian army, and murdered by them as he touched the land. Akhillas then hastened to Alexandria, to besiege Cæsar in the royal palace, and the burning of the great library was the atonement for Pompey's death.

Down even to the middle ages Pelusium was still the seaport of the eastern Delta. It held the place now occupied by Port Said. It was from its quays that the vessels started for the Syrian coast. In one that was bound for Tyre, Herodotos took his passage and ended his Egyptian tour.

But he had visited certain cities in the Delta into which we have been unable to follow him, owing to the uncertainty that still hangs over their exact position. Besides the places already described, we know that he saw Butô, which is coupled with Khemmis, as well as Paprêmis and Prosôpitis, and probably also Busiris.

Khemmis—which must be carefully distinguished from the other Khemmis, the modern Ekhmîm—was, he tells us, a floating island 'in a deep broad lake by the side of the temple at Butô,' where Lêtô, the Egyptian Uaz, was worshipped. Brugsch identifies this island of Khemmis with the town and marshes of Kheb, where the young Horus was hidden by his mother Isis out of the reach of Set. Kheb was in the nome called that of Menelaos by the Greeks, the capital of which seems to have been Pa-Uaz, 'the temple of Uaz,' transformed by Greek tongues into Butô, and of which another city was Kanôpos. Butô, or at least the twin-city where the great temple of the goddess stood, is probably now represented by Tel Fera'în, not far to the west of Fuah, at the extremity of the Mahmudîyeh canal. It was thus within easy distance of Kanôpos on the one side and of Sais on the other, and Herodotos might have visited it from either one of them.

But after all it is not certain that he did so. Butô is mentioned again by him in a passage which shows that it could not have been Pa-Uaz, but must have rather lain on the eastern side of the Delta, in the land of Goshen, where the desert adjoined the 'Arabian nome.' It is where he tells us about 'the winged serpents' which fly in the spring-time from Arabia to Egypt, on the confines of which they are met and slain by the sacred ibises. Anxious to learn something about them, he visited the spot where the yearly encounter took place, and there saw the ground strewn with the bones and spines of the slaughtered snakes. This spot, he further informs us, is in the Arabian desert, where it borders on 'the Egyptian plain,' 'hard by the city of Buto.'

Thanks to the excavations made by Mr. Griffith for the Egypt Exploration Fund at Tel en-Nebêsheh, near Salahîyeh, we now know where this eastern city of Buto stood. Its Egyptian name was Am, and it was the capital of the nineteenth nome of Am-pehu, but it was consecrated to the worship of the goddess Uaz, who was symbolised by a winged snake. The great temple of the goddess was built on the western side of the town, and the Pharaohs of the twelfth dynasty, as well as Ramses II. and his successors, and the Saites of the twenty-sixth dynasty, had all helped to endow and embellish it. When the Greek garrison was established in the neighbourhood at Daphnæ, a colony of Cyprian potters settled at Am. But in the age of the

Ptolemies it fell into decay, and by the beginning of the Roman era its magnificence belonged to the past.

Just beyond the precincts of the town was the Arabian desert, the realm of Set. The legend of Isis and Horus was accordingly transferred to it, and its patron goddess became Uaz of Butô, who, under the form of Isis, concealed Horus in its marshes. Was it here, therefore, in the Pa-Uaz of Am, that the Butô of Herodotos has to be looked for, rather than in the Menelaite nome?

We know that he must have passed the city of Am on his way from Bubastis to Daphnæ, and his expedition to the desert in search of the winged serpents shows that he stopped there. On the other hand, his account of the floating island of Khemmis was derived from his predecessor Hekatæos, and when he states that the Butô with which it was connected was built on the Sebennytic branch of the Nile, 'as one sails up it from the sea,' it would seem certain that his account of this Butô was also quoted from the older writer. And yet it is difficult to believe that his description of the monolithic shrine which stood there is not given at first-hand. Perhaps the best explanation would be that Herodotos really made an excursion to the city, but has so skilfully mingled what he himself saw there with the description of Hekatæos as to make it impossible to separate the two.

The site of Paprêmis is absolutely unknown, and we have no clue even to its relative position. But Prosôpitis may be the fourth nome, Sapi-ris or 'Sapi of the south.' In Byzantine times its capital bore the name of Nikiu, which Champollion long ago identified with the Coptic Pshati and the modern Abshadi, not far from Menûf. Menûf stands in a straight line due westward of Benha, and would have lain directly in the path of the traveller on his way from Naukratis to Memphis.

It was in the island of Prosôpitis that the Athenian fleet was blockaded by the Persians under Megabazus, and captured only when the river was turned into another channel, after the blockade had lasted for a year and a half. Immediately westward of Menûf, in fact, an island is formed by the Rosetta and Damietta branches of the Nile which unite at the southern end of it, and are joined together towards the north by the Bahr el-Fara'-unîyeh. But the island is twenty-seven miles long by fifteen wide, and it is difficult to understand how this could have been blockaded by the Persian army, much less defended by the crews of seventy vessels, for the space of a year and a half. Herodotos indeed asserts that the island of Prosôpitis was nine skhœnœ, or about sixty miles in circumference, and that it contained many cities; but this only makes the difficulty the greater.

Lastly, we come to Busiris, which is described by the Greek traveller as 'in the centre of the Delta.' This description exactly suits the position of Pa-Usar or Busiris, 'the temple of Osiris, the lord of Mendes,' and the capital of the Busirite nome. Its modern representative is Abusir, a little to the south of Semennûd or Sebennytos, on the railway line from Tanta to Mansûrah. If Herodotos really visited this place, he must have done so from Sais, to the west of which it lies in a pretty direct line. But the distance was considerable, and there is nothing in the language he uses in regard to it which obliges us to believe that he was really there. His description of the festival held there in honour of Isis is not that of an eye-witness; indeed, the remark he adds to it that 'all the Karians who live in Egypt slash themselves on the forehead with swords' in their religious exercises goes to show that it could not have been so. All he knows about the festival is that, after sacrificing, men and women strike themselves in honour of Osiris. The Karians, however, who cut their heads like the Persian devotees of Huseyn in modern Cairo, were not Egyptians, and therefore would not have been allowed to join in the mysteries of the worship of Osiris; moreover, they did not live in Busiris, but in the Karian quarter of Memphis. What Herodotos tells us about them plainly comes from his Karian dragoman, and refers to some native Karian festival.

There was more than one Pa-Usar or Temple of Osiris in Lower Egypt. Next to that in the Busirite nome, the most famous was that of the Ur-Mer or the bull Mnêvis, in the environs of Heliopolis. This latter Herodotos would have seen when he paid his visit to the city of the Sun-god, and this too was near Memphis, where the Karians lived.

There was yet another Busiris a little to the north of Memphis itself. According to Pliny, its inhabitants made their living by climbing the pyramids for the amusement of strangers, like the Bedouin of Gizeh to-day. Its name has been preserved in the village and pyramids of Abusir. But neither the Busiris of Memphis nor the Busiris of Heliopolis was 'in the centre of the Delta,' and it would seem that in this instance also Herodotos is either quoting from other travellers or is mixing their experiences with his own. With the Busiris of Memphis and the Busiris of Heliopolis he was doubtless acquainted: with the Busiris of the middle Delta we must conclude he was not. Hence his scanty notice of the festival that was celebrated there; hence also his reference to the Karian settlers in Memphis and their religious ceremonies. We must remember that Herodotos was not the first Greek tourist in Egypt, and that he too had his *Murray* and his *Baedeker* like the tourist of to-day.

CHAPTER VIII

MEMPHIS AND THE FAYYÛM

WE have followed Herodotos in his travels through the Delta, have seen him make his way from Kanôpos and Naukratis to Memphis and back again to Pelusium, and it is now time to accompany him through Memphis itself and the Fayyûm. There are no longer any uncertain sites to identify; from Memphis southward all is clear and determined.

To the visitor the interest of Memphis centred in its temple of Ptah. It was round the temple that the city had grown up, and as the city had been the capital of the older dynasties, so the temple had been their royal chapel. When the supremacy passed from Memphis to Thebes, it passed also from Ptah the god of Memphis to Amon the god of Thebes.

It is the great temple of Ptah, accordingly, about which Herodotos has most to tell us. Other localities in Memphis, such as the citadel and the palace, the Karian quarter, or 'the Tyrian Camp' with its shrine of Ashtoreth, are noticed only incidentally.

Memphis and the Fayyûm 243

But the great temple and its monuments are described as fully as was possible for an 'impure' foreigner, who was not permitted to enter its inner courts and who was unacquainted with the Egyptian language.

The history of Egypt known to Herodotos before the age when Greek mercenaries and traders were settled in the country by Psammetikhos is almost wholly connected with the monuments of the temple which were shown to him. And a very curious history it is — a collection of folk-tales, partly Egyptian, but mainly Karian or Greek in origin, and not always of a seemly character, which the dragomen attached to the various objects the visitor saw. Even the royal names round which they revolved were sometimes indiscoverable in the authentic annals of Egypt. But the stories were all gravely noted down by the traveller, and though they have lost nothing in the telling, it is probable that they have not always been reported by him correctly.

In one respect, at all events, this mythical history of Egypt is the creation of Herodotos himself and not of his guides. This is the order in which he has arranged the kings. It is the order in which he visited the monuments to which the dragomen attached their names, and it thus throws a welcome light on the course of his movements. With this clue in our hands we can follow him from one part of the temple of Ptah to another, and can trace his footsteps as far as the Fayyûm.

It is true he asserts that his list of kings was given on the authority of 'the Egyptians and the priests,' and that it was they who reckoned three hundred and forty-one generations from Menes, the founder of the kingdom, to Sethos, the antagonist of Sennacherib, the number of kings and high-priests during the period being exactly equal to the number of generations. But it can easily be shown that the calculation was made by Herodotos himself, and that neither the 'Egyptians,' whose language he did not understand, nor the sacristans, whom he dignifies with the title of priests, are in any way responsible for the absurd statement that a generation and a reign are equivalent terms. The number of kings whose names he heard from his dragoman is exactly eleven; in addition to these, he tells us, the names of three hundred and thirty kings were read to him from a papyrus roll by one of the temple scribes; so that the number three hundred and forty-one is obtained by adding the three hundred and thirty names to the eleven which were furnished him by his guides. Among the three hundred and thirty must have been included some of the latter, though the Greek traveller did not know it.

At Memphis Herodotos learned that Menes was

the first king of united Egypt, though the further statements he records in regard to him are not easily reconcilable one with the other. On the one hand he was informed that in his time all Egypt was a marsh except the Thebaic nome—a piece of information which seemed to Herodotos consonant with fact—on the other hand, that the land on which Memphis was built was a sort of huge embankment reclaimed from the Nile by Menes, who forced the river to leave its old channel under the plateau of Gizeh and to run in its present bed. Mariette believed that the dyke by means of which the first of the Pharaohs effected this change in the course of the river still exists near Kafr el-Ayyât, and it is geologically clear that the Nile once ran along the edge of the Libyan desert, and that the rock out of which the Sphinx was carved must have been one of those which jutted out into the stream.

But it was not on account of his engineering works that the name of Menes has been preserved in the histories of Herodotos. It was because he was the founder of the temple of Ptah and the city of Memphis. The temple which was the object of the tourist's visit owed its origin to him, and the traveller's sight-seeing naturally began with the mention of his name.

Before Herodotos could be shown round such

parts of the sanctuary as were accessible to strangers, it was necessary that he should be introduced to the authorities and receive their permission to visit it. Accordingly he was ushered into what was perhaps the library of the temple, and there a scribe read to him out of a roll the names of the three hundred and thirty kings, beginning with Menes and ending with Mœris. To three only does a story seem to have been attached, either by the scribe or by the interpreter, and only three names therefore did Herodotos enter in his note-book. The first of these was that of Menes, the second that of Nitôkris, the third that of Mœris. Nitôkris was celebrated not only because she was the one native woman who had ruled the country, but also because she had treacherously avenged the death of her brother and then flung herself into the flames. Neit-aker, as she was called in Egyptian, was actually an historical personage; she was the last sovereign of the sixth dynasty, but was very far from being the only queen who had reigned over Egypt. As regards Mœris the statements of Herodotos are only partially correct. He is said to have built the propylæa on the north side of the temple of Ptah, to have dug the great lake of the Fayyûm, and to have erected the pyramids which Herodotos believed he had seen standing in the middle of it. Mœris, however, was not the name of

Memphis and the Fayyûm 247

a king, but the Egyptian words Mi ur or 'great lake'; the Fayyûm was not created by the excavation of an artificial reservoir, but by banking out the water which had filled the oasis from geological times; and the monuments seen by Herodotos were not pyramids, but statues on pyramidal bases erected by Amon-em-hat III. of the twelfth dynasty in front of an ancient temple. Nor could any educated Egyptian have alleged that a king of the twelfth dynasty, who was not even the last monarch of that dynasty itself, closed the line of the Pharaohs. The whole account must rest on a combination of the Greek historian's own erroneous conclusions with the misinterpreted statements of the Egyptian 'priest.'

Mœris, in the topographical chronology of Herodotos, was followed by Sesostris, but this was because the tourist, after leaving the scribe's chamber, first visited the northern side of the temple. Here stood the two colossal figures of Ramses II. in front of the entrance, which, after centuries of neglect and concealment, have again become objects of interest. The larger one, forty-two feet in length, was discovered in 1820 and presented by Mohammed Ali to the British Government, but, as might have been expected, was never claimed. For years it lay on its face in the mud and water, but in 1883 Major Bagnold turned it round and raised it, and finally placed it in the shed, where it is now safe from further injury. The son and daughter of the Pharaoh were originally represented standing beside him. Major Bagnold also brought to light the companion statue, of lesser height and of a different stone. This is in a better state of preservation, and has been set up on a hillock by the side of a stêlê which was discovered at the same time. Fragments of papyri inscribed with Greek and demotic have been found at the north-eastern foot of the hillock, and it may be that they mark the site of the chamber where Herodotos listened to the words of the roll.

Northward of the colossi was the sacred lake, said to have been formed by Menes, and now a stagnant pond. At its south-eastern corner the foundations have recently been laid bare of small square rooms, the walls of which have been adorned with sculptures. But the waters of the inundation have followed the excavators, and the walls are fast perishing under the influence of moisture and nitrous salt.

About Sesostris the guides of Herodotos had a good deal to say. But nothing of it was history—not even his conquests in Europe and Scythia, his excavation of the canals which rendered Egypt unfit for horses and chariots, his equal division of the land among his subjects, or his having been the sole

Egyptian monarch who governed Ethiopia. How even a dragoman of Memphis could have imagined that it had ever been possible to cultivate the Egyptian soil without canals it is difficult to understand, and still more difficult to imagine how a traveller who had seen the Delta could have believed a statement of the kind. The only explanation can be that Herodotos never saw the Delta in its normal condition when the inundation had ceased to cover the land. That Sesostris should have been supposed to have been the only Pharaoh who established his power in Ethiopia is but a proof how little was known of the real history of Egypt by either Herodotos or his informants.

The origin of the name given to this Pharaoh of the dragoman's imagination is still a puzzle. The statues in front of the temple of Ptah, to which the name was attached, were set up by Ramses II., and in a papyrus we find the name Sesetsu given as the popular title of the same monarch. Perhaps it means 'the son of Set is he.' We know that Set, the ancient god of the Delta, was a special object of worship in the family of Ramses II., and his father Seti was named after the god. Sesetsu would correspond with fair exactitude to the Sesoôsis of Diodoros ; for Sesostris we should have to presuppose the form Sesetsu-Ra.

The son and successor of Sesostris, according to Herodotos, was Pherôn. The name is merely a mispronounced Pharaoh, the Egyptian Per-âa or 'Great House.' Pherôn undertook no military expedition, being blind in consequence of his impiety in hurling his spear at too high a Nile. After ten years of blindness an oracle came to him from Butô that he would be cured if he would wash his eyes in the urine of a woman who had been true to her husband. Trial after trial was made in vain, and when at last the king recovered his sight he collected all the women in whose case he had failed into 'a city now called the Red Mound,' and there burnt them, city and all. He then erected the two obelisks which stood in front of the temple of Ra at Heliopolis.

There are many 'Red Mounds' in Egypt, and the name Kom el-Ahmar or 'Red Mound' is accordingly very plentiful in a modern map of the country. Wherever kiln-baked bricks have been used in the construction of a building, or where the wall or houses of a city have been burnt, the mound of ruins to which they give rise is of a reddish colour. Such a mound must have existed in the neighbourhood of Heliopolis in the days of Herodotos. There is still a Kom el-Ahmar close to Tel el-Yehudîyeh, where the Jewish temple of Onias was built. But 'the Red Mound' of the guides was probably one that was visible from the pylon of the great temple of Heliopolis, where the obelisks stood with which the story of it was associated. The obelisks had indeed been erected by a 'Pharaoh,' but it was not a son of Ramses II. They been set up by Usertesen I. of the twelfth dynasty nearly fifteen centuries before Ramses II. was born.

As Pherôn was the son of Sesostris it was necessary for Herodotos to introduce him into his list immediately after his father, even though he had left no monument behind him in the temple of Memphis. But after Pherôn he returns to his series of 'Memphite' kings. This time it is 'a Memphite whose Greek name is Prôteus,' and whose shrine was situated in the midst of 'the Tyrian Camp' or settlement on the 'south side of the temple of Ptah.' The tourist, therefore, walked round the eastern wall of the great temple from north to south, and as the pylon on this side of the sanctuary was connected with the name of a king who was the builder of a brick pyramid seen on the way to the Fayyûm, an account of it is deferred till later. The next monument Herodotos came to was accordingly of Phœnician and not of Egyptian origin.

Prôteus in fact was a Phœnician god, worshipped, Herodotos tells us, along with the foreign Aphroditê, whom he suspects to be the Greek Helen in disguise.

The Phœnician Aphroditê, however, was really Ashtoreth, which the Greeks pronounced Astartê, the Istar of the Babylonians and Assyrians. But the 'priests,' or rather the guides of the traveller, were equal to the occasion, and on his asking them concerning Helen they at once gave him a long story about her arrival and adventures in Egypt. Prôteus was at the time the king in Memphis, and not the sea-god of ships and prophetic insight, as Homer had imagined, and he very properly took Helen away from Paris and kept her safely till Menelaos arrived after the Trojan war to claim his wife. Accordingly Prôteus, the Phœnician 'old man of the sea,' has gone down among the three hundred and forty-one Pharaohs of Egypt whose names were recounted to Herodotos by the 'priests.' There could not be a better illustration of the real character of his 'priestly' informants, or of the worthlessness of the information which they gave him.

When, however, Herodotos goes on to assert that 'they said' that Rhampsinitos succeeded Prôteus in the kingdom, he is dealing with them unjustly. The supposed fact must have come from his own notebook. After visiting the Tyrian Camp, on the south side of the great temple, the traveller was taken to its western entrance, where he was told that the propylæa had been erected by Rhampsinitos, as well as two colossal statues in front of them. The order in which he saw the monuments determined the order in which the names of Prôteus and Rhampsinitos occurred in his note-book, and the order in his notebook determined the order of their succession.

Rhampsinitos represents a real Egyptian king. He is Ramses III. of the twentieth dynasty, the last of the conquering Pharaohs, and the builder of Medînet Habu at Thebes. But Herodotos was never at Thebes, and had consequently never heard of the superb temple and palace Ramses had built there. All that he knows of the architectural works of the Pharaoh are the insignificant additions he made to the temple of Memphis. Of the real Pharaoh he is equally ignorant. In place of the vanquisher of the hordes of the north, the monarch who annihilated the invaders from the Ægean and captured or sunk their ships, the conqueror who carried his arms into Palestine and Syria, we have the hero of a folk-tale. Rhampsinitos and his treasury have become the subject of the story of the master-thief, a story which in various forms is found all over the world, and perhaps goes back to the infancy of mankind. Why this story should have been attached to Ramses III. it is just as impossible for us to know as it is to understand why the name of Neit, the goddess of Sais and the twenty-sixth dynasty, should have been combined with that of the Theban Pharaoh of the twentieth. Rhampsinitos, Ramessu-n-Neit or 'Ramses of Neit,' indicates the period in which alone the name could have been formed. It must have been the invention of the Karian dragomen who came into existence under the Saitic dynasty.

Ramses III. was, however, as we learn from the great Harris papyrus, one of the wealthiest of Egyptian princes. The gifts he made to the temples of the gods, more especially to that of Amon of Thebes, are almost fabulous in amount. His trading ships brought him the wares of the south and north; and the gold-mines of the eastern desert, as well as the copper and malachite mines of the province of Mafkat, the Sinaitic Peninsula of our modern maps, were actively worked in his reign. The chambers of one of his treasuries still exist at Medînet Habu, and we can still see depicted on their walls the vases of precious metal which he deposited in them.

The Rhampsinitos of folk-lore was similarly rich. He built a treasury for his wealth beside his palace, which should secure it against all attempts at robbery. But the architect left in it a stone which could be easily removed by any one who knew its secret, and before he died the secret was communicated to his two sons. To the amazement of the king, therefore, the gold began to disappear, though his seals remained unbroken and the doors fast locked. He set a trap, accordingly, by the side of the chests of gold; and one of the thieves was caught in it. He thereupon induced his brother to cut off his head, so that his body might not be recognised, and to decamp with it. Next morning Rhampsinitos found the headless corpse, which was thereupon exposed to public view under the protection of armed guards, who were ordered to arrest whoever showed any signs of recognising it. The mother of the dead man, frantic at the treatment of his body, which would deprive him of all hope in the next world, threatened to disclose the whole story unless her surviving son could secure his brother's corpse and give it honourable burial. Loading several asses with wine-skins, therefore, he drove them past the place where the guards sat over the corpse. There he allowed some of the wine to escape, accidentally as it were, and when the guards began eagerly to drink it he craftily encouraged them to do so until they had all fallen into a drunken sleep. He then seized the body and carried it to his mother. The king was now more than ever desirous of discovering such a master-thief, and ordered his daughter to adopt the Babylonian custom of sitting in public and admitting the attentions of any one who passed on condition that he told her the cleverest trick he had ever performed. The thief provided himself with the arm of a mummy, which he concealed under his cloak, and thus prepared presented himself to the princess and disclosed to her all he had done. As she tried to seize him, he left the dead man's arm in her hand and escaped. The king, struck with admiration, determined that so exceedingly clever a youth should be his own son-in-law, and issued a proclamation not only pardoning him but allowing him to marry his daughter. Such was the way in which Egyptian history was constructed by the combined efforts of the popular imagination, the foreign dragomen, and Herodotos!

After all, however, the master-thief did not succeed Rhampsinitos on the throne. After passing the western entrance of the temple of Ptah, Herodotos arrived again at the northern side, from which he had started, and, as he was not allowed to enter the sanctuary, there was nothing further for him to see. His next visit, accordingly, was to the pyramids of Gizeh, and the pyramidal builders—Kheops, Khephren, and Mykerinos of the fourth dynasty—are made to follow Ramses III. of the twentieth, who lived more than two thousand years after them. It does not say much for the judgment of our classical scholars that before the decipherment of the hieroglyphs they should have preferred the chronology of Herodotos to that of Manetho.

Herodotos, like a true sight-seer, found nothing in Memphis to interest him except the temple. About the city itself he has nothing to say, not even about the stuccoed city-wall which gave to it its name of 'the White Wall.' Portions of this wall are still standing at the northern end of the mounds which cover the site of Memphis. Like all the other city-walls of ancient Egypt, it is built of sun-dried bricks, bound together with the stems of palm-trees, and was once of great thickness. At the southern end of the mounds are the remains of the kilns in which the potters of the Roman and Byzantine age baked their vases of blue porcelain. Some of their failures still lie on the surface of the ground.

Herodotos went to the pyramids of Gizeh by water, across the lake on the western side of the city, which he states had been made by Menes, and then along a canal. At Gizeh his love of the marvellous was fully satisfied. He inspected the pyramids and the causeway along which the stones had been brought from the quarries of Turah for building them, and listened reverentially to all the stories which his guides told him about them and their builders. The measurements he gives were in most cases probably made by himself. But in saying that there were hieroglyphic inscriptions 'in the pyramid' he has made a mistake. There were no inscriptions either in it or outside it, unless it were a few hieratic records left by visitors on the lower casing-stones of the monument. At the same time it is certain that Herodotos saw the hieroglyphs, and that his guide pretended to translate them, since they contained, according to him, an account of the quantity of radishes, onions, and leeks eaten by the workmen when building the great pyramid, as well as the amount of money which it cost. But the vegetables represented Egyptian characters—the radish, for instance, being probably *rod*, 'fruit' or 'seed,' and the mention of them is a proof that it really was a hieroglyphic text which the dragoman proposed to interpret. It is even possible that the guide knew the hieroglyphic symbols for the numerals; if so, it would explain his finding in them the number of talents spent by Kheops upon his sepulchre, and it would also show that the inscriptions were engraved, not 'in the pyramid,' but in an adjoining tomb. In fact, this seems the simplest explanation of what Herodotos says about them; like many another traveller, he forgot to note where exactly the inscriptions were inscribed, and when he came to write his book assumed that they were in the pyramid itself.

According to the dragoman's legend, Kheops and

Khephren were cruel and impious tyrants, while their successor Mykerinos (Men-ka-Ra) was a good and merciful ruler. The key to this description of them is probably to be found in the statement of Diodorus Siculus that the people threatened to drag their bodies from their tombs after death and tear them in pieces, so that through fear of such a fate the Pharaohs took care to have themselves buried in a secret place. This secret place is the subterranean island, with its chambers, which Herodotos says was made under the great pyramid by means of a canal in order that the king might be entombed there. The myth must have originated in the fact that in the days of Herodotos the mummies of Kheops and Khephren were not to be found in their pyramids, which had been rifled centuries before, and the story of the cruelty and impiety of the two kings accordingly grew up to account for the fact.

The righteousness of Mykerinos was visited with the anger and punishment of the gods, since it had been destined that the Egyptians should be evil-entreated for one hundred and fifty years, and his piety and justice had averted from them part of their doom. This view of destiny and the action of the gods was as essentially Greek as it was foreign to the Egyptian mind, and it is not surprising therefore that the decree of heaven was announced to the unhappy Pharaoh through that thoroughly Greek institution, an oracle. We are reading in the story a Greek tragedy rather than a history of Egypt.

It was part of the punishment of Mykerinos that he should lose his daughter, and the dragomen thus managed to connect the pyramid at Gizeh with a gilded wooden image of a cow in the palace at Sais, which, since the reign of Psammetikhos, must have been well-known to them. The cow, which was really a symbol of Neit in the form of Hathor, with what Herodotos supposed to be the disk of the sun between its horns, though it was really the moon, was imagined to be hollow, and to be the coffin of the daughter of the Pharaoh. The wooden figures which stood beside it were further imagined to represent the concubines of the king. There were, however, other stories about both the figures and the cow, less reputable to the royal character, but equally showing how entirely ignorant Herodotos's informants were of Egyptian religion and custom. Though they knew that at the festival of Osiris the cow was carried out into the open air, they said this was because the daughter of Mykerinos when dying had asked her father that she might once a year see the sun. Can there be a stronger proof of the gulf that existed between the native

Egyptian and the 'impure' stranger, even when the latter belonged to the caste of dragomen? To us the representation of Hathor under the form of a cow with the lunar orb between its horns seems an elementary fact of ancient Egyptian religion; the modern tourist sees it depicted time after time on the walls of temples and tombs, and the modern dragoman has begun to learn something about its meaning. But in the fifth century before our era the dragoman and the tourist were alike foreigners, who were not permitted to penetrate within the temples, and there were neither books nor teachers to instruct them in the doctrines of the Egyptian faith.

Herodotos must have returned to Memphis after his visit to the pyramids, before setting forth on his voyage to the south. Had he gone straight from Gizeh to the Fayyûm along the edge of the desert, he would have passed the step-pyramid and the Serapeum at Saqqâra. It is difficult to believe that, had he done so, he would have told us nothing about the burial-place of the sacred bulls and the huge sarcophagi of granite in which they were entombed. The subterranean gallery begun by Psammetikhos was still open, and each Apis as he died was buried in it down to the end of the Ptolemaic period. At a later date, when the Persian empire had been overthrown, the Serapeum became a favourite place of pilgrimage for Greek visitors to Memphis. A Greek temple was built over the sepulchres of the bulls, Greek recluses took up their abode in its chambers, and Greek tourists inscribed their names on the sphinxes which lined the approach to the sanctuary.

Herodotos knew all about the living Apis, and the marks on the body of the bull which proved his divinity, as well as about the court in the temple of Ptah at Memphis, which Psammetikhos had built for the accommodation of the incarnate god. He was well acquainted also with the legend which made Kambyses slay the sacred bull and scourge its priests, and he tells us how the latter buried the body of their slaughtered deity in secret. But neither he nor his guides knew where the burial took place, or where the mummies of the bulls had been entombed from time immemorial. Had they done so we should have heard something about it. But, instead of this, we are told that the dead oxen were buried in the suburbs of the town where they had died, their horns being allowed to protrude above the ground in order to mark the spot. When the flesh was decayed the bones were conveyed in boats to a city in the island of Prosôpitis, called Atarbêkhis, and there deposited in their last resting-place.

It is evident, therefore, that the great cemetery of Memphis was not visited by travellers, and that the guides accordingly knew nothing about it. The Egyptians probably had the same feeling in regard to it as their Moslem descendants; the graves would be profaned if the 'impure' foreigner walked over them. The 'impure' foreigner, moreover, was usually satisfied with the three pyramids of Gizeh; he did not care to make another long expedition in the sun to the western desert in order to see there another pyramid. And, apart from the pyramid, there was little for him to visit. It is doubtful whether he would have been permitted to descend into the burying-place of the bulls, and the buildings above it were probably of no great size.

But whatever might have been the reason, Saqqâra and its Serapeum were unknown to the dragomen, and consequently to Herodotos as well. He must have started for the Fayyûm from Memphis and have sailed up the channel of the Nile itself. If he noticed the pyramids of Dahshûr and Mêdûm, they would have been in the far distance, and have appeared unworthy of attention after what he had seen at Gizeh. Soon after passing Mêdûm, however, it would have been necessary for him to leave the river and make his way inland by the canal which joined the Bahr Yûsuf at Illahûn. Here he would have been close to the great brick pyramid whose secret has been wrested from it by Professor Petrie, and here too he would have seen, a little to the south, the city of Herakleopolis, the Ahnas el-Medîneh of to-day, standing on the rubbish-mounds of the past on the eastern bank of the Bahr Yûsuf.

Herakleopolis, called Hininsu in Egyptian and the cuneiform inscriptions, was the capital of a nome which the Greek writers describe as an island. It was, in fact, enclosed on all sides by the water. On the east is the Nile; on the west the Bahr Yûsuf, itself probably an old channel of the river; northward a canal unites the two great streams, while southward another canal (or perhaps a branch of the river) once did the same in the neighbourhood of Ahnas. Strabo still speaks of it as a great 'island' which he passed through on his way to the Fayyûm from the north.

The route followed by Strabo must have been that already traversed by Herodotos. He too must have passed through the island of Hininsu on his way to the Fayyûm, and his scheme of Egyptian chronology ought to contain evidence of the fact.

And this is actually the case. Mykerinos, he teaches us, was succeeded by a king named Sasykhis or Asykhis, who built not only the eastern propylon of the temple of Ptah at Memphis, but also a brick pyramid, about which, of course, his guides had a characteristic story to tell him. That the story was of Greek origin is shown by the inscription, which they professed had been engraved by order of the Pharaoh, but which only a Greek could have invented. The brick pyramid must have been that of Illahûn. The two brick pyramids of Dahshûr would have been invisible from the river, and even to a visitor on the spot the state of ruin in which they are would have made them seem of little consequence. His attention would have been wholly absorbed by the massive pyramids of stone at the foot of which they stand.

The brick pyramid of Howâra, again, cannot be the one meant by Herodotos. It formed part of the buildings connected with the Labyrinth, the size and splendour of which overshadowed in his eyes all the rest. There remains, therefore, only the brick pyramid of Illahûn, by the side of which, as we have seen, the voyage of Herodotos would have led him.

The pyramid of Illahûn, when seen near at hand, is indeed a very striking object. It is the only one of the brick pyramids which challenges comparison with the pyramids of stone, and may well have given occasion for the story which was repeated to the Greek tourist. Its striking character is due to the fact that the brick superstructure is raised upon a plateau of rock, which has been cut into shape to receive it. The excavations of Professor Petrie in 1890 revealed the name of its builder. This was Usertesen II. of the twelfth dynasty, the king in the sixth year of whose reign the 'Asiatics' arrived with their tribute of antimony as depicted in the tomb of Khnum-hotep at Beni-Hassan. How the guides came to call him Sasykhis is difficult to explain. Perhaps it is the Egyptian Sa-Sovk, 'the son of Sovk' or 'Sebek' the crocodile-god of the Fayyûm, whom the Greeks termed Sûkhos. The Pharaohs of the twelfth dynasty, as creators and benefactors of the Fayyûm, the nome of the crocodile, were specially devoted to its worship, and in their inscriptions they speak of the works they had undertaken for their 'father Sovk.'

After Sasykhis, Herodotos continues, 'there reigned a blind man named Anysis, from the city of Anysis: while he was reigning the Ethiopians and Sabako, king of Ethiopia, invaded Egypt with a large force, so the blind man fled into the marshes, and the Ethiopian ruled Egypt for fifty years.' After his departure in consequence of a dream the blind man returned from the marshes, where he had lived in an artificial island called Elbô, which no one could rediscover until Amyrtæos found it again.

Memphis and the Fayyûm 267

Anysis, of course, is the name of a city, not of a man, and, in making it both, Herodotos has committed a similar mistake to that which he has made in transforming Pi-Bast, 'the temple of Bast,' and Pi-Uaz, 'the temple of Uaz,' into the names of his goddesses Bubastis and Butô. It is, in fact, merely the Greek form of the Hebrew Hanes, and the Hebrew Hanes is the Egyptian Hininsu, which, according to a well-known rule of Semitic and Egyptian phonetics, was pronounced Hinissu. We learn from the Book of Isaiah (xxx. 4) that Hanes was playing a prominent part in Egyptian politics at the very time when Sabako and his Ethiopians occupied the country. The ambassadors of Hezekiah who were sent from Jerusalem to ask the help of the Egyptian monarch against the common Assyrian enemy came not only to Zoan in the Delta, but to Hanes as well. Zoan and Hanes must have been for the moment the two centres of Egyptian government and the seats of the Pharaoh's court.

The intermittent glimpses that we get of Egyptian history in the stormy period that preceded the Ethiopian conquest show how this had come to be the case. Shishak's dynasty, the twenty-second, had been followed by the twenty-third, which Manetho calls Tanite, and which, therefore, must have had its origin in Zoan. While its second king, Osorkon II., was reigning at Tanis and Bubastis, the first sign of the coming Ethiopian invasion fell upon Egypt. Piankhi Mi-Amon, the king of Napata, descended the Nile, and called upon the rival princes of Egypt to acknowledge him as their head. Osorkon, who alone possessed a legitimate title to the supreme sovereignty, seems to have obeyed the summons, but it was resisted by two of the petty kings of Upper Egypt, those of Ashmunên and Ahnas, as well as by Tef-nekht or Tnêphakhtos, the prince of Sais. Ashmunên and Ahnas were accordingly besieged, and Ashmunên soon fell into the invader's hands. Ahnas and the rest of the south thereupon submitted, and Piankhi marched against Memphis. In spite of the troops and provisions thrown into it by Tef-nekht, the old capital of the country was taken by storm, and all show of resistance to the conqueror was at an end. From one extremity of the country to the other the native rulers hastened to pay homage to the Ethiopian and to accept his suzerainty.

Piankhi caused the account of his conquest to be engraved on a great stêlê of granite which he set up on Mount Barkal, the holy mountain of Napata. Here he gives a list of the seventeen princes among whom the cities of Egypt had been parcelled out, and each of whom claimed independent or semi-independent authority. Out of the seventeen four bear upon their foreheads the royal uræus, receive the title of kings, and have their names enclosed in a cartouche. Two of them are princes of the north, Osorkon of Bubastis and Tanis, and Aupet of Klysma, near Suez. The other two represent Upper Egypt. One is the king of Sesennu or Ashmunên, the other is Pef-dod-Bast of Hininsu or Ahnas. Thebes is wholly ignored.

The conquest of Piankhi proved to be but momentary. The Ethiopians retired, and Egypt returned to the condition in which they found it. It was a nation divided against itself, rent with internal wars and private feuds, and ready to fall into the hands of the first invader with military ability and sufficient troops. Two states towered in it above the rest; Tanis in the north and Ahnas in the south. Tanis had succeeded to the patrimony of Bubastis and Memphis; Ahnas to that of Thebes.

Sabako, therefore, fixed his court at Zoan and Hanes, simply because they had already become the leading cities, if not the capitals, of the north and the south. And to Zoan and Hanes, accordingly, the Jewish envoys had to make their way. The princes of Judah assembled at Zoan; the ambassadors went farther, even to Hanes. It is noteworthy that a century later the Assyrian king Assur-bani-pal still couples together the princes of Ahnas and Zoan in his list of the satraps of Egypt.

Anysis or Hanes was the extreme limit of Herodotos's voyage. As afterwards in the days of Strabo, it was the entrance to the Fayyûm, and the traveller who wished to visit the Fayyûm had first to pass through the city which the Greeks called Herakleopolis. The patron-god of the city was Hershef, whose name was the subject of various unsuccessful attempts at an etymology on the part of the Egyptians. But, like the names of several other deities, its true origin was lost in the night of antiquity. In Plutarch it appears in a Greek dress as Arsaphes. The god was invested with warlike attributes, and hence it was that he was identified by the Greeks with their own Hêraklês. His temple stood in the middle of the mounds of the old city, which the *fellahîn* call Umm el-Kimân, 'the mother of mounds.' In 1891 they were partially excavated by Dr. Naville for the Egypt Exploration Fund, but little was found to repay the expense and labour of the work. The site of the temple was discovered somewhat to the north-east of the four columns which are alone left of an early Coptic church. But hardly more than the site can be said still to exist. A few blocks of stone inscribed with the names of Ramses II. and Meneptah, and a fragment of a temple built by

Usertesen II., are almost all that survive of its past. Even the necropolis failed to produce monuments of antiquity. Its tombs had been ransacked by treasure-hunters and used again as places of burial in the Roman era, and Dr. Naville found in it only a few traces of the eighteenth dynasty.

And yet there had been a time when Herakleopolis was the capital of Egypt. The ninth and tenth dynasties sprang from it, and the authority of the tenth dynasty, at all events, was, as we now know, acknowledged as far as the Cataract. Professor Maspero and Mr. Griffith have shown that three of the tombs in the hill behind Assiout (Nos. III., IV., and V.) belong to that age. Hollowed out of the rock, high up in the cliff above the tombs of the twelfth dynasty, their mutilated inscriptions tell us of the ancient feudal lords of the nome, Tef-aba and his son Khiti, the latter of whom won battles for his master, the Pharaoh Mer-ka-Ra. Thebes was in open rebellion; so also was Herakleopolis itself, the home of the Pharaoh's family, and Khiti provided ships and soldiers in abundance for him. The fleet filled the Nile from Gebel Abu Foda on the north to Shotb on the south, and the forces of the rebels were annihilated. For awhile the authority of the Pharaoh was restored; but the power of the Theban princes remained unshaken, and a time came when the

Thebans of the eleventh dynasty succeeded to the heritage of the Herakleopolites of the tenth.

Who the 'blind' king of Anysis may have been we do not know. But he was certainly not the legitimate Pharaoh, although Herakleopolite vanity may have wished him to be thought so. According to Manetho, the Tanites of the twenty-third dynasty were followed by the twenty-fourth dynasty, consisting of a single Saite, Bokkhoris, whom the monuments call Bak-n-ran-f. Bokkhoris is said to have been burnt alive by his conqueror Sabako. In making the latter reign for fifty years, Herodotos has confused the founder of the dynasty with the dynasty itself. The length of his reign is variously given by the two copyists of Manetho—Africanus and Eusebius—as eight and twelve years; the last cypher can alone be the right one, as an inscription at the gold mines of Hammamât mentions his twelfth year. He was followed by two other Ethiopian kings, the second of whom was Tirhakah, and the whole length of the dynasty seems to have been fifty-two years. The Christian copyists, indeed, with their customary endeavour to reduce the chronology of the Egyptian historian, make it only forty and forty-four years; but the monuments show that Herodotos, with his round half century, is nearer the truth.

From a topographical point of view the

introduction of Sabako and the Ethiopian between Ahnas and the Fayyûm is out of place. But the story told to Herodotos prevented him from doing otherwise. The blind king is said to have fled to the marshes of the Delta, and there to have remained in concealment until the end of the Ethiopian rule, when he was once more acknowledged as Pharaoh. The legend of Sabako is thus only an episode in the history of the Herakleopolite prince.

From the blind Anysis we ought to pass to the kings of the twelfth dynasty who created the Fayyûm and erected the monuments which the Greek traveller saw there. We do not do so for two reasons. Herodotos had already mentioned king Mœris and the lake and pyramids he made when describing the list of kings which the sacred scribe had read to him in Memphis. He could not count the Egyptian monarch twice, at the beginning as well as the end of his eleven topographical Pharaohs. Then, again, the story told him about the Labyrinth connected its origin with Psammetikhos, with whom the Greek history of Egypt began. From this point forward Herodotos no longer derived his information from 'the Egyptians themselves,' that is to say, from his guides and dragomen, but 'from the rest of the world.' By 'the rest of the world' he means the Greeks. The story of the Labyrinth is accordingly relegated to what may be termed the second division of his Egyptian history, and forms part of his account of the rise of the twenty-sixth dynasty.

Between the blind king of Ahnas, therefore, and the supposed builder of the Labyrinth, a folk-tale is interposed which once more takes us back to the temple of Ptah at Memphis. It is attached to an image in the temple, which represents a man with a mouse in his hand, and it is evident that Herodotos heard it after his return from the Fayyûm. Had he heard of it when he was previously in Memphis, it would have been recorded in an earlier part of his book. Moreover, the statue stood within the temple, which the tourist was not allowed to enter, so that he would not have seen it at the time of his visit to the great Egyptian sanctuary. Whether he ever saw it at all is doubtful; perhaps he may have caught a glimpse of it through the open gate of the temple like the glimpses of sculptured columns in Mohammedan mosques which the older travellers in the East have boasted of securing. But more probably he heard about it from others, more especially from the dragoman he employed.

The story is a curious mixture of Egyptian and Semitic elements, while the inscription which the dragomen pretended to read upon the statue is a Greek invention. A priest of Ptah, so it ran, whose name was Sethos, became king of Egypt. His priestly instincts led him to neglect and ill-treat the army, even to the extent of robbing them of the twelve acres of land which each soldier possessed of right. Then Sennacherib, 'king of the Arabians and Assyrians,' marched against him, and the army refused to fight. In his extremity the priest-king entered the shrine of his god and implored him with tears to save his worshipper. Sleep fell upon the suppliant, and he beheld the god standing over him and bidding him be of good courage, for no harm should happen to him. Thereupon Sethos proceeded to Pelusium with such volunteers as he could find—pedlars, artisans, and tradesmen—and there found the enemy encamped. In the night, however, field-mice entered the camp of the Assyrians and gnawed their bowstrings and the thongs of their shields, so that in the morning they found themselves defenceless, and the Egyptians gained an easy victory. In memory of the event the stone image of the king was erected in the temple of Ptah with a field-mouse in his hand.

The statue must have been that of Horus, to whom alone, along with Uaz, the field-mouse was sacred. But it was apparently only in a few localities that such was the case. The figure of the animal is found on coins of Ekhmîm, and a bronze image of it discovered at Thebes, and now in the British Museum, is dedicated to 'Horus, the lord of Sekhem,' or Esneh. At 'Buto,' where the two deities were worshipped together, we may expect to find a cemetery of field-mice like that of the cats at Bubastis, and the Liverpool Museum possesses two bronze mice, both on the same stand, which were discovered in the mounds of Athribis near Benha. Horus was the god of Athribis, where he was adored under the name of Kheti-ti.

The priest-king of the folk-tale has taken the place of the historical Tirhakah. The name of his enemy, Sennacherib, however, has been remembered, though he is called king of 'the Arabians' as well as of the Assyrians. But the title must be of Egyptian origin. The 'Arabians' of the Greek writer are the Shasu, the Bedouin 'plunderers' of the Egyptian monuments, and none but an Egyptian would have described an Asiatic invader by such a name.

It was in B.C. 701, during his campaign against Hezekiah of Judah, that the Assyrian monarch met the forces of Tirhakah. The Ethiopian lord of Egypt had marched to the help of his Jewish ally, and at the little village of Eltekeh the battle took place. Tirhakah was defeated and driven back into Egypt, while Sennacherib was left to continue his campaign and reduce his rebellious vassal to obedience. In the insolence of victory he sent Hezekiah a letter declaring that, in spite of the promises of his God, Jerusalem should be delivered into the hands of its foes. Then it was that Hezekiah entered the sanctuary of the temple, and, spreading out the letter before the Lord, besought Him to save himself and the city from the Assyrian invader. The prayer was heard: Isaiah was commissioned to declare that the Assyrian king should never come into Jerusalem; and the Assyrian host perished mysteriously in a single night.

Half-a-century later a similar event happened in Assyria itself. Its king, Assur-bani-pal, surrounded by insurgent enemies, was suddenly attacked by Te-umman of Elam. While he was keeping the festival of the goddess Istar at Arbela, a message was brought to him from the Elamite monarch that he was on his march to destroy Assyria and its gods. Thereupon Assur-bani-pal went into the temple of the goddess, and, bowing to the ground before her, with tears implored her help. Istar listened to the prayer, and that night a seer dreamed a dream wherein she appeared and bade him announce to the king that Istar of Arbela, with quivers behind her shoulders and the bow and mace in her hand, would fight in front of him and overthrow his foes. The prophecy was fulfilled, and before long the Elamite army was crushed, and the head of Te-umman sent in triumph to Nineveh.

In Judah and Assyria we are dealing with history, in the story of Sethos with a folk-tale, and it is impossible therefore not to believe that the conduct of the priest of Ptah has been modelled upon that of Hezekiah and Assur-bani-pal. The basis of it is Semitic rather than Egyptian; it would have been told more appropriately of Sennacherib than of the Egyptian Pharaoh. Perhaps it had its source among the Phœnicians of the Tyrian camp at Memphis, or even among the Egyptianised Jews who carried Jeremiah into Egypt. Whatever may have been its origin, it does not belong to the realm of history.

Even with the appearance of Psammetikhos upon the stage, the Egyptian history of Herodotos does not yet commence. Before it can do so, he has to finish his wanderings and his sight-seeing, to be quit of his dragomen and of the topographical chronology that he built upon their stories. Through Herakleopolis lay the entrance to the Fayyûm, and the Fayyûm united the folk-lore of the guides with the sober history of the Greek epoch in Egypt.

Herodotos knows that Psammetikhos was king of Sais and that his father's name had been Necho.

But when he goes on to say that Necho had been slain by the Ethiopian Sabako, and that Psammetikhos himself had been driven in consequence into Syria, he takes us into the domain of fiction and not of fact. Necho had been one of twenty Egyptian satraps under Esar-haddon and Assur-bani-pal, and though he had once been carried in chains to Assyria on a charge of treason, he had returned to his government loaded with honours. Sabako had been dead long before, and Tirhakah was vainly endeavouring to drive the Assyrians and their vassal-satraps out of Egypt.

Still further from the truth was the legend which associated Psammetikhos with the Fayyûm. When the Egyptians had been 'freed,' we are told, after the reign of the priest of Ptah, there arose twelve kings who divided the country between them. They married into each other's families and swore an oath ever to remain friends. By way of leaving a monument of themselves they built the Labyrinth, with its twelve courts, each court for a king, six of them being on the north side and six on the south. But an oracle had announced that this friendly intercourse would be broken if ever one of them at their annual gathering in the temple of Ptah should pour a libation to the god from a bronze helmet. The prince who did so would become king of all Egypt. This untoward accident eventually occurred. Psammetikhos on one occasion accidentally used his helmet in place of the proper libation-bowl, and he was thereupon chased away by his colleagues, first into the marshes and then into Syria. An oracle, however, again came to his help. It declared that he would be avenged when men of bronze came from the sea, and, taking the hint, he hired some Ionian and Karian pirates, armed with bronze, who had landed for the sake of plunder, and with their assistance became undisputed master of Egypt. With this story of the foundation of the twenty-sixth dynasty, the Egyptian folk-lore of Herodotos came fitly to an end.

The twelve kings owe their origin to the twelve courts of the Labyrinth. They are a reminiscence of the twenty vassal-kings or satraps whom the Assyrians appointed to govern the country, and among whom Psammetikhos and his father had been included. But even the twelve courts are not altogether correct. We learn from Strabo that there were many more than twelve—as many, in fact, as were the nomes of Egypt. This makes us distrustful of the further statement of Herodotos that the halls contained one thousand five hundred chambers above the ground, and one thousand five hundred below. The information must have come from the guides, and it is not likely that he verified it. To count three thousand chambers would have occupied at least a day.

In the time of Strabo it was known that the real builder of the Labyrinth was Maindês, that is to say, Mâ(t)-n-Ra, or Amon-em-hat III. of the twelfth dynasty. The excavations of Professor Petrie at Howâra in 1888 have proved the fact. He succeeded in penetrating into the central chamber of the brick pyramid which formed part of the building, and there, deep in water, he found the sarcophagus and the shattered fragments of some of the funerary vases of the dead Pharaoh. They were all that had been left by the spoilers of a long-past age, but they were sufficient to show who the Pharaoh was. He had not been buried alone. In another chamber of the pyramid was the sarcophagus of his daughter Neferu-Ptah, who must have died before the pyramid was finally closed. The labyrinth itself has been used as a quarry or burnt into lime long ago. On its floor of hard plaster lie the chippings of the stones which composed it, six feet in thickness, and covering a far larger area than that of any other Egyptian temple of which we know. There was none other which could vie with it in size.

Amon-em-hat III. seems to have left another memorial of himself further north—at least, such is the natural interpretation of Mr. de Morgan's recent discoveries at Dahshûr. Though the pyramid did not repay his engineering skill with even a scrap of inscription, he found tombs on its northern side which prove that here also was a burial-place of the twelfth dynasty. Two long corridors had been cut out of the rock, one above the other, and at intervals along their northern walls square chambers had been excavated, in which were placed the sarcophagi of the dead. Inscriptions show for whom they were intended. Nofer-hont, Sont-Senebt, Sit-Hathor and Menit, were the royal princesses who had been entombed within them in the time of Amon-em-hat III. Their jewels had been hidden in two natural hollows in the stone floor of the corridors, and had thus escaped the eye of the ancient treasure-hunter. We can see them now in the Gizeh Museum, and thus learn to what an exquisite state of perfection the art of the goldsmith had already been brought.

Among them we may notice large sea-shells of solid gold, enamelled lotus-flowers and necklaces of amethyst, carnelian and agate beads. Of beautifully-worked gold ornaments there is a marvellous profusion. But nothing surpasses the golden pectorals inlaid with precious stones. The work is so perfect as to make it difficult to believe that we have before us a mosaic and not enamel. On one of the pectorals the cartouche of Usertesen III. is supported

Memphis and the Fayyûm

on the paws of two hawk-headed lions, crowned with the royal feathers, and trampling under their feet the bodies of the foe. On another Amon-em-hat III. is represented smiting the wild tribes of the Sinaitic Peninsula. By the side of this jewellery of the twelfth dynasty, that of Queen Ah-hotep of the seventeenth, found by Mariette at Thebes, looks formal and degenerate. In jewellery, as in all things else in ancient Egypt, the earlier art is the best.

From Amon-em-hat III. of the twelfth dynasty to the founder of the twenty-sixth, two thousand years later, is a far cry, and how the Labyrinth came to be connected with the latter by the guides of Herodotos it is hard to say. The bronze helmet of Psammetikhos indicates that the story is of Greek origin. That was a Greek head-dress; no Egyptian, much less an Egyptian Pharaoh, would ever have worn it. The head-dress of the Egyptian monarch was of linen, coloured red for Lower Egypt, white for the south.

Herodotos seems to have visited Howâra from the capital of the Fayyûm, much as a traveller would do to-day. At least, such is the inference which we may draw from his words. Its position is defined as being 'a little above Lake Mœris, near the city of the Crocodiles.' But we must remember that the Lake Mœris of the Greek tourist included not only the actual lake, but also the inundation, which covered at the time the cultivated land of the Fayyûm. Nor was it, as he supposed, an artificial piece of water excavated in a district which was 'terribly waterless,' the excavators of which were wasteful enough to fling all the earth they had extracted into the Nile twenty miles away. It was, on the contrary, an oasis reclaimed from marsh and water by the wise engineering labours of the kings of the twelfth dynasty and the embankments which they caused to be erected. So far from destroying the precious cultivable ground by turning it into a lake, they drained the lake so far as was possible, and thereby created a new Egypt for the cultivators of the soil.

From the walls of the city of the Crocodiles Herodotos looked out over a vast expanse of water, which he thought was the creation of the Pharaohs, but which was really the result of man's neglect. The dykes were broken which should have kept back the flood and prevented it from swamping the summer crops. It was with this view of almost boundless waters that the journey of Herodotos up the Nile came to an end. He returned to Memphis, and from thence pursued the way along which we have followed him to Pelusium and the sea. His note-book was filled with memoranda of all the

Memphis and the Fayyûm

wonders he had seen; of the strange customs he had observed among the Egyptian people; above all, with the folk-tales which his guides had poured into his ear. At a later day, when his eastern travels were over, and he had leisure for the work, he combined all this with the accounts written by his predecessors, and added a new book to the libraries of ancient Greece. From the outset it was a success, and though malicious critics endeavoured to condemn and supersede it, though Thukydides contradicted its statements in regard to Athens, though Ktêsias declared that its oriental history was a romance and Plutarch discoursed on the 'malignity' of its author, the book survived all attacks. We have lost the work of Hekatæos of Miletos, we have lost also— what is a more serious misfortune—that of the careful and well-informed Hekatæos of Abdera, but we still have Herodotos with us. And in spite of our own knowledge and his ignorance, in spite even of his innocent vanity and appropriation of the words of others, it is a pleasure to travel with him in our hand and visit with him the scenes he saw. Nowhere else can we find the folk-lore which grew and flourished in the meeting-place of East and West more than two thousand years ago, and in which lay the germs of much of the folk-lore of our own childhood. It may even be that some of the stories which the modern dragoman relates to the modern traveller on the Nile have no better parentage than the guides of Herodotos. Cairo is the successor of Memphis, and 'the caste' of the dragomen is not yet extinct.

APPENDICES

APPENDIX I

THE EGYPTIAN DYNASTIES ACCORDING TO MANETHO (AS QUOTED BY JULIUS AFRICANUS, A.D. 220), ETC.

[The excerpts of Africanus are known from George the Synkellos (A.D. 790) and Eusebius (A.D. 326): where Eusebius differs from Synkellos the fact is stated.]

DYNASTY I.—Thinites: 8 kings.

Reigned years.

1. Menes 62
2. Athôthis his son 57
3. Kenkenes his son 31
4. Ouenephes his son 23
5. Ousaphaidos his son (Ousaphaes, *Eus.*) . . 20
6. Miebidos his son (Niebaes, *Eus.*) . . . 26
7. Semempses his son 18
8. Biênakhes his son (Oubienthes or Vibethis, *Eus.*). 26

Sum 253
(*Eus.* 252
Really 263)

288 *The Egypt of the Hebrews and Herodotos*

DYNASTY II.—Thinites: 9 kings.   Reigned Years.

1. Boêthos (Bôkhos, *Eus.*) 38
2. Kaiekhôs (Khoos or Kekhous, *Eus.*) . . . 39
3. Binôthris (Biophis, *Eus.*) 47
4. Tlas (unnamed by *Eus.*) 17
5. Sethenês (unnamed by *Eus.*) 41
6. Khaires (unnamed by *Eus.*) 17
7. Nepherkheres 25
8. Sesôkhris 48
9. Kheneres (unnamed by *Eus.*) 30

                            Sum   302
                            (*Eus.* 297)

DYNASTY III.—Memphites: 9 kings.

1. Nekherophes (Nekherôkhis, *Eus.*) . . . 28
2. Tosorthros (Sesorthos, *Eus.*) 29
3. Tyreis (unnamed by *Eus.*) 7
4. Mesôkhris (unnamed by *Eus.*) 17
5. Sôyphis (unnamed by *Eus.*) 16
6. Tosertasis (unnamed by *Eus.*) 19
7. Akhes (unnamed by *Eus.*) 42
8. Sêphouris (unnamed by *Eus.*) 30
9. Kerpheres (unnamed by *Eus.*) 26

                            Sum   214
                            (*Eus.* 197)

DYNASTY IV.—Memphites: 8 kings. (*Eus.* 17.)

1. Sôris (unnamed by *Eus.*) 29
2. Souphis I. (3rd king of the dynasty, *Eus.*) . . 63
3. Souphis II. (unnamed by *Eus.*) 66

Appendix I.—*The Egyptian Dynasties*

Reigned Years.

4. Menkheres (unnamed by *Eus.*) 63
5. Ratoises (unnamed by *Eus.*) 25
6. Bikheris (unnamed by *Eus.*) 22
7. Seberkheres (unnamed by *Eus.*) . . . 7
8. Thamphthis (unnamed by *Eus.*) . . . 9

Sum 277
(*Eus.* 448
Really 284)

DYNASTY V.—Elephantines : 9 kings.
(*Eus.* 31 kings, including Othoês or Othius the First and Phiôps ; the others are unnamed.)

1. Ouserkheres 28
2. Sephres 13
3. Nepherkheres 20
4. Sisires or Sisikhis 7
5. Kheres or Ekheres 20
6. Rathoures 44
7. Menkheres 9
8. Tankheres 44
9. Ounos or Obnos 33

Sum 248
Really 218)

DYNASTY VI.—Memphites : 6 kings.
(No number in *Eus.*)

1. Othoês 30
2. Phios . . . . 53 (or 3)
3. Menthu-Souphis 7
4. Phiôps (lived 100 years) 94

290 *The Egypt of the Hebrews and Herodotos*

		Reigned Years
5. Menthe-Souphis	. . . . . .	1
6. Nitôkris, a queen	. . . . . .	12
	Sum	160
	(*Eus.*	245)

DYNASTY VII.—70 Memphites for 70 days.
(*Eus.* 5 kings for 75 days, or 75 years according to the Armenian Version.)

DYNASTY VIII.—27 Memphites for 146 years.
(*Eus.* 5 kings for 100 years, or 9 kings according to the Armenian Version.)

DYNASTY IX.—19 Herakleopolites for 409 years.
(*Eus.* 4 kings for 100 years.)

1. Akhthoes . . . . r

DYNASTY X.—19 Herakleopolites for 185 years.

DYNASTY XI.—16 Thebans for 43 years, after whom Ammenemes reigned 16 years.

End of Maretho's first book, the kings of the first eleven dynasties reigning altogether 2300 years (*Eus.* 2200) and 70 days (really 2287 years and 70 days).

DYNASTY XII.—Thebans : 7 kings.

1. Sesonkhôsis, son of Ammenemes 46
2. Ammanemes, slain by his eunuchs . . . 38
3. Sesôstris 48
4. Lakhares (Lamaris or Lambares, *Eus.*), the builder of the Labyrinth 8

Appendix I.—The Egyptian Dynasties

		Reigned Years.
5.	Ammeres (unnamed by *Eus.*)	8
6.	Ammenemes (unnamed by *Eus.*)	8
7.	Skemiophris his sister (unnamed by *Eus.*)	4
	Sum	160
	(*Eus.*	245)

DYNASTY XIII.—Thebans: 60 kings for 453 years

DYNASTY XIV.—Xoites: 76 kings for 134 years.
(*Eus.* 484 years).

DYNASTY XV.—Shepherds: 6 Phœnician strangers at Memphis for 284 years. (*Eus.* Thebans for 250 years).

1.	Saites	19
2.	Bnôn	44
3.	Pakhnan	61
4.	Staan	50
5.	Arkles	49
6.	Aphôbis	61
	Sum	284

DYNASTY XVI.—Shepherds: 32 kings for 582 years.
(*Eus.* 5 Thebans for 190 years).

DYNASTY XVII.—Shepherds: 43 kings for 151 years and 43 Thebans for 151 years.
(*Eus.* Shepherds, Phœnician strangers for 103 years:

1.	Saites	19
2.	Bnôn	40
3.	Arkles (Arm. Version)	30
4.	Aphôphis (Arm. Version)	14
	Sum	103)

292 *The Egypt of the Hebrews and Herodotos*

DYNASTY XVIII.—Thebans: 16 kings.
(*Eus.* 14 kings.)

Reigned Years.

1. Amôs[is] 25
2. Khebrôs (Khebrôn, *Eus.*) 13
3. Amenôphthis (Amenôphis for 21 years, *Eus.*) . 24
4. Amensis or Amersis (omitted by *Eus.*) . . 22
5. Misaphris (Miphris for 12 years, *Eus.*) . . 13
6. Misphragmouthôsis 26
7. Touthmôsis 9
8. Amenôphis Memnôn 31
9. Horos (Oros, *Eus.*) 37
10. Akherres (Akhenkheres or Akhenkherses for 16 or 12 years, *Eus.*) 32
11. Rathôs (omitted by *Eus.*) 6
12. Khebrés (Akherres for 8 years, *Eus.*) . . . 12
13. Akherres (Kherres for 15 years, *Eus.*) . . 12
14. Armeses (Armais Danaos, *Eus.*) . . . 5
15. Ramesses (Ramesses Ægyptos for 68 years, *Eus.*) . 1
16. Amenôphath (Amenôphis for 40 years, *Eus.*) . 19

Sum 263
(*Eus.* 348
Really 287)

DYNASTY XIX.—Thebans: 7 kings. (*Eus.* 5 kings.)

1. Sethôs (for 55 years, *Eus.*) 51
2. Rapsakes (Rampses for 66 years, *Eus.*) . . 61
3. Ammenephthes (for 8 years, *Eus.*) . . . 20
4. Ramesses (omitted by *Eus.*) 60
5. Ammenemmes (for 26 years, *Eus.*) . . . 5
6. Thouôris or Polybos 7

Sum 209
(*Eus.* 194
Really 204)

Appendix I.—The Egyptian Dynasties 293

DYNASTY XX.—Thebans: 12 kings for 135 years.
(*Eus.* 172 or 178 years.)

Among the 12 kings were:— Reigned Years.

Nekhepsôs	19
Psammouthis	13
...	4 (*Eus.* 15)
Kêrtos	16 (*Eus.* 12)
Rampsis	45
Amenses or Ammenemes	26
Okhyras	14
Sum	137

DYNASTY XXI.—Tanites: 7 kings.

1. Smendes	26
2. Psousennes (for 41 years, *Eus.*)	46
3. Nephelkheres (Nepherkheres, *Eus.*)	4
4. Amenôphthis	9
5. Osokhôr	6
6. Psinakhes	9
7. Psousennes (for 35 years, *Eus.*)	14
Sum	130
(*Eus.*	130
Really	114)

DYNASTY XXII.—Bubastites: 9 kings. (*Eus.* 3 kings.)

1. Sesonkhis (Sesonkhôsis, *Eus.*)	21
2. Osorthôn	15
3, 4, 5. Unnamed (omitted by *Eus.*)	25
6. Takelôthis	13
7, 8, 9. Unnamed (omitted by *Eus.*)	42
Sum	120
(*Eus.*	44
Really	116)

294   *The Egypt of the Hebrews and Herodotos*

DYNASTY XXIII.—Tanites; 4 kings.
(*Eus.* 3 kings.)   Reigned ears.

1. Petoubates (Petoubastes for 25 years, *Eus.*) . . 40
2. Osorkhô Hêraklês (Osorthôn for 9 years, *Eus.*) . 8
3. Psammous 10
4. Zêt (omitted by *Eus.*) 31

                                      Sum 89
                                     (*Eus.* 44)

DYNASTY XXIV.—One Saite.

1. Bokkhôris the legislator (for 44 years, *Eus.*) . 6

DYNASTY XXV.—Ethiopians: 3 kings.

1. Sabakôn (for 12 years, *Eus.*) 8
2. Sebikhôs his son (for 12 years, *Eus.*) . . . 14
3. Tearkos (Tarakos for 20 years, *Eus.*) . . . 18

                                      Sum 40
                                     (*Eus.* 44)

DYNASTY XXVI.—Saites: 9 kings.
(*Eus.* 1, Ammeris the Ethiopian for 18 or 12 years.)

1. Stephinates (Stephinathis, the 2nd king, *Eus.*) . 7
2. Nekhepsôs (the 3rd king, *Eus.*) 6
3. Nekhaô (for 6 years, *Eus.*) 8
4. Psammêtikhos (for 44 or 45 years, *Eus.*) . . 54
5. Nekhaô II. 6
6. Psammouthis II. (or Psammitikhos, for 17 years, *Eus.*) 6
7. Ouaphris, (for 25 years, *Eus.*) 19
8. Amôsis (for 42 years, *Eus.*) 44
9. Psammekherites (omitted by *Eus.*) . . . $\frac{1}{2}$

                                      Sum $150\frac{1}{2}$
                                     (*Eus.* 167)

Appendix I.—The Egyptian Dynasties

DYNASTY XXVII.—Persians : 8 kings.

		Yrs.	Mths
1.	Kambyses, in the 5th year of his reign (for 3 years, *Eus.*)	6	0
2.	Dareios, son of Hystaspes	36	0
3.	Xerxes I.	21	0
4.	Artabanos (omitted by *Eus.*)	0	7
5.	Artaxerxes	41	0
6.	Xerxes II.	0	2
7.	Sogdianos	0	7
8.	Dareios, son of Xerxes	19	0
	Sum	124	4
	(*Eus.*	120	4)

DYNASTY XXVIII.—One Saite.

		Reigned Years.
1.	Amyrtaios	6

DYNASTY XXIX.—Mendesians : 4 kings.
(*Eus.* 5 kings.)

		Yrs.	Mths.
1.	Nepherites I. or Nekherites	6	0
2.	Akhôris	13	0
3.	Psammouthes	1	0
	(*Eus.* inserts Mouthis here, 1 year.)		
4.	Nepherites II.	0	4
	Sum	20	4
	(*Eus.*	21	4)

DYNASTY XXX.—Sebennytes : 3 kings.

		Reigned Years.
1.	Nektanebes I. (for 10 years, *Eus.*)	18
2.	Teôs	2
3.	Nektanebes II. (for 8 years, *Eus.*)	18
	Sum	38
	(*Eus.*	20)

DYNASTY XXXI.—Persians : 3 kings.   Reigned Years.
1. Okhos, in his 20th year (for 6 years, *Eus.*) . . 2
2. Arses (for 4 years, *Eus.*) 3
3. Dareios (for 6 years, *Eus.*) 4

                                    Sum   9
                                 (*Eus.* 16)

THE DYNASTIES OF MANETHO ACCORDING TO JOSEPHUS:—

DYNASTY XV.—Hyksôs or Shepherds.

After the overthrow of Timaios, the last king of the fourteenth dynasty, a period of anarchy.

	Yrs.	Mths.
1. Salatis at Memphis	13	0
2. Beon	44	0
3. Apakhnas	36	7
4. Apôphis	61	0
5. Yanias or Annas	50	1
6. Assis	49	2

DYNASTIES XVIII. and XIX.—Thebans.

	Yrs.	Mths.
1. Tethmôsis	25	4
2. Khebrôn his son,	13	0
3. Amenôphis I.	20	7
4. Amesses his sister	21	9
5. Mephres	12	9
6. Mephramouthôsis	25	10
7. Thmôsis	9	8
8. Amenôphis II.	30	10
9. Oros	36	5
10. Akenkhres his daughter	12	1
11. Rathôtis her brother	9	0

Appendix I.—The Egyptian Dynasties 297

		Yrs.	Mths.
12.	Akenkheres I.	12	5
13.	Akenkheres II.	12	3
14.	Armais	4	1
15.	Ramesses	1	4
16.	Armesses Miamoun	60	2
17.	Amenôphis III.	19	6
18.	Sethôsis Ægyptos and Ramesses (or Hermeus) Danaos	59	0
19.	Rhampses his son	66	0
20.	Amenôphis his son	?	
21.	Sethôs Ramesses his son	?	

[The order ought to be: 15, 18, 19 (identical with 16), 20 (identical with 17).]

THE THEBAN KINGS OF EGYPT ACCORDING TO ERATOSTHENES.

Reigned Years.

1. Mênes, a Thênite of Thebes, interpreted 'of Amon' 62
2. Athôthes, son of Mênes, interpreted 'born of Thoth' 59
3. Athôthes II. 32
4. Diabiês his son, interpreted 'loving his comrades' 19
5. Pemphôs his brother, interpreted 'son of Hêraklês' (Semempsis) 18
6. Toigar the invincible Momkheiri, a Memphite, interpreted 'with superfluous limbs' (Tosorthros) 79
7. Stoikhos his son, interpreted 'insensate Arês' [? Set] 6
8. Gosormies (perhaps Tosertasis) 30
9. Mares his son, interpreted 'Sun-given' 26
10. Anôyphis his son, interpreted 'promiscuous' or 'festive' 20
11. Sirios, interpreted 'son of side-locks' or 'unenvied' 18
12. Khnoubos Gneuros, interpreted 'the golden son of the golden' 22

298 *The Egypt of the Hebrews and Herodotos*

	Reigned Years
13. Rauôsis, interpreted 'chief ruler' (Ratoises)	13
14. Biyrẹs (Bikheres)	10
15. Saôphis, interpreted 'long-haired' or 'tradesman' (Kheops)	29
16. Saôphis II. (Khephren)	27
17. Moskheres, interpreted 'given to the Sun' (Mykerinos)	31
18. Mousthis	33
19. Pammes Arkhondes (Pepi I.)	35
20. Pappos the Great (Pepi II.)	100
21. Ekheso-Sokaras (Sokar-m-saf)	1
22. Nitôkris, a queen, interpreted 'Nit the victorious'	6
23. Myrtaios the given to Amon	22
24. Thyosi-mares, interpreted 'the strong Sun'.	12
25. Thirillos or Thinillos, interpreted 'who has increased his father's strength' (Nefer-ka-Ra Terel)	8
26. Semphroukrates, interpreted 'Hêraklês Harpokrates'.	18
27. Khouthêr Tauros the tyrant (perhaps Akhthoês).	7
28. Meures	12
29. Khômaephtha, interpreted 'a world loving Ptah'	11
30. Soikouniosokhos the tyrant	60
31. Pente-athyris	16
32. Stammenes III. (Amen-m-hat II.)	23
33. Sistosi-khermes, interpreted 'Heraklês the strong' (Usertesen II.)	55
34. Maris (Amen-m-hat III.)	43
35. Siphyas (Siphthas), interpreted 'Thoth the son of Ptah' (Si-Ptah)	5
36. Name lost	14
37. Phrourôn or Neilos (Sebek-neferu-Ra)	5
38. Amouthantaios	63

Appendix I.—The Egyptian Dynasties

THE EGYPTIAN KINGS ACCORDING TO THE MONUMENTS.

DYNASTY I.

	ABYDOS.	SAQQÂRAH.	TURIN PAPYRUS.	MANETHO.
1.	Meni	...	Meni	Menes
2.	Teta	...	Atut	Athothis
3.	Atota			Kenkenes
4.	Ata	...	...	Ouenephes 1.
5.	Husapti	...	Husapti	Ousaphaidos
6.	Mer-ba-pa	Mer-ba-pen	Mer-ba-pen, 73 yrs.	Miebidos
7.	Samsu	...	Samsu, 72 yrs.	Semempses
8.	Qabh(u)	Qabhu	Qabhu, 83 yrs.	Bienekhes.

DYNASTY II.

1.	Buzau	Bai-nuter	(Buzau), 95 yrs.	Boêthos
2.	Kakau	Kakau	Kakau	Kaiekhos
3.	Ba-nuter-en	Ba-nuter-en	Ba-nuter-en, 95 yrs.	Binothris
4.	Uznas	Uznas	(Uznas), 70 yrs.	Tlas
5.	Senda[1]	Send	Senda, 74 (?) yrs.	Sethenes
6.	...	Nefer-ka-Ra	(Nefer-ka-Ra), 70 yrs.	Nepherkheres

DYNASTY III.

		Nefer-ka-Sokar	Nefer-ka-Sokar (? 2) 8 yrs. 4 mths. 2 dys.	Nekherophes
2.		Zefa ...	Hu-Zefa, 25(?) yrs. 8 mths. 4 dys.	Tosorthros
3.	...	Babai	...	...
4.	Zazai	...	Zazai, 37 yrs. 2 mths. 1 day	Tyreis

[1] The inscription of Sheri, the prophet of Send, part of which is in t Ashmolean Museum at Oxford and part at Cairo, makes Per-ab-sen t successor of Send. He will have corresponded to the Khaires of Manetho.

300 *The Egypt of the Hebrews and Herodotos*

ABYDOS.	SAQQÂRAH.	TURIN PAPYRUS.	MANETHO.
5. Neb-ka	...	Neb-ka-(Ra), 19 yrs.	Mesokhris
6. Zoser-Sa	Zoser	Zoser, 19 yrs. 2 mths.	Sôyphis
7. Teta II.	Zoser-teta	Zoser-teta, 6 yrs.	Tosertasis
8. Sezes	Neb-ka-Ra	...	Akhes
9. Nefer-ka-Ra I.	...	(Nefer-ka-Ra), 6 yrs.	Sephouris
10.	Huni	Huni, 24 yrs.	Kerpheres.

DYNASTY IV.

1. Snefru	Snefru	Snefru, 24 yrs.	Soris
2. Khufu	Khufuf	(Khufu), 23 yrs.	Souphis I.
3. Ra-dad-f	Ra-dad-f	(Ra-dad-f), 8 yrs.	Ratoises
4. Khâ-f-Ra	Khâ-f-Ra	...	Souphis II.
5. Men-kau-Ra	...	[Men]-kau-[Ra]	Menkheres
5. Shepseskaf	...	Shepseskaf	Seberkheres (

DYNASTY V.

1. User-ka-f	User-ka-f	(Userkaf), 28 yrs.	Ouserkheres
2. Sahu-Ra	Sahu-Ra	(Sahu-Ra), 4 yrs.	Sephres
3. Kaka	...	(Kaka), 2 yrs.	...
4. Nefer-Ra	Nefer-ar-ka-Ra[1]	(Nefer-ar-ka-Ra), 7 yrs.	Nepherkhere
5.	Shepses-ka-Ra	(Shepses-ka-Ra), 12 yrs.	Sisires
6.	Khâ-nefer-Ra	...	Kheres
7. ...	...	Akau-Hor, 7 yrs.[2]	Rathoures
8. Ra-n-user (An)	...	(Ra-n-user-An), 25 yrs.	...

[1] In an inscription now at Palermo a King Ahtes is mentioned by t side of Nefer-ar-ka-Ra.

[2] In the tomb of Mera, discovered by Mr. de Morgan at Saqqârah in 189 Akau-Hor stands between Unas and Teta.

Appendix I.—The Egyptian Dynasties

ABYDOS.	SAQQÂRAH.	TURIN PAPYRUS.	MANETHO.
9. Men-kau-Hor	Men-ka-Hor	Men-ka-Hor, 8 yrs.	Menkheres
10. Dad-ka-Ra (Assa)	Mâ-ka-Ra	Dad(-ka Ra Assa), 28 yrs.	Tankheres
11. Unas	Unas	Unas, 30 yrs.	Obnos.

Dynasty VI.

ABYDOS.	SAQQÂRAH.	TURIN PAPYRUS.	MANETHO.
1. Teta III.	Teta	..	Othoes
2. User-ka-Ra	...	(Ati?)	...
3. Meri-Ra (Pepi I.)	Pepi I.	(Pepi I.), 20 yrs.	Phios
4. Mer-n-Ra Miht-m-saf I.	Mer-n-Ra I.	(Miht-m-saf I.), 14 yrs.	Methousoup
5. Nefer-ka-Ra (Pepi II.)	Nefer-ka-Ra	(Pepi II), 9[4] yrs.	Phiops
6. Mer-n-Ra Miht-m-saf II.	...	(Miht-m-saf II.), 1 yr. 1 mth.	Menthesouph
7.	...	Neit-aker, a queen	Nitokris.

Dynasties VII. and VIII.[1]

TURIN PAPYRUS.	ABYDOS.
1. Nefer-ka, 2 yrs. 1 mth. 1 dy.	1. Nuter-ka-Ra
2. Neferus, 4 yrs. 2 mth. 1 dy.	2. Men-ka-Ra
3. Ab-n-Ra I., 2 yrs. 1 mth. 1 dy.	3. Nefer-ka-Ra III.
4. ... 1 yr. 8 dys.	4. Nefer-ka-Ra IV. Nebi
5 Ab-n-Ra II.	5. Dad-ka-Ra Shema
6. Hanti	6. Nefer-ka-Ra v. Khondu

[1] One of the kings of the seventh dynasty was Dad-nefer-Ra Dudumes, whose name is conjoined with those of the sixth dynasty kings at El-Kab, and who built at Gebelên.

TURIN PAPYRUS.	ABYDOS.
7. Pest-sat-n-Sopd	7. Mer-n-Hor
8. Pait-kheps	8. Snefer-ka I.
9. Serhlinib.[1]	9. Ka-n-Ra.
	10. Nefer-ka-Ra VI. Terel
	11. Nefer-ka-Hor
	12. Nefer-ka-Ra VII. Pepi-Seneb
	13. Snefer-ka II. Annu
	14. [User-]kau-Ra
	15. Nefer-kau-Ra
	16. Nefer-kau-Hor
	17. Nefer-ar-ka-Ra.

DYNASTY IX.

MONUMENTS.

Khiti (or Khruti) 1. Mer-ab-Ra (the Akhthoes of Manetho)	Âa-hotep-Ra
	Skhâ-n-Ra
...	Aah-mes(?)-Ra
Mâa-ab-Ra	Se-n(?)-mu-Ra[2]
Khâ-user-Ra	...

DYNASTY X.

MONUMENTS.	TURIN PAPYRUS.
Mer-ka-Ra	
...	
Nefer-hepu-Ra	
...	Nefer-ka-Ra

[1] The last five names are thus given by Lauth.

[2] The names of these six kings are found only on scarabs, and are placed here by Professor Petrie.

Appendix I.—The Egyptian Dynasties

MONUMENTS.	TURIN PAPYRUS.
Ra-hotep-ab Amu-si-Hor-nez-hirtef	Khiti II.
	Se-heru-herri
	[Ameni?][1]
	Mer . . .
	Meh . . .
	Hu . . .[2]

Dynasty XI.[3]

	KARNAK.	OTHER MONUMENTS.
1.	Antef I., Prince (of Thebes)	Seshes-Hor-ap-mâa-Ra Antuf-Aa
2.	Men[tu-hotep I.] the Pharaoh	Neb-hotep Mentu-hotep I.
3.	Antef II.	Uah-ânkh [Ter?]-seshes ap-mâa-Ra Antef-Aa, his son
4.	Antef III.	Seshes-herher-mâa-Ra Antef, his brother
5.		Nuter-nefer Neb-taui-Ra Mentu-hotep II.
6.	Antef IV.	Nub-kheper-Ra Antauf (more than 50 yrs.)
7.	Neb-[khru]-Ra	Neb-khru-Ra Mentu-hotep III. (more than 46 yrs.)
8.		Queen Aah
9.	. . .	Antef v. her son
10.	S-ânkh-ka-Ra	S-ânkh-ka-Ra[4]

[1] Ameni is mentioned in a papyrus along with Khiti.
[2] According to Lauth, the Turin papyrus gives nineteen kings to the tenth dynasty, and 185 years.
[3] According to Petrie's arrangement. Lieblein further includes in the dynasty, Ra-snefer-ka, Ra . . ., User-n-Ra, Neb-nem-Ra, and An-âa.
[4] According to Lieblein the Turin papyrus makes the sum of the eleventh dynasty 243 years, Neb-khru-Ra reigning 51 years.

DYNASTY XII.

MONUMENTS.	TURIN PAPYRUS.	MANETHO.
1. Amen-m-hat I. S-hotep-ab-Ra alone, 20 yrs. With Usertesen I., 10 yrs.	S-hotep-ab-Ra, 19 yrs	Ammenemes
2. Usertesen I. Kheper-ka-Ra alone, 32 yrs. With Amen-m-hat II., 3 yrs.	... 45 yrs. 7 mths.	Sesonkhosis
3. Amen-m-hat II. Nub-kau-Ra alone, 29 yrs. With Usertesen II., 6 yrs.	... 3[2] yrs.	Ammanemes
4. Usertesen II. Khâ-kheper-Ra	... 19 yrs.	Sesostris
5. Usertesen III. Khâ-kau-Ra (more than 26 yrs.)	... 3[8] yrs.	Lakhares
6. Amen-m-hat III. Mâat-n-Ra, 43 yrs.	... 4[3] yrs.	Ammeres
7. Amen-m-hat IV. Mâ-khru-Ra	Mâ-khru-[Ra], 9 yrs. 3 mths. 27 dys.	Ammenemes
8. Sebek-nefru-Ra (a queen)	Sebek-nefru-Ra, 3 yrs. 10 mths. 24 dys. Sum of years of twelfth dynasty: 213 years 1 mth. 17 days.	Skemiophris

Appendix I.—The Egyptian Dynasties

DYNASTIES XIII. and XIV.
TURIN PAPYRUS.[1]

1. Sebek-hotep I.[Sekhem]-khu-taui-Ra (son of Sebek-nefru-Ra), 1 yr. 3 mths. 24 dys.
2. Sekhem-ka-Ra, 6 yrs.
3. Ra Amen-m-hat v.
4. S-hotep-ab-Ra II.
5. Aufni, 2 yrs.
6. S-ânkh-ab-Ra [Ameni Antuf Amen-m-hat], 1 yr.
7. S-men-ka-Ra
8. S-hotep-ab-Ra III.
9. S-ânkh-ka-Ra
10, 11. Destroyed
12. Nezem-ab-Ra
13. Ra Sebek-hotep II.
14. Ran-seneb
15. Autu-ab-Ra I. (Hor)[2]
16. Sezef-[ka]-Ra
17. Sekhem-khu-taui-Ra II. Sebek-hotep III.
18. User-n-Ra
19. S-menkh-ka-Ra Mermenfiu
20. . . . ka-Ra
21. S-user-set-Ra
22. Sekhem-uaz-taui-Ra Sebek-hotep IV.
23. Khâ-seshesh-Ra Neferhotep, son of Haânkh-f
24. Si-Hathor-Ra
25. Khâ-nefer-Ra Sebekhotep v.
26. [Khâ-ka-Ra]
27. [Khâ-ânkh-Ra Sebekhotep VI.]
28. Khâ-hotep-Ra Sebekhotep VII., 4 yrs. 8 mths. 29 dys.
29. Uab-Ra Aa-ab, 10 yrs. 8 mths. 29 dys.
30. Mer-nefer-Ra Ai, 23 yrs.[3] 8 mths. 18 dys.
31. Mer-hotep-Ra Ana, 2 yrs. 2 mths. 9 dys.
32. S-ânkh-n-s-uaztu-Ra, 3 yrs. 2 mths.
33. Mer-sekhem-Ra Anran,[4] 3 yrs. 1 mth.
34. S-uaz-ka-Ra Ur, 5 yrs. . . . mth. 8 dys.
35. Anemen . . . Ra

---

[1] According to Brugsch.
[2] His name has been found by Mr. de Morgan at Dahshûr.
[3] According to Maspero, thirteen years.
[4] Maspero: Andû.

306 *The Egypt of the Hebrews and Herodotos*

36-46. Destroyed
47. Mer-kheper-Ra
48. Mer-kau-Ra Sebek-hotep VIII.
49-53. Destroyed
54. ... mes-Ra
55. ... mât-Ra Aba
56. Nefer-uben-Ra I.
57. ... ka-Ra
58. S-uaz-n-Ra.
59-60. Destroyed
61. Nehasi-Ra[1]
62. Khâ-khru-Ra
63. Neb-f-autu-Ra, 2 yrs. 5 mths. 15 dys.
64. S-heb-Ra, 3 yrs.
65. Mer-zefa-Ra, 3 yrs.
66. S-uaz-ka-Ra, 1 yr.
67. Neb-zefa-Ra, 1 yr.
68. Uben-Ra I.
69-70. Destroyed
71. [Neb-]zefa-Ra II., 4 yrs.
72. [Nefer-]Uben-Ra II.
73. Autu-ab-Ra II.
74. Her-ab-Ra
75. Neb-sen-Ra
76-79. Destroyed
80. S-kheper-n-Ra
81. Dad-khru-Ra
82. S-ânkh-ka-Ra
83. Nefer-tum-Ra
84. Sekhem ... Ra
85. Ka ... Ra
86. Nefer-ab-Ra
87. A ... ka-Ra
88. Khâ ... Ra, 2 yrs.
89. Nez-ka ... Ra
90. S-men ... Ra
91-111. Destroyed.
112. Sekhem ... Ra
113. Sekhem ... Ra
114. Sekhem-us ... Ra
115. Sesen ... Ra
116. Neb-ati-uzu-Ra
117. Neb-aten-uzu-Ra
118. S-men-ka-Ra
119. S-user-[aten]-Ra
120. Khâ-sekhem-[hent]-Ra
Some 37 more names are illegible.

[DYNASTIES XIII. and XIV.

KARNAK.

1. ... ka.
2. S-uaz-n-Ra (Nefer-ka-Ra)
3. S-ankh-ab-Rá (T. P. 6)
4. Sekhem-khu-taui-Ra (T. P. 17)

[1] Monuments of Nehasi, 'the negro,' have been found at Tel Mokdam and San.

Appendix I.—*The Egyptian Dynasties* 307

5. Sekhem-s-uaz-taui-Ra.
   (T. P. 22)
6. Khâ-seshesh-Ra (T. P. 23)
7. Khâ-nefer-Ra (T. P. 25)
8. Khâ-ka-Ra (T. P. 26)
9. Khâ-ânkh-Ra (T. P. 27)
10. Kha-hotep-Ra
11. S-nefer-Ra
12. ... Ra
13. Ses-user-taui-Ra
14. Mer-sekhem-Ra
15. Sekhem-uaz-khâu-Ra
    (Sebek-m-saf I.)
16. S-uah-n-Ra
17. [Sekhem]-uah-khâu-Ra
    (Sebek-m-saf II.)
18. Za ... Ra
19. S-uaz-n-Ra
20. S-nefer ... Ra
21. ... Ra.

OTHER MONUMENTS.

Men-khâu-Ra An-ab
Sekhem-ap-taui-Ra
Nefer-kheper-ka-Ra
Mut-r-ka-n-Ra
Ta-neb-n-Ra
Sekhem-nefer-khâu-Ra
   Apheru-m-saf

Mâa-nt-n-Ra Ter-n-Ra
Senb-in-mâ
Uazd
Khâ-nefrui
Men-nefer-Ra (Menophres)
Sekhem-sheddi-taui-Ra Sebek-
   m-saf II.

Ra-seshes-men-taui Tehuti].

·DYNASTIES XV. and XVI.

TURIN PAPYRUS.

1. Abehnas ... (?)
2. Apepi
3. A ..

OTHER MONUMENTS.

Shalati (?)
Banân (?)
Ya'qob-hal ('Jacob-el')
Khian S-user-(Set-)n-Ra

Apepi I. Aa-user-Ra (reigned more than 33 years)
Apepi II. Aa-ab-taui-Ra.

308 *The Egypt of the Hebrews and Herodotos*

DYNASTY XVII.

Skenen-Ra Taa I. (contemporary with Apepi II.)
Skenen-Ra Taa II. Aa

Skenen-Ra Taa III. Ken Uaz-kheper-Ra Ka-mes, and wife Aah-hotep.

Other kings of the seventeenth dynasty were:—
Aah-hotep   Kheper-ka-n-Ra
S-khent-neb-Ra   S-nekht-n-Ra
Amen-sa

DYNASTY XVIII.

		MANETHO.
1.	Neb-pehuti-Ra Aahmes (more than 20 yrs.), and wife Nefert-ari-Aahmes[1]	Amosis
2.	Ser-ka-Ra Amen-hotep I., his son (20 yrs. 7 mths.); his mother at first regent	Amenophis I.
3.	Aa-kheper-ka-Ra Tehuti-mes I., his son, and wife Aahmes Meri-Amen, and Queen Amen-sit.	Chebron (?)
4.	Aa-kheper-n-Ra Tehuti-mes II., his son (more than 9 yrs.), and wife (sister) Hashepsu I. Mâ-ka-Ra	Amensis
5.	Khnum Amen Hashepsu II. Mâ-ka-Ra, his sister (more than 16 yrs.)	Amensis (?)
6.	Ra-men-kheper Tehuti-mes III., her brother, (57 yrs. 11 mths. 1 dy., B.C. 1503, March 20-1449, Feb. 14[2])	Misaphris

[1] In the eighteenth year of Aahmes, Queen Amen-sit is associated with him on a stêlê found at Thebes.

[2] According to Dr. Mahler's astronomical determination. Thothmes counted sixteen years of his sister's reign as part of his own. Hashepsu was only his half-sister, his mother being Ast, who was probably not of royal blood. The mother of Hashepsu was Hashepsu I.

Appendix I.—*The Egyptian Dynasties* 309

		MANETHO.
7.	Aa-khepru-Ra Amen-hotep II., his son (more than 5 yrs.)	Misphragmuthosis
8.	Men-khepru-Ra Tehuti-mes IV., his son (more than 7 yrs.)	Touthmosis
9.	Neb-mâ-Ra Amen-hotep III., his son, (more than 35 yrs.), and wife Teie	Amenophis II.
10.	Nefer-khepru-Ra Amen-hotep IV. Khu-n-aten[1], his son (more than 17 yrs), and wife Nefrui-Thi S-âa-ka-khepru-Ra	Horos
11.	Ankh-khepru-Ra, and wife Meri-Aten	Akherres
12.	Tut-ânkh-Amen Khepru-neb-Ra, and wife Ankh-nes-Amen	Rathotis
13.	Aten-Ra-nefer-nefru-mer-Aten	
14.	Ai Kheper-khepru-ar-mâ-Ra and wife Thi more than 4 yrs.	
15.	Hor-m-hib Mi-Amen Ser-khepru-Ka (more than 3 yrs.)	Armais

DYNASTY XIX.

1.	Men-pehuti-Ra Ramessu I. (more than 2 yrs.)	Ramesses
2.	Men-mâ-Ra Seti I. Mer-n-Ptah I. (more than 27 yrs.), and wife Tua	Sethos
3.	User-mâ-Ra (Osymandyas) Sotep-n-Ra Ramessu II. Mi-Amen (B.C. 1348-1281)	
4.	Mer-n-Ptah II. Hotep-hi-ma Ba-n-Ra Mi-Amen	Ammenephthes

[1] Called Khuri[ya] in one of the Tel el-Amarna tables. Hence the Horos of Manetho.

310 *The Egypt of the Hebrews and Herodotos*

                                              MANETHO.

5. User-khepru-Ra Seti II. Mer-n- Sethos Ramesses
Ptah III.
6. Amen-mesu Hik-An Mer-kha-Ra Amenemes
Sotep-n-Ra
7. Khu-n-Ra Sotep-n-Ra Mer-n- Thouoris
Ptah IV. Si-Ptah (more than 6 yrs.),
and wife Ta-user

DYNASTY XX.

1. Set-nekt Merer Mi Amon (recovered the kingdom from the Phœnician Arisu)
2. Ramessu III. Hik-An (more than 32 yrs.)
3. Ramessu IV. Hik-Mâ Mi-Amen (more than 11 yrs.)
4. Ramessu V. User-mâ-s-kheper-n-Ra Mi-Amen (more than 4 yrs.)
5. Ramessu VI. Neb-mâ-Ra Mi-Amen Amen-hir-khopesh-f (Ramessu Meri-Tum in northern Egypt)
6. Ramessu VII. At-Amen User-mâ-Ra Mi-Amen
7. Ramessu VIII. Set-hir-khopesh-f Mi-Amen User-mâ-Ra Khu-n-Amen
8. Ramessu IX. Si-Ptah S-khâ-n-Ra Mi-Amen (19 yrs.)
9. Ramessu X. Nefer-ka-Ra Mi-Amen Sotep-n-Ra (more than 10 yrs.)
10. Ramessu XI. Amen-hir-khopesh-f Kheper-mâ Ra Sotep-n-Ra
11. Ramessu XII. Men-mâ-Ra Mi-Amen Sotep-n-Ptah Khâ-m-uas (more than 27 yrs.)

Appendix I.—The Egyptian Dynasties 311

DYNASTY XXI. ILLEGITIMATE.

1. Hir-Hor Si-Amen, High-priest of Amon at Thebes, and wife Nezem-mut
2. Piankhi, High-priest, and wife Tent-Amen
3. Pinezem I., High-priest, and wife Hont-taui
4. Pinezem II., King, and wife Mâ-ka-Ra
5. Men-kheper-Ra, High-priest, and wife Isis-m-kheb
6. Pinezem III., High-priest.

DYNASTY XXI. LEGITIMATE.

		MANETHO.
1.	Nes-Bindidi Mi-Amen	Smendes
2.	P-seb-khâ-n I. Mi-Amen Aa-kheper-Ra Sotep-n-Amen	Psousennes I.
3.	[Nefer-ka-Ra]	Nephelkheres
4.	Amen-m-apt	Amenophthis
5.	...	Osokhor
6.	Pinezem (?)	Psinakhes
7.	Hor P-seb-khâ-n II.	Psousennes II.

DYNASTY XXII.

1. Shashanq I. Mi-Amen Hez-kheper-Ra Sotep-n-Ra, son of Nemart (more than 21 yrs.), and wife Ka-râ-mât — Sesonkhis
2. Usarkon I. Mi-Amen Sekhem-kheper-Ra (married Mâ-ka-Ra, daughter of P-seb-khâ-n II.) — Osorkon
3. Takelet I. Mi-Amen Si-Isis User-mâ-Ra Sotep-n-Amen (more than 23 yrs.)
4. Usarkon II. Mi-Amen Si-Bast User-mâ-Ra (more than 23 yrs.)

	MANETHO.
5. Shashanq II. Mi-Amen Sekhem-kheper-Ra	...
6. Takelet II. Mi-Amen Si-Isis Hez-kheper-Ra (more than 15 yrs.)	Takelothis
7. Shashanq III. Mi-Amen Si-Bast User-mâ-Ra (52 yrs.)	
8. Pimai Mi-Amen User-mâ-Ra Sotep-n-Amen	...
9. Shashanq IV. Aa-kheper-Ra (more than 37 yrs.)	...

DYNASTY XXIII.

1. S-her-ab-Ra Petu-si-Bast	Petoubastes
2. Usarkon III. Mi-Amen Aa-kheper-Ra Sotep-n-Amen	Osorkho
3. P-si-Mut User-Ra Sotep-n-Ptah	Psammos
4. ...	Zet.

INTERREGNUM.

Egypt, divided between several princes, including Tefnekht (Tnephakhthos), father of Bak-n-ran-f. It is overrun by Piankhi the Ethiopian, while Usarkon III. reigns at Bubastis. The son and successor of Piankhi is Mi-Amen-Nut.

DYNASTY XXIV.

	MANETHO.
1. Bak-n-ran-f Uah-ka-Ra (more than 16 yrs.)[1]	Bokkhoris

---

[1] There is a contract in the Louvre drawn up at Thebes in the sixteenth year of his reign.

Appendix I.—The Egyptian Dynasties

DYNASTY XXV.

		MANETHO.
1.	Shabaka Nefer-ka-Ra, son of Kashet (12 yrs.)	Sabako
2.	Shabataka Dad-ka-Ra	Sebikhos
3.	Taharka Nefer-tum-khu-Ra or Tirhakah (26 yrs.)	Tearkos

INTERREGNUM.

The Assyrian conquest and division of Egypt into twenty satrapies, B.C. 672-660. Taharka and his successor Urdamanu (Rud-Amen), or, as the name may also be read, Tandamane (Tanuath-Amen), make vain attempts to recover it. In Manetho the period is represented by Stephinates (Sotep-n-Nit), Nekhepsos and Nekhao, the last of whom is called in the Assyrian inscriptions Niku, the father of Psammetikhos, and vassal-king of Memphis and Sais.

DYNASTY XXVI.

		MANETHO.
1.	Psamtik I. Uah-ab-Ra and wife Mehet-usekh (B.C. 664-610)	Psammetikhos
2.	Nekau Nem-ab-Ra and wife Mi-Mut Nit-aker (B.C. 610-594)	Nekhao
3.	Psamtik II. Nefer-ab-Ra, and wife Nit-aker (B.C. 594-589)	Psammouthis
4.	Uah-ab-Ra Haa-ab-Ra and wife Aah-hotep (B.C. 589-570)	Ouaphris
5.	Aah-mes Si-Nit Khnum-ab-Ra and wife Thent-kheta (B.C. 570-526)	Amosis
6.	Psamtik III. Ankh-ka-n-Ra (B.C. 526-525)	Psammekherites

DYNASTY XXVII.

	MANETHO.
1. Kambathet Sam-taui Mestu-Ra (B.C. 525-519)	Kambyses
2. Ntariush I. Settu-Ra (B.C. 521-485)	Dareios I.
3. Khabbash Senen Tanen Sotep-n-Ptah (B.C. 485)	...
4. Khsherish (B.C. 484)	Xerxes I.
Artakhsharsha (B.C. 465-425)	Artaxerxes
Ntariush Mi-Amen-Ra (B.C. 424-405)	Dareios II.

DYNASTY XXVIII.

Amen-ar-t-rut[1] (more than 6 yrs.), B.C. 415	Amyrtaios

DYNASTY XXIX.

1. Nef-âa-rut I. Ba-n-Ra Mi-nuteru (more than 4 yrs.)	Nepherites I.
2. Hakori Khnum-mâ-Ra Sotep-n-Ptah (13 yrs.)	Akhoris
3. P-si-Mut User-Ptah-sotep-n-Ra (1 yr.)	Psammouthes
4. Hor-neb-kha (1 yr.)	Mouthes
5. Nef-âa-rut II. (1 yr.)	Nepherites II.

DYNASTY XXX.

1. Nekht-Hor-hib Ra-snezem-ab Sotep-n-Anhur, son of Nef-âa-rut I. (19 yrs.)	Nektanebes I.
2. Zihu (1 yr.)	Teôs
3. Nekht-neb-f Kheper-ka-Ra (18 yrs.)	Nektanebes II.

[1] According to Wiedemann.

APPENDIX II.—THE PTOLEMIES.

PTOLEMY I., SOTER, son of Lagôs (B.C. 306)

Leontiskos. Lagôs. Ptolemy Keraunos. Lysandra. PTOLEMY II., PHILADELPHUS (B.C. 284). Arsinoë. Argaios. Philotera.

PTOLEMY III., EUERGETES I. (B.C. 246). Lysimakhos. Berenikê.

PTOLEMY IV., PHILOPATOR (B.C. 221). Magas. Arsinoë.

PTOLEMY V., EPIPHANES (B.C. 204).

PTOLEMY VI., Philomêtor (B.C. 180). Kleopatra. PTOLEMY VIII., EUERGETES II. (B.C. 145).

PTOLEMY EUPATOR (?). Kleopatra. Kleopatra Kokkê (B.C. 116). PTOLEMY VII., PHILOPATOR II. (B.C. 145). Kleopatra. PTOLEMY X., ALEXANDER I. (B.C. 106). Ptolemy, King of Cyprus. Ptolemy Apion.

Kleopatra. Memphitês. PTOLEMY IX., SOTER II. (B.C. 145). Kleopatra. Arsinoë. PTOLEMY XI., ALEXANDER II. (B.C. 80). Ptolemy.

Kleopatra Berenikê (B.C. 81). PTOLEMY XII., NEOS DIONYSOS (B.C. 80). Kleopatra (B.C. 51). Alexander Helios. Kleopatra Selênê. Ptolemy.

Kleopatra Tryphaina (B.C. 57). Berenikê (B.C. 57). Ptolemy. Drusilla

Cæsarion. Ptolemy, King of Mauritania.

APPENDIX III

BIBLICAL DATES

	B.C.
Ramses II., the Pharaoh of the Oppression, and builder of Pithom	1348-1281
Campaign of Ramses III. in Judah and Moab,	cir. 1200
Solomon marries the daughter of the Tanite Pharaoh, and receives Gezer	cir. 960
Shishak (Shashanq I.) invades Palestine and takes Jerusalem	cir. 925
Invasion of Judah by Zerah (Osorkon II.)	cir. 900
Hoshea of Israel makes alliance with So of Egypt	725
Sargon defeats the 'Pharaoh' and Sibe his general at Raphia	720
Defeat of Tirhakah by Sennacherib at Eltekeh	701
Invasion of Egypt by Esar-haddon	674
Tirhakah driven from the frontier to Memphis and thence to Ethiopia	670
Revolt of Egypt suppressed by Assur-bani-pal	668
Destruction of Thebes (No-Amon) by the Assyrians	665
Necho invades Asia; defeat and death of Josiah	609
Necho defeated at Carchemish by Nebuchadrezzar; loss of Asiatic possessions	605
The Jews fly to Egypt, carrying Jeremiah with them	cir. 585
Egypt invaded by Nebuchadrezzar	567

Appendix III.—Biblical Dates

	B.C.
Palestine seized by Ptolemy I.; many Jews settled by him in Egypt	320
The Greek translation of the Old Testament commenced	cir. 280
Onias permitted by Ptolemy Philometor to build the temple at Onion	167
Flight of the Holy Family into Egypt	4
Vespasian orders the prefect Lupus to close the temple at Onion	A.D. 70

APPENDIX IV

EGYPTIAN.	GREEK.	EGYPTIAN CAPITA.
I. To-khonti 'the frontier'	...	Abu or Qebh
IA. ...	Ombítes	Nubi 'the golden'
II. Utes-Hor	Apollinopolites	Debu or Hat-Hor
III. Ten (?)	Latopolites	Nekheb
		(1) Nekhen
		(2) Sni
		(3) On of the South or On-Mentu
IV. Uas	Diospolites	[T]-Apt or Nu, 'the city' (including Nes-taui or Karnak, Asher, or the temple of Mut, and Aa-Zamut on the W. bank)
		(1) Pa-Hathor
		(2) Kesui
V. Horui	Koptites	Qebti
VI. Aa-du (?)	Tentyrites	Ta-n-terer

[1] The Ombos, the combat of whose inhabitants with those of Den-Juvenal (*Sat.* xv.), was not Kom Ombo, but another Nubti behind em-Medîneh, Professor Petrie has found the remains of a temple dedi-the Gizeh Museum it is called 'the place of Nubt'

THE NOMES (HESEPU). UPPER EGYPT

GREEK CAPITAL.	MODERN NAM	GODS.
(Elephantinê)	Gezîret-Assuan	Khnum, Sati, and Anukit
Ombos	Kom Ombo	Sebek
Apollinopolis Magna	Edfu	Horus
Eileithyia	El-Kab	Nekhbit
Hierakonpolis	Kom el-Ahmar	Aroeris
Latopolis	Esneh	Khnum and Nit
Hermonthis	Erment	Mentu
Thebai or Diospolis Magna	Luxor, etc.	Amon (-Ra), Mut, and Khonsu
Pathyris	Qurnah	Hathor
Apollinopolis Parva	Qûs	Aroeris and Hakit
Koptos	Qoft	Min
Tentyris [1]	Denderah	Hathor

derah, on account of their worship of the crocodile, is celebrated by Zawaydah, a little south of Ballas. In the mounds now called Kôm cated by Thothmes III. to Set. On a statue from Denderah now in

EGYPTIAN.	GREEK.	EGYPTIAN CAPITAL.
VII. Seshesht	Diospolites	Ha(t)-seshesht, 'house of the sistrum,' or Ha(t)
VIII. Abez	Thinites	Teni
IX. Men (?)	Panopolites	(1) Nshit or Psi Apu or Khent-Min
X. Uazt	Aphroditopolites	Thebu
XA. ...	Antaiopolites	Du-qa
XI. Set	Hypselites	Shas-hotep
XII. Duf	Hierakopolites	Nu(t)-nti-Bak or Pa-Hor-nub
XIII. Atef-khonti	Lykopolites	Siaut
XIV. Atef-peh ('hinder Atef')	...	Qesi or Kerst
XV. Un-t	Hermopolites	Khmunu
XVI. Mah(ez)	N. part of Hermopolites	Hebnu
XVII. Anpu	Kynopolites	Kasa
XVIII. Sep	...	Sep-t or Ha(t)-Benu
XIX. Uab	Oxyrrhynkhites	Pa-Maza
XX. Am-khonti	Herakleopolites	Khninsu
XXI. Am-peh	...	{ Shen-âkhun or Smen-Hor
XXIA. ...	Arsinoites	Shed
XXII. Mâtenu	Aphroditopolites	Tep-ahe or Pa-ki, 'cow's city'

Appendix IV.—The Nomes

GREEK CAPITAL.	MODERN NAME.	GODS.
Diospolis Parva	Hû	Hathor and Osiris (Nefer-hotep)
Thinis or This	Girgeh	Anhur
Ptolemais	Menshîyeh	...
Khemmis or Panopolis	Ekhmîm	Min
Aphroditopolis	Etfeh	Uaz (Hathor)
Antaiopolis	Qau	Horus
Hypsele	Shotb	Khnum and Uaz
Hierakopolis	North of Benûb	Osiris and Isis (as lions)
Lykopolis	Siût	Upuat (Anubis)
Cusai	Qusîyeh	Hathor
Hermopolis	Eshmunên	Thoth
Theodosiopolis	Taha el-Medîneh (?)	Horus
Kynopolis	El-Qais	Anubis
Hipponon (?)	El-Hîbeh	Anubis
Oxyrrhynkhos	Behnesa	Set
Herakleopolis Magna	Ahnas el-Medîneh	Hor-shefi (Hârsaphes)
...	N. of Beni-Suef	Khnum
Arsinoê-Krokodilopolis	Medînet el-Fayûm	Sebek
Aphroditopolis	Atfîh	Hathor

X

	EGYPTIAN.	GREEK.	LOWER EGYPTIAN CAPITAL.
I.	Anbu-hez 'the white wall'	Memphites	Men-nefer (Men-fi) or Ha(t)-ka-Ptah
II.	Khonsu	Letopolites	Sekhem
III.	Ament 'the West'	Libya	Amu or Nu(t)-nti-Hapi
IIIA.	...	Andropolis	Aa-za (?)
IV.	Sap of the South	Prosopites	Zeqâ and Pa-ari-sheps (?)
V.	Sap of the North	Saites	Sai (1) Dema-n-Hor
VA.	...	Kabasites	...
VI.	Ka-khas (?)	Xoites	Khasuu
VII.	Nefer(?)-amenti	Metelites	Senti-nefer or Pa-khas-neb-amenti
VIIA.	...	Menelaites	Pequat or Kanup (1) Ta-nuha
VIIB.	...	Khemmites	Khebu
VIIC.	Pe-to-n-Uaz	Pthenotes	Pe and Dep
VIID.	Pe-tosh-n-Pa-Uaz	Buticas	Pa-Uaz(t)
VIII.	Nefer (?)-abti	Heroopolites	Pa-Tum (Pithom) in Thuku (Succoth)
IX.	Ati	Busirites	Pa-Usir-neb-dad
X.	Ka-kem	Athribites	Hâ(t)-to-hir-ab
XI.	Ka-heseb	Pharbaithites	Sheden or Pa-Mâqa
XII.	Theb-Aht	Sebennytes Superior	Theb-nuter (1) Pa-khebit
XIII.	Hiq-ames	Heliopolites	Anu (On)

Appendix IV.—The Nomes

EGYPT.

GREEK CAPITAL.	MODERN NAME.	GODS.
Memphis	Tel Monf	Ptah and Sekhet
Letopolis	Usîm	Aroeris
Apis	Kom-el-Hisn (?)	Hathor
Andropolis	Kherbatah	...
Prosopis or Nikiu	Shebshir (?) and Abshadi	Sebek and Amon-Ra
Sais	Sâ el-Hagar	Nit
...	Damanhur	Horus
Kabasa	Shabas	...
Xois	Sakhâ	Ra
Metelis (?)	Atfeh	Amon-Ra, Osiris, Horus, Isis, and Sebek
Kanôpos	Abukir	Sebek
Thônis (?)	Edku (?)	..
Khemmis	Sengar (?)	...
Leontopolis	Ko mel-Dantua	Horus and Uaz
Buto	Tel Fera'în	Uaz
Ero or Heroopolis or Patumos	Tel-el-Maskhutah	Tum
Busiris	Abusir	Osiris
Athribis	Tel Atrib	Horus-Kheti
Pharbaithos	Horbeit	Set
Sebennytos	Semennûd	Anhur
Iseum	Behbeit	Isis-Rennt
Heliopolis	Tel Hisn	Ra

324 *The Egypt of the Hebrews and Herodotos*

EGYPTIAN.	GREEK.	EGYPTIAN CAPITAL.
XIV. Khent-abt	Sethroites (?)	Zaru or Hud of the North
XV. Thoth or Heb	Hermopolites	Khmunu or Bah
XVI. Ha-Mehit	Mendesios-Thmuites	Pa-Ba-neb-dad (Bindidi) (1) Ta-Ha-Biu
XVII. Sam-behed	Diospolites or Sebennytes Inferior	(Pa-Khen-n-Amon) ...
XVIII. Am-khonti	Bubastites	Pa-Bast
XIX. Am-pehu	Butikos (?)	Am-t or Pa-Uaz
XX. Sopd-qemhes	Arabia	Kosem (Goshen) or Pa-Kos or Pa Sopd

Mafkat ('the malachite land') or the Sinaitic Peninisula, is still reckoned as an Egyptian province in the time of

THE OASES.

OASIS.	CAPITAL.
(1) Kenem or Uaht-ris, 'the Oasis of the South'	Hib (1) Kasht (2) Usekh
(2) Zes-zes, 'the two swords'	Ast-Abt
(3) To-Aht, 'Cow-land'	...
(4) Uaht, 'the Oasis'	
(5) Sekhet-amu, 'Palm-grove'	
(6) Uaht-meht, 'Oasis of the North'	..
(7) Sekhet-demam, 'Salt-field'	Serp

Appendix IV.—The Nomes

GREEK CAPITAL.	MODERN NAME.	GODS.
Sethroê (?)	Kantarah (?)	Horus
Hermopolis	Tel-Baqlîyeh	Thoth, Nehemaui, and Nefer-Hor
Mendes	Tmei el-Emdid	Osiris-Mendes (Ba-n-dad) and Isis
Thmuis (Pakhnamunis)	Do. (Tida)	Amon-Ra, Mut, and Khonsu
Diospolis	Belqas	
Bubastis	Tel el-Bast	Bast
Buto	Tel en-Nebêsheh	Uaz
Phakussa	Saft el-Henneh	Horus-Sopd

which was subject to Egypt as early as the third dynasty, the Ptolemies.

The Oases.

GREEK NAME.	MODERN NAME OF OASIS.	GODS.
Hibis	El-Khargeh	Amon
Kysis	Dush	Osiris-Yui
..	Gêtah	...
...	El-Dakhleh	Amon
...	El-Farâfrah	Min
...	?	...
City of Ammon	Sîwah	Amon
The little Oasis	El-Bâharîyeh	...
Skyathis	Wadi en-Natrûn	Khonsu & Month

APPENDIX V

THE GREEK WRITERS UPON EGYPT

(1) HEKATAIOS of Miletos, tyrant, statesman, and writer, B.C. 500-480. Sent as ambassador to the Persians after the suppression of the Ionic revolt. Travelled in Egypt as far as Thebes. His account of Egypt contained in his great work on geography, now lost.

(2) Thales of Miletos, philosopher, B.C. 500. Wrote on the causes of the inundation of the Nile.

(3) Hellanikos of Mytilênê, historian, B.C. 420. Wrote an account of Egypt and a journey to the oasis of Ammon, now lost.

(4) Herodotos of Halikarnassos, historian, B.C., 445-430. Travelled in Egypt as far as the Fayyûm. His account of Egypt chiefly contained in the second book of his histories.

(5) Demokritos of Abdera, philosopher, B.C. 405. Spent five years in Egypt, and wrote books on geography and on the Ethiopic hieroglyphics, now lost.

(6) Aristagoras of Miletos, B.C. 350. Wrote a history of Egypt in at least two books, now lost.

(7) Eudoxos of Knidos, philosopher. Visited Egypt in B.C. 358, and wrote an account of it in his work on geography, now lost.

(8) Leo of Pella, B.C. 330. Wrote a book on the Egyptian gods, now lost.

(9) Hekataios of Abdera, B.C. 300. Lived at the court

Appendix V.—The Greek Writers

of Ptolemy I., travelled up the Nile and examined the Theban temples. Wrote a history of Egypt, the first book of which was on Egyptian philosophy, now lost. The account of the Ramesseum (the temple of Osymandyas or Usir-mâ-Ra) given by Diodôros is derived from his work.

(10) Manetho, Egyptian priest of Sebennytos, B.C. 270. Compiled the history of Egypt in Greek from the records contained in the temples. Corrected many of the errors of Herodotos, according to Josephus. The work was divided into three parts, and Josephus quotes from it the account of the Hyksos conquest, the list of the kings of the eighteenth dynasty, and the Egyptian legend of the Israelitish Exodus. An epitome of the history was probably added at the end of the work. We know it from the list of dynasties quoted by the Christian writers Julius Africanus (A.D. 220) and Eusebius, both of whom endeavoured to harmonise its chronology with that of the Old Testament. The work of Africanus is lost, but the list of dynasties has been preserved by Georgios the Synkellos or Coadjutor of the Patriarch of Constantinople (A.D. 792), who has added two other lists professedly from Manetho, but really from post-Christian forgeries ('The Old Chronicle' and 'The Book of Sôthis'). Eusebius quotes from a copyist of Africanus, or some unknown copyist of Manetho himself, and his list has been preserved (like that of Africanus) by George the Synkellos, as well as in an Armenian translation. Manetho also wrote (in Greek) on Egyptian festivals and religion, but all his works are lost.

(11) Eratosthenes of Kyrênê, geographer, chronologist, astronomer and mathematician, B.C. 275-194. Librarian of the Alexandrine Museum under Ptolemy IV. First fixed the latitude of places by measuring the length of the sun's shadow at noon on the longest day in Alexandria and then

calculating the distance to Assuan, where there was no shadow at all In his work on chronology (now lost) he gave a list of Theban kings, selected from the various dynasties, like the lists of Karnak or Abydos. This has been preserved, along with an attempt to translate the meaning of the names. The translations, however, are erroneous, as they are made from the Greek forms of the names compared with words then current in the decaying Egyptian of the day.

(12) Ptolemy of Megalopolis, B.C. 200. Wrote a history of Ptolemy Philopator, now lost.

(13) Kallixenos of Rhodes, B.C. 210. Wrote a description of Alexandria in four or more books, now lost.

(14) Philistos of Naukratis, B.C. 225. Wrote a description of Naukratis, a history of Egypt in twelve books, and an account of Egyptian religion in three books: all lost.

(15) Kharôn of Naukratis, B.C. 160. Wrote on Naukratis and on the succession of the Ptolemaic priests; the works are lost.

(16) Lykeas of Naukratis, B.C. 160. Wrote an account of Egypt, now lost.

(17) Agatharkhides of Knidos, geographer and historian, B.C. 120. Gave an account of the working of the Egyptian gold-mines (in his geographical work on the Red Sea) which has been preserved by Photios.

(18) Lysimakhos of Alexandria, B.C. 50. Wrote a history of Egypt containing the Egyptian legend of the Hebrew Exodus, which has been preserved by Josephus.

(19) L. Cornelius Alexander Polyhistor, B.C. 82-60. Wrote an account of Egypt in three books; now lost.

(20) Diodôros of Sicily (Diodorus Siculus), historian, travelled in Egypt, B.C. 57, published his great historical work, called *Bibliothêkê*, B.C. 28. The first book of it devoted

Appendix V.—The Greek Writers 329

to Egypt and Ethiopia. Quoted largely from Herodotos, Hekataios of Abdera, Ephoros and other authors now lost. We are dependent on him for a connected history of Egypt during the Persian period.

(21) Ptolemy of Mendes, historian, A.D. 1. Wrote a history of Egypt in three (?) books, now lost.

(22) Strabo of Amasia, geographer, A.D. 20. Travelled in Egypt. The last (17th) book of his great work on geography is devoted to Egypt.

(23) Apion of El-Khargeh, grammarian and historian, A.D. 40. Pleaded for the Alexandrines against Philo and the Jews before Caligula. Wrote a history of Egypt in five books, the third of which discussed the Hebrew Exodus; now lost.

(24) Khairêmôn of Naukratis, stoic philosopher, A.D. 50. Was Nero's teacher. Wrote an account of Egypt and an explanation of the hieroglyphics; now lost.

(25) Josephus, son of the Jewish priest Matthias, born A.D. 37, received his freedom and the name of Flavius, A.D. 69. Quotes from Manetho, Lysimakhos, etc., in his *Antiquities of the Jews* and *Contra Apionem*.

(26) Plutarch of Khaironeia, moralist, A.D. 125. Wrote at Delphi his treatise on Isis and Osiris, which is of great value for the history of the Osiris-myth.

(27) Ptolemy of Alexandria, geographer, A.D. 160. Egypt is thoroughly and scientifically treated in his great work on geography.

(28) St. Clement of Alexandria, head of the Alexandrine (Christian) School, A.D. 191-220. Many references to Egyptian history and religion in his *Strômateis*. He divides Egyptian writing into hieroglyphic, hieratic and epistolographic (or demotic), the first being further divided into alphabetic and symbolic, and the symbolic characters into imitative, figurative and rebus-like.

(29) Julius Africanus, Christian apologist, wrote in A.D. 221 his *Chronology*, in five books; now lost.

(30) Porphyry of Batanea, A.D. 233-305, wrote a history of the Ptolemies; now lost.

(31) Eusebios, bishop of Cæsarea, published in A.D. 326 his *Chronicle*, containing a list of Manetho's dynasties. The work has been preserved in an Armenian translation.

(32) Horapollo of Nilopolis, grammarian, A.D. 390, wrote a work on the hieroglyphics in Coptic, which was translated into Greek by Philippos. Only the ideographic values of the characters are given, but they are mostly correct.

APPENDIX VI

ARCHÆOLOGICAL EXCURSIONS IN THE DELTA

(1) TEL el-Yehudîyeh or Onion.—Take the train from Cairo at 10 A.M., reaching Shibîn el-Qanâter at 12.25. Leave Shibîn el-Qanâter at 5.57 P.M., reaching Cairo at 6.50. Donkeys can be procured at Shibîn, but it is a pleasant walk of a mile and a half through the fields (towards the south-east) to the Tel. There is a *café* at Shibîn adjoining the station, but it is advisable to take lunch from Cairo.

(2) Kôm el-Atrib or Athribis.—The mounds lie close to the station of Benha el-'Asal, north-east of the town, and can easily be explored between two trains. All trains between Cairo and Alexandria stop at Benha.

(3) Naukratis.—The mounds of Naukratis (Kôm Qa'if) lie nearly five miles due west of the station of Teh el-Barûd on the line between Cairo and Alexandria, where all trains stop except the express. The first half of the walk is along a good road under an avenue of trees, but after a village is reached it leads through fields. Donkeys are not always to be had at Teh el-Barûd. The low mounds west of the station are not earlier than the Roman period.

(4) Kanopos or Aboukir.—A train leaves the Ramleh station at Alexandria at 7.40 A.M., and reaches Aboukir at 10.42 A.M., returning from Aboukir at 4.42 P.M. It is a short walk northwards from the station to the temple of Zephyrion discovered by Daninos Pasha in 1891. Then

walk eastward along the shore, where the rocks have been cut into baths and numerous relics of antiquity lie half-covered by the waves.

(5) *The Monument of Darius, near Suez.*—A ride of rather more than five miles through the desert north of Suez along the line of the Freshwater Canal brings us to the fragments of one of the granite stelæ erected by Darius to commemorate his re-opening of the Canal between the Red Sea and the Nile. Traces of the cuneiform and hieroglyphic inscriptions can still be detected upon some of them. The stelæ were erected at certain intervals along the line of the Canal, and the remains of three others of them have been found, on a mound one kilometre south of Tel el-Maskhûtah or Pithom, a little to the east of the station of the Serapeum on the Suez Canal, and on the side of a mound between the 61st kilometre of the Canal and the telegraphic station of Kabret. From Ismailîyeh to Tel el-Maskhûtah is a ride across the desert of eleven miles.

(6) *Tanis or Zoan.*—The easiest way of visiting Tanis or Sân is to sleep at Mansûrah, where there is a very tolerable hotel, and go by the morning train (at 9.15) to the station of Abu 'l-Shekûk, arriving there at 10.55 A.M. One of the small dahabiyehs which ply on the Mo'izz canal, which passes the station and runs to Sân, should have been previously engaged, and a servant sent with food the day before from Mansûrah to get it ready. It is advisable also to send cantine and bedding. A few hours (8 to 10) will take the traveller to Sân, where he can remain as long as he wishes. There is sufficient water in the canal all the year round to float the dahabiyeh. On the way to Abu 'l-Shekûk the station of Baqlîyeh is passed (at 9.41 A.M.), close to which (to the east) is Tel el-Baqlîyeh or Hermopolis Parva. The twin mounds of Tmei el-Amdîd (Mendes and Thmuis) are not far to the east of the station of

Appendix VI.—Archæological Excursions 333

Simbellauên, which is reached at 10.11 A.M. (or by the 6.45 A.M. train from Mansûrah at 7.30 A.M.). Donkeys should be telegraphed for beforehand. The great monolithic granite shrine of Amasis still stands on the mounds. Tel en-Nebêsheh is only eight miles south-east of Sân.

(7) Horbêt or Pharbaithos.—Leaving Mansûrah at 9.15 A.M., the train reaches Abu-Kebir at 11.55, where donkeys can be easily procured. It is a pleasant ride of three miles through the fields to Horbeit and the gigantic monoliths of Nektanebo. The train leaves Abu-Kebir for Zagazig and Cairo at 4 P.M., reaching Zagazig at 4.32 and Cairo at 6.50 P.M.

(8) Behbit (Egyptian Hebit, Roman Iseum).—The granite ruins of the temple of Isis, built by Ptolemy II., lie eight miles by river north of Mansûrah, and are less than half-an-hour's walk from the eastern bank of the river. Delicate bas-reliefs have been carved on the granite blocks. The ruins are a favourite object of picnic parties from Mansûrah.

(9) Bubastis or Tel Bast.—The ruins of the ancient city are a few minutes' walk from the railway station and can be visited between two trains. The site of the temple is in the middle of the mounds, the ruins of the old houses rising up on all sides of it. There is a poor hotel in Zagazig, kept by a Greek.

(13) Sais or Sâ el-Hagar.—This has become difficult of access since the construction of the railway from Alexandria to Cairo. The nearest railway station is Kafr ez-Zaiyât, from which it is distant (by donkey) about five hours. The voyage by river involves the passage of several bridges.

(11) Tel ed-Deffeneh.—Tents and camels are necessary, as well as drinking water, for that of the canal and Lake Menzaleh is brackish. Either go by train to Salahîyeh

(leaving Cairo at 5 P.M., arriving at 9.35 P.M.), or, better, sleep at Ismailîyeh, and go thence by tramway to Kantara. The distance across the desert to Tel ed-Deffeneh from Salahîyeh and Kantara is about the same (eleven miles), but donkeys are more easily procurable at Kantara than camels. At Kantara (on the east side of the canal) are monuments and a *Tel* (perhaps that of Zaru). The excursion may be combined with one to Pelusium, passing Tel el-Hir on the way. From Kantara to Pelusium is rather more than half-a-day's journey. Encamp at the edge of the sand-dunes, one-and-a-half miles from the mounds of Pelusium, walking to them over the mud, which sometimes will not bear the weight of a camel. No fresh water is procurable there.

INDEX

A

abrêk, 33.
Ab-sha, 19.
Abshadi, 238.
Abu, 203.
Abukîr, 208.
Abu-Simbel, 48, 186.
Abusir, 240.
Abutig, 194.
Abydos, 75, 153, 186, 196, 216.
Achæans, 84.
Adapa or Adama, 66.
Æginetans, 214.
Africanus, 16, 40, 286.
Ah-hotep, Queen, 283.
Ahnas el-Medîneh, 36, 192, 264, 269.
Aigyptos, 206.
Akhæmenes, 178.
Akhillas, 234.
Akhilleus, 167.
Alexander Ægos, 139, 140.
Alexander's Tomb, 138.
Alexandria, 140, 147.
Am, Am-pehu, 236, 237.
Amasis (Ahmes II.), 130 *sqq.*, 215, 216, 230, 232.
Ameni, 94.
Amenôphis III., 53, 58, 196.
—— IV. (Khu-n-Aten), 53.
Amon, 12, 53, 88, 122, 228, 242.
Amon-em-hat III., 13, 189, 247, 281-3.
—— IV., 208.
Amorites, 82, 88, 101, 110.

Amyrtæos, 178, 179, 181, 266.
Anaxagoras, 183.
Antiochus, 153 *sqq.*
Anthylla, 215.
Anysis, 204, 266 *sqq.*
Apis, 118, 223, 261.
Apopi, 15, 23, 42, 45, 228.
Apries, 128 *sqq.*, 216.
Arabian nome, 236.
Arabians, 276.
Arad, 108.
Aram-Naharaim (Mitanni), 58, 82
Arioch, 1.
Armais (Hor-m-hib), 73.
Arisu, 84, 94.
Arkhandropolis, 215.
Arsaphes (Her-shcf), 270.
Arvad, 81.
Ashdod, 125.
Ashkelon, 90.
Ashmunên, 268, 269.
Ashtoreth, 242, 252.
Asshurim, 81.
Assur-bani-pal, 118, 120, 269, 277.
Assyria, 59, 82, 275.
Asykhis or Sasykhis, 264.
Atarbekhis, 262.
Aten (-Ra), 55.
Athêna, 217.
Athenians, 179, 181, 238.
Athribis, 118, 276.
Aupet, 269.
Avaris, 15, 39, 41, 92, 233.

B

Baba, 36.
Babylonians, 33, 60, 61.
Bagnold, Major, 4, 247.
Bah, 210.
Bahr Yûsuf, 263, 264.
Bashan, 72.
Bast, 224 *sqq.*
Bata, 25 *sqq.*
Benha, 238, 276.
Beni-Hassan, 19, 194, 266.
Berenikê, 146.
Bes, 225.
Biahmu, 185, 188.
Bigeh, 200, 203.
Blemmyes, 167.
Bokkhoris, 272.
Book of the Dead, 222.
Bouriant, M., 171.
Brugsch, 26, 35, 77, 335.
Bubastis, 45, 110, 112, 193, 204, 224 *sqq.*, 267.
Busiris, 205, 239 *sqq.*
Butô, 193, 204, 225, 235 *sqq.*, 250, 267.

C

Cæsar, 165, 234.
Cæsarion, 166.
Cairo, 220.
Canaan, 60, 67 *sqq.*
—— libraries in, 67.
camel, 21.
canal, 77, 125, 146.
Carchemish, 126.
Canopus, Decree of, 150.
cats, 193, 225, 230.
Cilicia, 81.
Champollion, 109, 238.
Christianity, 168 *sqq.*
circumnavigation of Africa, 125.
Cleopatra, 140, 165.
colossus at Memphis, 3, 247.

colossi of Fayyûm, 188 *sqq.*
Coptos, 167.
Coptic alphabet, 169.
cuneiform, 60-65.
—— tablets, 61 *sqq.*
Cyprian potters, 236.

D

Dahabiyeh voyage, 194.
Dakkeh, 152.
Dahshûr, 204, 263, 265, 282.
Damanhur, 193, 204, 210.
Danaans, 86.
Daninos Pasha, 208.
Daphnæ, 129, 131, 205, 230.
Dead Sea, 87.
Debod, 152.
De Cara, Dr., 39.
De Morgan, Mr., 281, 300.
Demetrius Phalereus, 147.
Denderah, 197.
Dêr Abu Hannes, 173.
Diocletian, 167.
Diodoros, 247, 259.
Diospolis (Thebes), 163.
dreams, 30.
Dudu, 60.

E

Ebed-Asherah, 72.
Ebed-tob, 71.
Ecclesiasticus, 145.
Edom, 43, 72, 88, 96, 101-103.
Egypt, etymology of, 4, 206.
Ekhmîm, 197, 235, 275.
Elbo, 266.
Eleazar, 148.
Elephantinê, 201 *sqq.*
El-Hibeh, 105.
El-Kab, 14, 36, 41.
El-Khargeh, 10

Eltekeh, 276.
Enna, 25.
Enoch, book of, 162, 170.
Erman, Professor, 17, 25.
Esar-haddon, 113, 116, 118, 279.
Esneh, 276.
Ethiopians, 112, 122, 149, 152, 249, 266.
Eusebius, 17, 40, 286.
Exodus, 38, 40, 45, 51, 91.
Ezer, 72.

F

Fayyûm, 13, 137, 141, 142, 186, 188, 194, 196, 246.
famines, 34-38.
Fenkhu, 107.

G

Gardner, Mr. E., 212, 214.
Gaza, 80, 87, 88, 90, 95, 107, 126, 128, 139.
Gebal (Byblos), 72.
Gebel Abu Foda, 194, 271.
Gebelên, 105.
Gezer, 105.
Goshen, 43, 44, 96, 120, 236.
Golénischeff, M., 94.
Grant-Bey, Dr., 221.
Greeks, 123, 131.
Griffith, Mr., 11, 236, 271.
Gyges, 122.

H

Hadashah, 90.
Hamath, 88.
Hammamât, 272.
Hanes (Ahnas), 267
Hapi (Nile), 200.
Hathor, 31, 260.
hawks, 193.

Hebron, 72, 87, 89.
Hekatæos, 176, 177, 183, 186, 223, 237, 285.
Helen, 251.
Heliopolis, 204, 220 *sqq.*, 240, 250.
Hellanikos, 183.
Hellenion, 213.
helmet, bronze, 283.
Hephæstion, 138
Herakleopolis (Ahnas), 192, 195, 204, 264, 270-271.
Hermes, 227.
Hermopolis, 193, 204, 210.
Her-shef (Arsaphes), 270.
Hezekiah, 115, 276.
Hierakon, 194.
Hininsu (Ahnas), 264, 267.
hippopotamus, 177, 193.
Hittites, 63, 74, 82, 86, 88.
Homer, 182.
Hont-mâ-Ra, 208.
Hophra, *see* Apries.
Hor-m-hib, 73, 75.
Horus, 201, 222, 235, 237, 275.
Howâra, 191, 265, 281, 283.
Huseyn, feast of, 239.
Hyksos, 14, 23, 38, 39, 40, 42, 227.
Hypatia, 170.

Iannas, 228.
ibises, 193, 210.
Illahun, 263, 265.
Inaros, 178, 181.
inundation, 184.
Ionians, 213, 230, 280
Isis, 219, 235, 239.
Istar, 277.

J

Jaddua, 144, 150

Jason, 156.
Jerahmeel, 108.
Jeroboam, 106.
Jerusalem, 71, 80, 87, 106, 116, 126, 127, 134, 139.
Jews, 141, 144, 148, 152, 153, 155, 159, 162, 164.
Joseph, 24 *sqq.*, 93, 221.
Josiah, 126.
Judah, 87, 88, 107.

K

Kadesh, 82.
Kambyses, 132, 149, 262.
Ka-meri-Ra, 11.
Kanôpos, 207-209, 235.
Kanôpic arm of Nile, 206, 209, 211.
Karians, 123, 183, 187, 218, 230, 239, 242, 254, 280.
Kafr el-Ayyât, 245.
Kellogg, Dr., 99.
Kerkasoros, 185.
Khabiri, 71.
Khabbash, 134
Khal, 72, 100.
Khaf-Ra (Khephren), 256, 259.
Kheb, 235.
Khemmis, 197, 235, 237.
Kheops (Khufu), 8, 227, 256, 258.
Khephren (Khaf-Ra), 256, 259.
Kheti-ti, 276.
Khian (Iannas), 228.
Khita-sir, 82.
Khiti, 271.
Khri-Ahu, 220.
Khu-n-Aten (Amenôphis IV.), 53 *sqq.*
Kimon, 179, 181.
Kirjath-sepher, 67, 68.
Kleomenes, 137, 138.
Klysma, 269.
Kokkê (Cleopatra), 161.
Kom el-Ahmar, 250.
Kôm Qa'if, 211.
Krophi, 199-201.
Ktêsias, 285.
Kyrênê, 130.

L

Labai, 71.
Labyrinth, 186, 273, 279.
Leku, 84.
Leontopolis, 158.
Lepsius, 76.
Leto, 235.
Libyans, 84, 106, 123, 130.
Lisht, 191.

M

Maccabees, the, 160.
Mafkat (Sinai), 254.
Mahanaim, 108.
Mahler, Professor, 17, 308.
Maindes, 281.
Manasseh, 116.
Manetho, 14, 16, 18, 73, 92, 100, 148, 228, 257, 272.
Mariette, 39, 78, 245, 283.
Mark Antony, 166.
Maspero, Professor, 39, 107, 191, 271
Master-thief, tale of, 253.
Maxyes, 84, 85, 87.
Medînet Habu, 87, 89, 102, 253, 254.
Mêdum, 7, 263.
Megabyzos, 179, 181.
Megabazus, 238.
Megiddo, 72, 107.
Melchizedek, 71.
Memnon, 196.
Memphis, 2, 5, 41 *sqq.*, 219, 242 *sqq.*
Mendes, 239.
Menelaus (the Jew), 153.
Menelaite nome, 235, 237.
Menes, 2, 190, 244, 246

Index

Meneptah, 40, 43, 45, 49, 83, 92, 96, 97, 270.
Menshîyeh (Ptolemais), 143.
Menzaleh, Lake, 231.
Menûf, 238.
Mer-ka-Ra, 271.
Merom, 80.
Messianic prophecy, 94.
mice, 193, 275, 276.
Miletus, 126.
Milesians, 214, 215.
Min, 197.
Mitanni (Aram Naharaim), 58, 82, 88.
Mnevis, 222, 240.
Moab, 81.
Mohar, Travels of a, 68.
Moph (Memphis), 3.
Mophi, 201.
Mœris, 188, 189, 246 *sqq.*, 273, 283
Museum, the, 141, 147, 165.
Mut, 201.
Mykerinos (Men-ka-Ra), 256, 259, 264.

N

Nahum, 121.
name, change of, 31.
Napata, 112, 119, 268.
Naville, Dr., 43, 44, 76, 78, 110, 158, 211, 225, 226, 270, 271.
Naukratis, 131, 132, 204, 209 *sqq.*, 232.
Neapolis (Qeneh), 197.
Nebuchadrezzar, 127, 129, 130.
Necho of Sais, 117, 118, 120, 278.
—— II., 125 *sqq.*
Neferu-Ptah, 281.
Neit, 199, 216, 218, 253, 260.
Nektanebo I., 229.
—— II., 135, 211, 221.
Nikanor, 139.
Nikiu, 238.

Nile, 31, 34, 183, 184.
—— sources of, 198 *sqq.*
Nineveh, 124.
Nitokris, 11, 246.
No-Amon (Thebes), 121
Noph (Memphis), 3.
Norden, 187.
Nut-Amon, 30.

O

On (Heliopolis), 31, 131.
Onias, 157 *sqq.*, 162, 250.
—— II., 151.
Onion, 157.
Osarsiph, 92.
Osiris, 216, 239.
Osorkon I., 227.
—— II., 110, 225, 226, 228, 268.
ostraka, 144.
Osymandyas, 196.

P

Pausiris, 179.
Papias, 173.
Paprêmis, 178, 180, 193, 205, 238.
Pa-Uaz (Butô), 235.
Peguath, 207.
Pelusiac arm of Nile, 224.
Pelusium, 178, 232.
Pepi I., 227.
Perdikkas, 138.
Pergamos, library of, 166.
Perseus, 198.
Peter, Apocalypse of St., 171.
—— Gospel of St., 171.
Petrie, Professor W. F., 7, 9, 11, 48, 54, 57, 65, 78, 129, 137, 185, 188, 191, 211, 230, 266, 281.
Phanês, 132, 214, 233, 234.
Phakussa, 43.

340 *The Egypt of the Hebrews and Herodotos*

Pharaoh, meaning of, 22, 250.
Pharos, 147, 182.
Pherôn, 250.
Philæ, 200.
Philistines, 80, 84, 86, 88, 90.
Philotera (Qoseir), 146.
Phut, 130.
phœnix, 177, 223.
Pi-ankhi, 112, 268.
Pi-Sopd, 120.
Pithom, 43, 169.
Plato, 224.
Plutarch, 270, 285.
Polybos, 182.
Polykratês, 176.
Pompey, 164, 234.
Potiphar, 24.
Probus, 167.
Prosôpitis, 238, 262, 335.
Proteus, 182, 251.
Psalms of Solomon, 164.
Psammetikhos I., 118, 120, 122 *sqq.*, 231, 243, 278 *sqq.*
—— II., 127.
—— III., 132, 234.
Ptah, 4, 196, 204, 242 *sqq.*, 274, 279.
Ptolemais, 143.
Ptolemy I., Lagos, 138 *sqq.*
—— II., Philadelphus, 146 *sqq.*, 213.
—— III., 148 *sqq.*
—— IV., 151.
—— V., 152.
—— VI., 154.
—— Physkôn, 154.
—— Lathyrus, 162.
Pyramid, the great, 8, 190, 256.

Q

Qebhu, 203.
Qerti, 200, 202.
Qoseir, 146.

R

Ra, 12, 24, 29, 56, 222.
Raamses (city), 76, 98.
Ra-men-kheper, 105.
Ramses I., 75.
—— II., 3, 16, 18, 43, 47, 68, 76, 78, 80 *sqq.*, 117, 196, 206, 208, 228, 236, 247, 250, 270.
—— III., 85-90, 101, 102, 157, 253, 254.
Ra-nefer, 7.
Raphia, 114.
Red Mound, 250.
Retennu, 111.
Rhampsinitos (Ramses III.), 252 *sqq.*
Rhodopis, 214.
Rome, 153, 155, 164.
Rosetta Stone, 153.

S

Sabako, 110, 229, 266, 269, 270.
Sadducees, 151.
Sa el-Hagar (Sais), 217.
Saft el-Henneh (Goshen), 43.
Sais, 204, 215 *sqq.*
Samaritans, 137, 159, 162.
Samians, 214.
Sapi-ris, 238.
Sappho, 214.
Sardinians, 84.
Sargon, 114.
Sasykhis or Asykhis, 264, 266.
Satrapies, Assyrian, in Egypt, 117, 122, 279.
Satuna, 82.
Schumacher, Dr., 81.
Scyths, 123.
sebah, 212.
Sebek, 266.
Sebennytic arm of Nile, 237.
Sehêl, stela of, 35.
Sekhem (Esneh), 276.

Index

Sekhet, 225.
Semennûd (Sebennytos), 239.
Send, 6.
Senem (Bigeh), 200.
Sennacherib, 114, 244, 275 *sqq.*
Septimius, 234.
Septuagint, 145.
Serapeum, 261.
Serapis, 207.
serpents, winged, 236.
Sesetsu (Sesostris), 249.
Sesostris (Ramses II.), 47, 196, 229, 247 *sqq.*
Set, 75, 222, 235, 237, 249.
Sethos, 244, 275.
Seti I., 75, 228.
—— II., 84, 97-100.
Set-nekht, 100.
Shasu (Bedouin), 276.
Shechem, 72.
Shed-festival, 226.
Shepherd kings, 14.
Sheri, 6.
Shishak, 106, 228.
Sib'e (So), 114.
Siculians, 86.
Sidon, 91, 128.
Simon the Just, 150.
Sin, 233.
Sinai, 7, 89, 254, 283.
Singar, 82.
Si-Ptah, 84, 99.
Smendes, 105.
Snefru, 6.
So (Sib'e), 114.
Solomon, 105.
Solon, 183, 217.
Sostratos, 147.
Sphinx, 5, 30, 191, 245.
St. John, J. A., 192.
Strabo, 223, 264, 281.
Succoth, 43, 77, 96.
Sumerian, 64, 65.

Suphah, 101.
Sutekh, 23, 39, 228.

T

Tahpanhes, 129, 131.
Tand-Amon, 119.
Tanis (*see* Zoan), 104 *sqq.*, 232.
Tantah, 226.
Ta-user, Queen, 99.
Teie, Queen, 57, 58.
Tel el-Amarna, 52 *sqq.*
Tel el-Baqlîyeh, 210.
Tel ed-Deffeneh, 129, 231 *sqq.*
Tel el-Yehudîyeh, 157, 250.
Tel en-Nebêsheh, 236.
Tel Fera'in, 235.
Tel Mokdam, 39.
Thannyras, 179.
Thebes, 12, 50, 163, 182, 186, 194, 196
This (Girgeh), 2.
Thothmes III., 18, 58, 80, 196, 222.
Thukydides, 285.
Tirhakah, 114 *sqq.*, 272, 276.
Tnêphakhtos, 268.
Tunip, 82.
Turah, 257.
Turin Papyrus, 16.
Tut-ankh-Amon, 73.
Two brothers, Tale of, 25 *sqq.*
Tyre, 72, 205, 234.
Tyrian camp, 242, 251.
Tyrsenians, 84.

U

Uaz, 235, 236, 237, 275.
Urd-Amon, 119.
Ur-mer, 240.
Usertesen I., 221, 251.
—— II., 19, 266, 270.
—— III., 282.

W

Wadi Tumilât (Goshen), 43.
Wiedemann, Professor, 39, 223.
Wilbour, Mr., 35.

X

Xanthos, 176.

Y

Yaud-hamelek, 109.

Z

Zagazig, 224.
Zahi, 72.
Zakkur, 84, 86, 88.
Zaphnath-paaneah, 32.
Zemar, 72.
Zenodotos, 147.
Zephyrion, 207.
Zerah, 111.
Zoan (Sân, Tanis), 15, 19, 39, 41, 42, 48, 78, 267.

THE END